On the Biology of Learning

ON THE BIOLOGY

Under the General Editorship of
Jerome Kagan
Harvard University

Harcourt, Brace & World, Inc.

OF LEARNING

Karl H. Pribram, Editor

Holger Hydén
University of Göteborg

Konrad Lorenz
Max-Planck-Institut

H. W. Magoun
University of California at Los Angeles

Wilder Penfield
Montreal Neurological Institute

Karl H. Pribram
Stanford University

New York   Chicago   San Francisco   Atlanta

ON THE BIOLOGY OF LEARNING
Karl H. Pribram, Editor

© 1969 by HARCOURT, BRACE & WORLD, INC.

ISBN: 0-15-567520-6

Library of Congress Catalog Card Number: 75-96911

Printed in the United States of America

Foreword

The essays in this book appeared first in 1966–67 as public lectures sponsored by the Graduate School of Education of Harvard University. One of the objectives of the School's annual lecture series is to anticipate issues of fundamental importance to education before they become "popular." The neurophysiology and biochemistry of learning seemed to be such a topic. Our request to the speakers was that they address the research on learning in their specialties and comment on its social utility. Our hope for the series in this respect was expressed in a phrase of Penfield's: "to draw from physiological facts some meaning that will serve the purposes of wisdom." This volume must speak for itself on the degree to which it realizes these substantial objectives.

The book, however, cannot communicate certain things about the original lectures. The wide response to the series in the academic faculties of biology and psychology as well as in the professional faculties of medicine and education was gratifying to the sponsors. The public audience too was large. It is difficult to characterize the response of such a diverse audience. Thoughtful analysis of the lectures, excitement generated by the powerful personal presence of a Lorenz or a Penfield, interest in the confrontation between the East Coast school of neurophysiology and the West Coast neurophysiologists, the simple attempt by the lay listener to understand—all were evident in that response.

Lectures (even good ones) do not necessarily make systematic or complete books. The lectures in this book should be seen as discrete statements by five scholars who were selected partly because their approaches to the biology of learning differ. The Committee on Lectures of the Harvard Graduate School of Education feels that the original intention of the lecture series was substantially realized. Thanks to Professor Pribram's efforts as editor, we feel that the series has also become a worthwhile book.

Ralph L. Mosher
Cambridge, Massachusetts

Contents

Introduction

During the twentieth century the psychological sciences have burgeoned under the impetus of behaviorism. Much has been learned, but a gnawing dissatisfaction remains, stemming in part from the very condition that ensured growth: a wealth of data, often contradictory, that begs for meaning. Today a new phase is in the making, an era that takes its cues from biology. As with all new departures, it is bound at the beginning to declare its independence—which in this case means to denounce the sins of behaviorism, much as behaviorism once flaunted the errors of the physiology from which it sprang. Already there are those who give lusty voice to the infant (see, for instance, Koestler [13, 14]). But a mature reading will come with the development of a set of biobehavioral sciences in which the meaning of data obtained at any one level of investigation is culled against the perspective of knowledge at other levels.

This volume is composed of essays written by pioneers. Each in his own way has, over a lifetime of research, charted meaningful directions in the biobehavioral sciences. Each has made distinguished contributions of fact by employing his skills in the solution of riddles left by his predecessors. In addition, each does something strict behaviorists usually feel constrained not to do (because they think it "unscientific"): each of the contributors continues to reflect on the riddles that gave rise to his research. Each asks whether his data clarify or whether, indeed, the enigma has deepened because the question asked was inappropriate and must therefore be rephrased. Some of the authors are in their forties and have two decades or so of research and publications behind them; others are in their seventies and have been active for a half-century. Yet it is hard to decide which have the more youthful approach to their subject matter. All show a remarkable record of continued growth—perhaps just because of this process of reflection on the primal riddles that haunt them.

The first essay, by Konrad Lorenz, admirably illustrates these issues. Lorenz is responsible for the introduction and wide application of behavioral techniques to zoological investigation. This pursuit became so widespread that its practice developed into a separate science —ethology. Lorenz's influence aimed ethology at one of the fundamental problems posed by evolutionary theory—that of how adaptation and selection take place. But, though a wealth of fascinating evidence has been harvested, the data uncovered by the strictly behaviorally oriented ethologists have not as yet come to grips with this riddle. Why is this?

My view is that the narrow devotion to behaviorism led to a rejection of fundamental issues conceptualized by earlier investigators under the rubrics "innate" and "learned." The behavioral answer to the riddle is that behavior is inexorably composed of both innate and learned factors and that these continuously interact (see, for instance, Beach [6] and Hinde [10]). A "scientific" ethology can hope only to define and perhaps fully describe the occasions for the occurrence of "species-specific behaviors," these investigators claim.

I have always been puzzled by the category "species-specific." In man, for example, the most characteristic species-specific behavior is the making of propositional utterances (to use Hughlings Jackson's unambiguous term to describe human language). For me, the important problem is to discern the mechanism that allows us to make propositional utterances when this appears precluded in the apes. We inherit something that *structures* our communication and that other creatures do not share. Yet the *content* of our language is obviously learned: some of us discourse in English, others in Arabic, still others in Chinese. For me and for many linquists (7, 11), the question is to define the innate structure or structures of this species-specific behavior; for others, the goal might well be to come to grips with the ease or difficulty of acquisition of one or another manifestation of language.

Lorenz clearly presents this issue in the essay included here. Many of his ethological colleagues currently accuse him of turning the clock back, and in a way he does—back to the riddles that spawned their discipline. The argument made by these critics of Lorenz is that there is no hard evidence for Lorenz's views, an argument reminiscent of that levied during the thirties, forties, and fifties against cognitivists by those of a stimulus-response persuasion. But in the sixties the outstanding researches in experimental psychology have devolved from the cognitive approach: the problems of structure, coding, and patterning, and of expectancy, memory, and categorizing have become amenable to experimental analysis.

Lorenz moves with this *Zeitgeist* and exhorts his own science to return to the problems that gave it birth. He meets the issues squarely: he does not hesitate to use the term "innate *basis* of learning" [italics mine]; to discuss life as a *knowledge* process; and so on. More than any of his contemporaries, he sees clearly the future of his science precisely because he returns to and reflects on its fundamental riddles. However, as with any vision expressed, a certain one-sidedness is unavoidable. Examples are perhaps colored, evidence too often preliminary and nonquantitative to give assurance. But then that leaves something to be accomplished by those who want to make the vision endure.

For me the most exciting part of Lorenz's essay, aside from the general "cognitive" approach, is the chapter on learning. His remarks on imprinting, habituation, and success and failure learning are provocative and raise in my mind several questions. For example, might not all perceptual learning follow the time course of imprinting? Is not this what we mean by insight? Patrick Bateson's carefully performed experiments (5) have shown that imprinting follows the laws of perceptual learning. The question can therefore be posed: Is indeed *all* perceptual learning characterized by "discontinuity" (that is, seeming suddenness) and relative permanence? Does not all learning of this type affect perceptions and behaviors remote in time and type? Interestingly, support for just such a possibility is discussed by Penfield in his sections on "Second-Language Learning" and "The Blank Slate."

Lorenz's questions concerning the importance and nature of the process of habituation fascinate me. He states that "the motor side of the response is not affected; habituation is *stimulus-specific desensitization.*" Here, from an entirely different set of data, an entirely different field of inquiry, comes a conclusion close to that reached in Sokolov's (22) and my own research (1, 2, 3, 4, 9, 12) on the basis of neurobehavioral and psychophysiological findings and by Richard Thompson (23), who used a neurophysiological approach. Such convergences give validity to the questions asked, even though the particular answers may be modified as the results of continued experimental explorations become available.

Success and failure learning is what Lorenz calls conditioning—

that is, learning through reinforcement. I have also come to the conclusion that reinforcement is essentially an organizing process (18) and even venture a possible mechanism for its occurrence in my contribution here. My proposal does not seem out of place in a volume that contains Lorenz's description of embryological induction, and so I am heartened. Again, the fact that disparate disciplinary frames converge in interest and in the questions asked (as well as in the solutions currently tendered) attests to the vigor of the biohehavioral approach.

One final comment on Lorenz's contribution. Early in the essay he invokes a systems approach and discusses hierarchies of structure and function in the organism. Some, unless they read further, might wonder whether Lorenz is espousing a reductionist view of the learning problem. The later chapters, especially those sections that deal with tradition, culture, and science itself make it abundantly clear that here speaks no reductionist. Yet the apparent paradox persists. My solution to this paradox is that the reductionist fallacy stems from a confusion of hierarchies. Just because a recognizable entity is made up of parts is no assurance that the parts are indeed "simpler" than the whole—for example, try to give an anatomical description of the face of a loved one. Anatomical and functional hierarchies do not necessarily parallel each other—nor do those of content and form. And, in the biobehavioral realm, the mind-body relationship takes on an apparent dual perspective: greater complexities and simplicities of one kind—the descriptive—are discovered as one searches the biological continuum, while those of a different sort—the normative—emerge as one reaches out into the psychosocial world (19). Lorenz, the biobehavioral scientist, takes both directions and handles his excursion into the biobehavioral paradox skillfully.

The authors of this volume are all controversial figures, the controversies they engender attest to their leadership. Perhaps, however, none is more controversial at the moment than Holger Hydén. In this case the argument rages not directly about inheritance and learning but about the possibility of a common substrate for both. The focus is on a molecule: ribonucleic acid. Molecular biologists have over the past two decades unraveled the mystery of the construction of the gene—the mechanism by which an individual can pass on his own inheritance to his offspring. The molecules involved are deoxyribonucleic acids (DNA), which, by the way of ribonucleic acids (RNA), instruct (that is, give structure to) the proteins and other large molecules that make up the substance of our bodies.

Hydén discovered that nerve cells "secrete" large amounts of RNA when stimulated. Until this discovery, the biochemical activities of the brain had for the most part eluded investigation; most of the evidence had suggested that nervous tissue was metabolically relatively inert, a finding unattractive and unlikely to *Homo sapiens*. Activity of any sort was therefore welcome news. That the activity should take the form of massive amounts of RNA secretion held special promise: since DNA and RNA function as the carriers of genetic memory, the proposal went, perhaps these same molecules serve as substrates of experiential memory as well.

The imagination of scientists was captured, and, as Hydén's review of their activities indicates, considerable headway has been made in delineating what is, what is not to be, and what might be expected from this line of attack on the memory problem. Obviously, Nature does not relinquish her answers unambiguously. Also obviously, the notion of a separate molecule for every separate memory is altogether too naive a statement of the issue. But by no means need this mean, as so many of his detractors would have it, that the approach engendered by Hydén's discovery and his own meticulous follow-up experiments should be discounted. For, even today, the picture being composed by these researches is not that unclear. Very specific alternatives are being explored; RNA may act as an inductor (20), derepressing the genetic potential of glia to divide, so as to allow new connections to be made; protein or other macromolecular configurations may be altered by neural activity; or the increased metabolic activity signaled by RNA secretion may indicate a change in the amount of chemical substance activated at neural synapses. Of course, a combination of these effects may occur to impart the more or less permanent changes in brain that must occur if we are to possess memory. Hydén proposes one such combination in the paper presented here. At the moment, he hypothesizes a three-step learning mechanism: (1) neural-glial couplets that share a characteristic protein response to a stimulus situation, constituting (2) a selective mechanism, which results in a derepression of the local genome to produce a specific RNA, which in turn activates the local synaptic mechanism so that (3) a permanent change takes place in local information-rich molecules.

But more lasting than any currently held views are the solid data that continue to be produced by Hydén's laboratories and those of others excited by the discovery of the importance of the RNA molecule in the economy of the central nervous system. RNA has been the key that unlocked the doors; explorations of what lies beyond have barely begun. The prospect continues to be an exciting one, and Hydén's chapter may be taken as an authoritative and current progress report on these researches. But more than that, it is a written record of the thinking of a competent investigator who shares Lorenz's primal questions and has approached them with his own exquisite technical competence. Both of these men view the problem of memory as "of a piece"—the genetic and the experiential forming a continuum that must be delineated not obfuscated by denying its existence as a problem.

With Wilder Penfield's contribution we enter a somewhat different world. Though Lorenz and Hydén pay tribute to the brain's mechanisms and tissues, their biology centers on the theory of evolution—mechanisms of heredity, adaptation, and selection at the individual, social, and molecular levels. Lorenz and Hydén take biology's great synthesis—its second law (the first having been cell theory)—another crucial step forward. Penfield, by contrast, looks toward a barely charted biological synthesis-to-come: the resolution of the mind-brain problem. This is the world of neuropsychology, a world beset as much by issues of how to state the question's as by those of how to seek the answers in discovery. It is to Penfield's credit that he faces the issues squarely. Again, the contrast is staggering beween this treatment and the earlier behavioristic taboo against concepts derived from subjective experience (and verbally reported). Penfield's experiments on man, experiments with the naked brain, are telling.

Even strict behaviorists, however, allow inconsistencies to enrich their science. Today the concept "attention" is in vogue—partly because it can be more or less behaviorized in terms of "observing responses." Penfield's argument should therefore fall on receptive ears. He draws toward his conclusions slowly and carefully by giving anatomical and physiological detail, which reviews briefly much of his lifelong experimental contribution. In essence, this becomes a discourse on how the brain may work.

Central to this presentation is the dictum, which is repeated on several occasions, that a child learns *only* when he is paying attention. Penfield suggests that attention is initiated in the diencephalon—an issue that will recur in somewhat different form in both of these two subsequent presentations. As an hypothesis, the importance of attention to learning is a challenging notion. The evidence for it is not at all conclusive, however. Much of the process of operant conditioning may well occur in the absence of awareness on the part of the organism conditioned. This has led me and my colleagues to view learning as possible in at least two modes: in one, attention is crucial, while in the other, a more probabilistic, rote memorization mechanism is involved. Here the critical point is that Penfield has recognized and detailed one—if only one—of the forms the learning process can take

6   *Introduction*

and has made a good case for some of the brain mechanisms that may be involved.

Another important mind-brain issue Penfield illuminates early on is the importance of the *patterning* of neural activity. His exercises in the interruption of speech by electrical excitation of certain cortical areas are well known; his use of these findings to argue the importance of pattern in the brain's machinery is often not sufficiently appreciated.

But throughout Penfield's essay the dominant riddle is that of the relationship between mind and brain. He comes very close to deciphering the riddle in his heading "Duality of Approach"; yet to my mind he reverts, albeit only temporarily, to sounding like a simple dualist in his discussions of the issue: "Physicians must make a double approach to the problem of man, for there is no thoroughfare of cause and effect between brain and the mind of man and there will be none until a new bridge is built." There is, of course, the possibility that the question of cause and effect between brain and mind may be the wrong question, that the two approaches he heralds may be conceptual ones and that the *events* we variously *call* neural and psychological are *identical* (see, for example, 8, 15, 19). Nonetheless, the issues are staked out clearly. Penfield's research results are redirected toward the primal questions that intrigued him sufficiently as a young man to make him undertake the exacting, albeit exciting, training necessary to allow him direct access to man's most prized possession —his brain. A lifetime of such research has led him to conclude simply that "each man uses his mind to . . . program his brain." Can we ask for our labors any greater harvest?

H. W. Magoun, the fourth contributor to this book, carries into detail the examination of brain processes begun by Penfield. Magoun's focus is on learning per se. He derives his approach from the empiricist tradition, quoting from John Locke that the mind is given to us as a "white paper, void of all characters, without any ideas; how comes it to be furnished? . . . To this I answer in one word, from experience." Magoun, like Penfield, hedges his empiricism by emphasizing the dependence of learning on attention—but the hedge is a minor one. He reviews and amplifies Hydén's molecular studies within the framework of "the fixation of experience," referring to Adey's suggestion that *inter*cellular protein occurring in the brain may be altered by neural activity. But Magoun focuses mainly on the problems of novelty and reinforcement: "obviously, the promotion of novelty rather than repetition should become a primary law of learning." Magoun bases this statement on the fact that simple repetition of input signals promotes habituation of neural processes. He locates both the orienting mechanism and habituation in the reticular formation of the mesencephalon—and it will be recalled that Penfield suggests a higher-level core brain structure, the diencephalon, for this attention function. My own view as described in my chapter differs somewhat more radically: habituation itself has been shown to be an initial step in the learning process, giving rise to a "neuronal model," an expectancy against which to test further inputs. As such, initial expectancies can be built into the organism, and these actively guide all subsequent experience. On this basis and on that of the fact of ubiquitous efferent control of receptor function by the central nervous system, the brain becomes a more assertive structure than that conceived by Locke.

In detail, I differ with both Magoun and Penfield. Not only the mesencephalon and diencephalon but also the amygdala (a portion of the limbic forebrain), and even the frontal cortex, have been found to be involved in generating the neuronal model upon which expectancies are based. The emphasis on novelty is not misplaced. But novelty must be recognized for what it is—a modest departure from the expected: that is, information. As studies in my laboratory have demonstrated, until habituation has taken firm root, novel stimuli only perturb—they fail to register. In short, the work on novelty and habituation has confirmed the old saying that "education is what remains after all that was learned has been forgotten."

Magoun's analysis of the reinforcement problem is also of interest. Magoun takes as his point of departure the discovery by Olds and Milner of the central self-stimulation procedure and views reinforcement as an "arousal" process, which is similar to that obtained in response to novelty but is "far more persistent and, unlike that of the orienting reflex, does not attenuate or habituate upon repetition. . . ." As already noted, I view reinforcement more as an organizing reaction that synchronizes neural processes (8). In fact, I do not consider even the orienting reaction and its habituation in terms of simple arousal; rather, I see them as manifestations of the lateral and self-inhibition of neurons—Pavlov's mechanisms of external and internal inhibition.

But these differences only point to the closeness in kind that characterizes the questions we neurobehavioral scientists are asking. Whether (as some feel) the cortex is the locus of learning or whether (as Magoun holds) the process takes place in the reticular core of the nervous system will be resolved by experiment. As already indicated, I have found evidence for at least two types of learning, one more related to the classical cortical analyzer systems, the other more linked to the core structures of the brain.

Like all pioneers, Magoun looks ever to a future rooted firmly in the past. He ends his essay with a three-stage description of the *development* of learning. Whatever one may feel about the particulars of his stages, the important point is that he calls attention to a newly won research opportunity: study the maturation of neural structure and function concomitant with behavioral development, and you will achieve new insights into learning. Until recently, such studies could be effected only at the gross level. Now that sophisticated techniques have become available, we are no longer limited to studies of the course of myelization. Today we can make measurements of cortical thickness, extent of dendritic arborization, numbers and health of dendritic spines, configurations of receptive fields of unit electrical responses, patterns of the slower electric potential changes, and concentrations of RNA and of neural transmitter substance. All these techniques can be applied in longitudinal studies. Furthermore, behavioral development has by now been minutely characterized in such a way that correlations, when they are obtained, are more likely to prove meaningful. This is the promising field of inquiry heralded by Magoun's summary statement.

To turn now to my own contribution. I had originally been asked to present a summary critique such as the one written here, but certain circumstances precluded this. Though Hydén's and Penfield's essays were available to me early, Magoun's was not, nor was Lorenz's. Moreover, Magoun's paper proved to be a bombshell. I had just presented an invited address at the Eastern Psychological Association meetings in which I proposed a memory-based information processing theory of emotion. Much of the work of my laboratory over the past decade has been devoted to experiments on the registration of novelty and on the brain's control over its own input. I had intended to describe this work and weave it together with that presented by Hydén, Penfield, and Magoun. But Magoun "scooped" me; he not only used the same threads I had in mind but also produced a most provocative, memorable, and beautifully executed tapestry. Nor did it help that he called by other names parts of the brain in which I had invested heavily.

The paper I presented was therefore forged in the heat of conflicting emotions: not a little frustration, some self-doubt, yet firm confidence in what had been accomplished. The overriding factor was an acute awareness that on the basis of my research I had a vision of the way the brain works that was in some respects clearer than that held by the other contributors. The question was whether I could communicate this vision. The essay must speak for itself on this point. Its full impact did not become clear even to me until several months after the writing—until I reread it in preparation for a conference on the pathology of memory (21). By then the import of its message was clear: *learning and remembering are critically dependent on coding.* Novelty, information processing, and item storage and retrieval are all secondary in importance. We must crack the codes (please note the plural) by which the brain transmutes difficult-to-process, all-or-none signals into more easily managed patterns. I have described some of the encoding and decoding possibilities; but perhaps more important than the particulars are the findings that lead to the conclusion that both spatial (that is, holographic) and temporal (that is, programmed) coding processes are distinguishable, necessary, and possible.

What then are educators to gain from this interchange among biobehavioral scientists? Most important, perhaps, is the adventure that awaits—similar, indeed, to that undertaken by reading a Faulkner or a Hemingway or perhaps a Byrd or an Amundsen. In this volume are exposed the lifelong, arduous endeavors of some—sleuths of biobehavioral science. An accounting of these endeavors and their inherent risk should be shared by those to whom is entrusted the task of relating the strivings of earlier generations to the new.

More specifically, educators are in a position to actively reevaluate their own views on the basis of the challenges presented. Do we really store items of information, as Hydén would have it, and if so, to what extent? Or do we more properly mind the way in which we program our brains, as Penfield says we must? Or is it imperative that we find the rightful place of novelty in a more enduring world, as I would have it? Does the insight that the brain's *codes* are the crucial sites for illumination of the memory mechanism only make the problem harder? Or does this insight into how the brain regulates human affairs render Lorenz's bridges from chemistry to culture more understandable? The answers lie with the reader—not only in the perusal of this volume but in continued sampling of research to come. For my part, the journey has been, and is, as exciting and rewarding an adventure as any.

Karl H. Pribram

REFERENCES

1. Bagshaw, M. H., and Benzies, S. "Multiple measures of the orienting reaction to a simple non-reinforced stimulus after amygdalectomy." *Exp. Neurol.*, 20 (1968) 175–87.
2. Bagshaw, M. H., and Coppock, H. W. "GSR conditioning deficit in amygdalectomized monkeys." *Exp. Neurol.*, 20 (1968).
3. Bagshaw, M. H., Kimble, D. P., and Pribram, K. H. "The GSR of monkeys during orienting and habituation and after ablation of the amygdala, hippocampus and inferotemporal cortex." *Neuropsychologia*, 3 (1965) 111–19.
4. Bagshaw, M. H., and Pribram, J. D. "The effect of amygdalectomy on shock threshold of the monkey." *Exp. Neurol.*, 20 (1968).
5. Bateson, P. P. G. "Changes in chicks' responses to novel moving objects over the sensitive period for imprinting." *Anim. Behav.*, 12 (1964) 479–89.
6. Beach, F. A. "The descent of instinct." *Psychol. Rev.*, 62 (1955) 401–10.
7. Chomsky, N. "Formal properties of grammar," in Luce, R. D., Bush, R. R., and Galanter, E. (eds.), *Handbook of mathematical psychology*. New York: John Wiley and Sons, 1963, pp. 323–418.
8. Feigl, H. Mind-body: Not a pseudoproblem. In Hook, S. (ed.), *Dimensions of mind*. New York: Collier Books, 1960, pp. 33–44.
9. Greuninger, W., Kimble, D. P. Greuninger, J., and Levine, S. "GSR and corticosteroid response in monkeys with frontal ablations." *Neuropsychologia*, 3 (1965) 205–16.
10. Hinde, R. In Kimble, D. P. (ed.), *Experience and capacity* (Fourth Conference on Learning, Remembering and Forgetting). New York: New York Academy of Sciences, 1968.
11. Jakobsen, R. "Linguistic types of aphasia," in Carterette, E. C. (ed.), *Brain function, Vol. 4: speech, language and communication*. Los Angeles: University of California Press, 1966, pp. 67–91.
12. Kimble, D. P., Bagshaw, M. H., and Pribram, K. H." The GSR of monkeys during orienting and habituation after selective partial ablations of the cingulate and frontal cortex." *Neuropsychologia*, 3 (1965) 121–28.
13. Koestler, A. *The act of creation*. New York: Macmillan, 1964.
14. Koestler, A. *The ghost in the machine*. London: Hutchinson, 1967.
15. Mackay, D. M. "The epistemological problem for automata," in *Automata studies*. Princeton: Princeton University Press, 1956, pp. 235–52.
16. Pribram, K. H. "Concerning three rhinencephalic systems." *Electroencephalog. clin., Neurophysiol.*, 6 (1954) 708–09.
17. Pribram, K. H. "Toward a science of neuropsychology: method and data," in Patton, R. A. (ed.), *Current trends in psychology and the behavioral sciences*. Pittsburgh: University of Pittsburgh Press, 1954, pp. 115–42.
18. Pribram, K. H. "Reinforcement revisited: a structural view," in Jones,

M. (ed.), *Nebraska symposium on motivation*. Lincoln: University of Nebraska Press, 1963, pp. 113–59.

19. Pribram, K. H. "Proposal for a structural pragmatism: some neuropsychological considerations of problems in philosophy," in Wolman, B., and Nagle, E. (eds.), *Scientific psychology: principles and approaches*. New York: Basic Books, 1965, pp. 426–59.

20. Pribram, K. H. "Some dimensions of remembering: steps toward a neuropsychological model of memory," in Gaito, J. (ed.), *Macromolecules and behavior*. New York: Academic Press, 1966, pp. 165–87.

20a. Pribram, K. H. "A neuropsychological analysis of cerebral function: an informal progress resport of an experimental program." *Canadian Psychologist*, 7a (1966) 324–67.

21. Pribram, K. H. "The amnestic syndromes: disturbances in coding," in Waugh, N. (ed.), *The psychopathology of memory*. New York: Academic Press. In press.

22. Sokolov, E. N. "Neuronal models and the orienting reflex," in Brazier, M. A. B. (ed.), *The central nervous system and behavior*. New York: Josiah Macy, Jr. Foundation, 1960, pp. 187–276.

23. Thompson, R. F., and Spencer, W. A. "Habituation: a model phenomenon for the study of neuronal substrates of behavior." *Psych. Rev.*, 173 (1966) 16–43.

Innate Bases of Learning

by Konrad Z. Lorenz

Chapter 1. Life as a Knowledge Process

The greatest wonder of organic life is that it develops, in seeming defiance of all the laws of probability, from the simple to the complicated, from systems of lower to systems of higher harmony. However, infractions of the second law of thermodynamics simply do not occur, and, to achieve what it does, life is dependent on a gradient in the general, all-pervading flow of energy dissipation. Life lives on negative entropy. Any living species is a system that, very much like a prairie fire, greedily gathers energy and, in a positive feedback cycle, becomes able to gather the more energy, and to do it the quicker, the more it has already acquired.

What distinguishes the organism from this and other inorganic systems that also gather energy with a positive feedback is its special structure, which is molded by evolution to make probable the gain of energy and to exploit highly specific sources of energy. The process of this molding is called adaptation, and, thanks to the old Darwinian theory of natural selection and to the recent findings of biochemistry, we have a pretty good idea of the mechanisms achieving it. These insights not only justify but demand our asking a question unknown to physics and chemistry, the question, "what for?" This is not the *teleological* question concerning the ultimate aims and reasons of creation; it is just shorthand for the Darwinian question: "which is the function whose survival value exerted the selection pressure *causing* the species to evolve the characteristics that our question concerns?" Colin Pittendrigh suggested the term *teleonomy* for this kind of approach, hoping, by analogy, to divorce the concept of teleonomy from that of teleology as strictly as the concepts of astronomy and astrology are divided.

Every process of adapting a species to a certain given in its environment creates a new correspondence between the properties of the organism and those of its ambience. By virtue of its causation by selection, this change of the organism is one that increases the chances of its gaining energy—in other words, the probability of its survival. As it is the organism that changes in the process and not (or not to an appreciable degree) the environment, it is the former that develops a mold, in fact an image, of its natural environment. The fin of a fish reflects the properties of water, much as a horse's hoof reflects those of the hard, even ground of a steppe, or as an eye reflects the properties of light emanating from the sun.

In the parlance of information theory, it is correct to say that the process of adaptation increases the transinformation between the living system and its environment. However, the concept of information, as defined by information theorists, is formed in intentional disregard of the semantic level, consciously abstracting from the *meaning* that information concerning the environment may have for the organism in the interest of its survival. In the parlance of information theorists, it is impossible to speak of information *about* something. If I should confine myself to their terminology, I should have to forgo the important teleonomic aspects by which the biological concept of adaptation is determined. I shall, therefore, use the term "information" as it is used in common parlance and as it has been exactly defined by Bernhard Hassenstein (27). To define this concept in the terms of information theory, one might say that it is that kind of transinformation, between an organism and its environment, that is effected by the adaptation of the former to the latter. "Information" in common parlance means relevant, teleonomically organized information that has a meaning for the organism receiving or possessing it. In other words, it means *knowledge*. After long and somewhat bitter experience in the attempt to avoid misunderstanding, I shall speak of "information" when discussing cognitive functions of lower organisms, in order to avoid the reproach of ascribing to them human, conscious knowledge processes; and I shall speak of "knowledge" when dealing with the latter, in order not to countenance the pernicious error of equating knowledge with information in the sense of information theory. However, *the terms "information" and "knowledge" will be used synonymously* in this paper, both meaning relevant, teleonomically meaningful information. This will facilitate our approach to the all-important question of how, by creating in itself a progressively detailed image of its environment, the organism improves its chances of gaining energy and thereby surviving.

Any relevant information that the living system acquires concerning its environment improves its chances of increasing its capital of energy—in other words, its rate of propagation. Otto Rössler (73) was the first to formulate clearly that this positive feedback of energy-gain (which in itself is paying compound interest!) is linked with another cycle of positive feedback—that of information-gain—because the increased rate of propagation made possible by newly acquired information, in its turn, opens new possibilities for further gain of information, since among an increased progeny there also are increased chances of successful new mutations and recombinations of genes.

This twin cycle of positive feedback is characteristic of all that is alive, even of the "borrowed life," as Weidel (93) calls it, of a virus. Though true, it is misleading to say that evolution proceeds solely by random change and by weeding out the unfit. What life really does is conduct a closely knit and active enterprise, in which research and gain of capital collaborate to each other's advantage. The way a modern commercial concern continuously spends a certain proportion of its financial gains on further research is not a model, but a special case of this essential life process.

Thus viewed, life itself is a knowledge process. Donald Campbell, in his essay on "Evolutionary Epistemology" (8), argues that "the natural selection paradigm for such knowledge increments can be generalized to other epistemic activities, such as learning, thought and science." This is entirely true; in fact it is more or less what I propose to do here, though keeping in mind that life is, on the other side, an economical (one is tempted to say a commercial) process. It is the economic advantages of having more knowledge about environment that, since the very beginning of life, have exerted the selection pressure responsible for the progressively higher evolution of all knowledge-acquiring organic structures and functions. The general trend to more complex, "higher" organization, discernible in most evolutionary processes, is explicable on this principle; in my opinion, there is no need to assume a "demiurgic intelligence," as J. G. Bennett does in his *Dramatic Universe* (4). In fact, the levels of what, in living creatures, we call "lower" and "higher" organization cannot be better or more objectively defined than by the amount of relevant, teleonomically organized information they possess—and this applies as well to information contained in the genome as to that which an individual or, for that matter, a human culture has acquired in its life span. In our emotional estimate of the lower and the higher, we are also swayed by the potential ability of an organism to acquire new information, new knowledge.

Chapter 2. Origin of New Systemic Properties

A condensed survey of the physiological functions that have been evolved to acquire information can serve, simultaneously, to furnish impressive illustrations of how evolution in general proceeds and also to give us an unbiased view of the position that *learning* holds in the frame of reference of all the other knowledge processes.

In describing evolution, we are forever hampered by the fact that our vocabulary was created by a culture not yet aware of phylogeny. All the existing terms (development, evolution, *Entwicklung,* etc.) imply the unfolding of something preexisting, wrapped closely into a tight bundle, as a flower is in its bud. They are wonderfully expressive of what they are made to express, the processes of ontogeny, but they fail miserably to do justice to what is the essence of evolution, the coming-into-existence of *something entirely new, which simply did not exist before.* Even the German word *Schöpfung* implies etymologically that some preexisting substance is being ladled out of a great reservoir. Some philosophers of evolution, feeling the inadequacy of these words and groping for a new one, have rather pathetically hit on the term "emergence," which, worse than any other, suggests that an entirely preexisting thing, like a surfacing walrus, puts in an appearance above the water, which previously, to a literally superficial view, had seemed empty. Some theistic philosophers have coined, for the act of creating something entirely new, the term *fulguratio* "lightning," which implies that a creative stroke of lightning emanates from an all-knowing and eternal god. By an etymological fluke of coincidence, this term is more descriptive of what really happens than are all those aforementioned. To us, the thunderbolt of Zeus is an electric spark like any other, and the first thing that comes to our mind on seeing a spark at an unexpected point in a system is a short circuit. When the beginning and the end of a one-way chain of causation establish a connection, so that the end effect influences the first cause, a feedback cycle is established; in other words, the previously linear chain is transformed into a system possessing entirely new systemic properties.

Cybernetics and general systems theory have relieved the coming-into-existence of entirely new properties and functions of the odium of being a miracle. It is no miracle if a preexistent linear chain of causes and effects becomes closed into a circle, though the consequences may be truly epoch-making. One of the events that must

Konrad Z. Lorenz

have happened at the origin of life is the "fulguration" of a feedback cycle containing, in its chain of causation, one link whose effect on the next one bore a negative sign. If all the effects in a feedback circle are positive, they inevitably result in a snowballing of events that must sooner or later spell destruction to the system. The better the prairie fire burns, the sooner it burns itself out; the avalanche is of still shorter duration. If the great twin cycle of positive feedback of which I have spoken has not, as yet, led to a dangerous disturbance of the equilibrium between life and its environment, this is exclusively due to the overpowering odds against which life has to contend in a pitiless, inorganic universe. In fact, with man's increasing mastery of our planet, the positive feedback cycle under discussion may still lead to destruction.

No permanent equilibrium of an open system can be established in a variable environment without the aid of the negative, or self-regulating, feedback cycle. It is all but impossible to construe even a thought model of life without reference to this principle. Very probably, the first regulating cycles, the principle of homeostasis, must have come into being simultaneously with, or even before, the molecular structure performing self-reduplication and the trial-and-success procedure of gaining information. Indeed, the regulating cycle itself can be regarded as the most primitive (or at least the simplest) form of a knowledge process, because, as I shall explain later, it is able, quite by itself, to feed into the organic system relevant information about the environment.

The establishment of a regulating cycle is perhaps the most important, but it is far from being the only possible, "fulguration" of new systemic properties coming into existence at the integration of several independently preexisting subsystems into a functional whole of higher order. Hassenstein's (27) electric model, represented in Figure 1, is sufficient to explain the principle. The cryptic-sounding statement of gestalt psychologists that the whole is more than its parts contains exactly that amount of truth.

Very many and very different scientists and philosophers have recognized the role that this type of integration has played in evolution. Goethe defined "development" as differentiation of the parts and as their subordination to the whole. W. H. Thorpe (92), in his book *Science, Man and Morals,* has given many examples of how "unity out of diversity" constitutes a creative principle in evolution; L. von Bertalanffy, in his book on theoretical biology (5), has discussed it with great exactitude; and Teilhard de Chardin (88) has expressed it in the shortest and most poetic way in saying, *"Créer, c'est unir."*

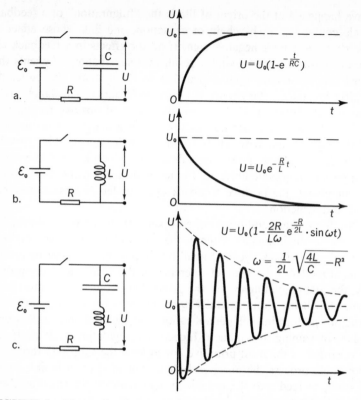

In the figure, the equations shown:

Circuit a:
$$U = U_0(1 - e^{-\frac{t}{RC}})$$

Circuit b:
$$U = U_0 e^{-\frac{R}{L}t}$$

Circuit c:
$$U = U_0\left(1 - \frac{2R}{L\omega} e^{\frac{-R}{2L}} \cdot \sin \omega t\right)$$

$$\omega = \frac{1}{2L}\sqrt{\frac{4L}{C} - R^2}$$

FIGURE 1 Three circuits, among them an oscillating cycle, illustrate the concept of "systemic property." The poles of a battery with the electromotoric power E_o and with the potential tension U_o are joined by a conduit. The resistance of the circuit, in ohms, is supposed to be concentrated in R. In circuit a, there is a condenser of the capacity C; in circuit b, an induction coil L; and in c, both condenser and coil together. At two terminals, the voltage U can be measured. The diagrams at the right represent the changes occurring in this tension after the circuit is shut. In a, the condenser is gradually charged up, until the tension U_o is reached. In b, the current, which at first had to overcome the resistance offered by the self-induction of the coil, increases until the current intensity determined by E_o and R is reached, the tension U then being theoretically zero—the resistance of the circuit being thought of as concentrated in R. In c, the closing of the switch causes an oscillation of decreasing amplitude. It is apparent that the systemic properties of c are not the result of an additive superposition of those characteristic of a and b. The diagram is valid for the following values: $c = 0,\ 7 \cdot 10^{-9}\ F;\ L = 10^{-3}$ $Hy;\ R = 10^3\ \Omega;\ \lambda \approx 1,\ 2 \cdot 10^{-6}$ sec. The last value also defines the temporal axis, which is identical for all three curves. (SOURCE: B. Hassenstein, *Kybernetik und biologische Forschung.* Frankfurt: Akad. Verlagsgesellschaft Athenaion, 1966. Calculations by E. U. v. Weizsäcker.)

Konrad Z. Lorenz

Although this unification, in itself, certainly implies an increase in the system's complication, it is in further evolution very often followed by processes of simplification. The progressive division of labor among the subsystems permits each of them to restrict its function to the part allotted to it in the context of the whole. Even our own brain cells, which together and as an integrated supracellular unit perform all the highest functions of the human mind, are vastly inferior to an amoeba or a paramecium in regard to the individual function performed by each of them and to the adaptive knowledge underlying these functions. This simplification of any primarily independent subsystem in the course of its integration into a superimposed greater unit is a phenomenon to be found on every level of evolution. In the psychosocial evolution of mankind in general and of science in particular, it poses a difficult problem. Progressive specialization has the unavoidable consequence that the individual "knows more and more about less and less"—as an old joke has it—until finally the specialist loses his bearings and ceases to know what place his special knowledge holds in the frame of reference of supraindividual, collectively human culture and science. I shall come back to the problem of the specialist's stultification in the chapter on pathology of knowledge and dehumanization.

A different type of simplification consists in arranging the relationship of the integrated parts in the most efficient manner. Anybody who has ever constructed some sort of apparatus for a certain purpose will have noticed that the moment one has finished the work, he is struck by the realization that there was a simpler way to do it. Causal concatenations as well as the exchange of information between the parts of a system may, in this manner, be simplified and, at the same time, rendered more efficient. When this type of improvement is achieved in social systems of human culture, we usually speak of "better organization."

It is, then, not too difficult to understand how, with the integration of preexisting subsystems into a functional whole, entirely new systemic properties come into existence. Also, it is easy to see that in consequence of this, there arises a one-sided stratification of lower and higher systems, a relationship that exists, not only between the subsystem and the whole, but between lower organisms and their more highly evolved descendants as well. This relationship is highly characteristic of the whole world of organisms. When examining a living system of a higher level, we must constantly keep in mind that it possesses, for the most part, all the systemic properties of the subsystems of which it is composed, and that none of the natural laws, down to those of chemistry and physics, which prevail in its components, suffer any infraction in the functioning of the whole. The one-sidedness of the relationship between the higher and the lower levels of integration lies in the fact that, conversely, the properties of the superimposed, integrated system are not contained in any of its components and are certainly not predictable on the basis of a knowledge that comprehends only the single subsystems and does not include the way in which they are put together. In other words, one must know the *structure* of the whole in order to understand its systemic properties.

In this sense, the higher system is not "reducible" to its elements, as Michael Polanyi (65, 66) has emphasized again and again. Living systems are not reducible to inorganic matter and processes; nor, for that matter, are man-made machines. However, this does not mean that the higher system cannot be *explained* and *understood* on the basis of a thorough level-by-level analysis of the components subsystems *and the structure* in which they are put together. Polanyi does not imply that supranatural vitalistic factors are necessary to explain the existence of living systems, and, to avoid this suspicion, I prefer to say that the higher system is not *deducible* from the knowledge of its subsystems. Though it is indeed *made* of them, this making consisted in a historically unique event of "fulguration," which is the evolutionary counterpart of what, in cultural development, we call an *invention*.

This stratified building of organisms has the important consequence that the living system, in the course of its evolutionary progress, *remains* what it was in respect to practically everything it was before, while simultaneously becoming something entirely different in respect to new, *additional* properties and faculties. Life processes are still physical and chemical processes and something very different besides; man is still an animal and a primate, while, additionally, he is everything he claims to be in his proudest moments. From their ontological aspects, all these facts have been recognized with superlative clarity by the German philosopher Nicolai Hartmann (24, 25, 26). A number of definitely nonvitalistic biologists—some of whom, I am quite sure, never have read Hartmann—have said the same, emphasizing that living beings comprise a whole series of levels, each of which we must study in terms of its own distinctive conceptions without for a moment forgetting its relationship to the levels below it.

An amazing number of scientists, otherwise biologically minded people among them, seem unable to grasp the fact that the stratified structure of the whole world of organisms absolutely forbids the conceptualization of living systems or life processes in terms of "disjunctive"—that is to say, mutually exclusive—concepts. It is nonsense to oppose to each other "animal" and "man," "nature" and "culture," "innate programming" and "learning," as if the old logical diagram of alpha and nonalpha were applicable to them. Man, as I have just said, is still an animal; human nature persists in and is the basis of culture; and all learning is very specifically innately programmed. The fallacy of disjunctive conceptualization is characteristic of philosophical anthropologists of a certain type and has given rise to endless and fruitless discussions of the question, "in what way is man different from other living creatures?" These authors fail to understand that *any* "fulguration" of a new systemic property, however small and unimportant, produces a difference that cannot by any effort of conceptualization be described as a difference only in degree. Our system c in Figure 1 is indubitably different in kind, not only in degree, from systems a and b. Failing to grasp the principle of stratified and integrated levels, and interested only in the properties by which man is distinctly set off from and raised above "the animal," philosophers of this type remain blissfully ignorant of the fact that differences at least as fundamental as those between chimpanzee and man are to be found anywhere, between any two steps in the evolutionary ladder. Whenever one of these people used the disjunctive concepts of "man" and "the animal," my teacher Oskar Heinroth very kindly interrupted with the question: "Excuse me, please. When you speak of the animal, are you thinking of an amoeba or of a chimpanzee?"

An example of the fallacy under discussion being spun out to its last bitter consequences is furnished by Mortimer J. Adler's book *The Difference of Man and the Difference It Makes* (1). Understanding neither that differences "in kind," however great and trenchant, do not contradict the continuity of life, nor that speciation can be explained in a natural way, the author unavoidably arrives at the conclusion that man is radically different in kind from other animals, and that, besides possessing the well-known peculiarities of conceptual thought and syntactic language, he possesses "contra-causal freedom of choice by virtue of having a nonphysical or immaterial factor in his make-up, a factor that has a certain measure of autonomy and causal efficacy."

The analogous, but inverse, fallacy lies in ascribing to the lower and simpler subsystems or ancestral forms systemic properties that come into existence only at a specific, higher level of integration. A typical example of this error is the persistent attempt of psychologists and even ethologists to find adaptive modifiability through learning, not only in lower animals that simply do not learn, but worse, in those subsystems that, in higher organisms, not only are not programmed to learn but are specifically programmed to be resistant to any modification. To a psychologist, most of whose knowledge of behavior stems from the study of human beings or mammals, and who, furthermore, was brought up in the firm conviction that the conditioned response is a simple and elementary mechanism of behavior, it may seem natural to assume that at least oriments or phylogenetical precursors of conditioning must be discernible in protozoa and the lowest invertebrates. This erroneous assumption accounts for the almost pathetic persistence with which many scientists have tried to demonstrate true conditioning in these animals and also for the great number of self-deceptions that occurred in this research.

Chapter 3. Cognitive Processes Not Involving Learning

Like all life processes, the mechanisms gathering and storing information are stratified, many layered, and closely interwoven. Even a preliminary attempt to analyze their relationship may be helpful in clearing away a number of current conceptual confusions. In the following survey of simpler and of more complicated examples of these mechanisms and of their functions, I want to emphasize three points that, in fact, already emerge from what has been said in the preceding pages.

First: A new and more complex function very often, if not always, arises from the integration of several preexisting simpler ones, which, so far from disappearing or losing their importance, persist as indispensable parts of the new systemic whole.

Second: Simpler systems are perfectly able to function on their own and indeed do so in lower organisms, which otherwise could not live or produce more highly organized descendants.

Third: It is entirely in vain to search, in the independent functioning of simple and primitive mechanisms, for traces or oriments of those systemic properties that come into existence only after these mechanisms have been integrated into a system of higher order.

The basic process of acquiring and storing information is that performed by the chain molecules of DNA and RNA in the genome. I need not bother to explain its mechanism. No limit is known to the quantity of information it can acquire and retain; it by far surpasses all that a human culture, with all its libraries, can achieve in that respect. No organic structure, including that of the human brain, has been devised by any other method than the trial-and-success procedure of the genome. It has not lost any of its importance on the way from the first beginnings of life to the greatest achievements of humanity.

Its enormous range and capability notwithstanding, the trial-and-success procedure employed by the genome to gather information does not seem able, by itself, to keep up a state of adaptedness that is continuous enough to guarantee survival. The obvious reason for this is that it cannot cope with *quick* changes in the environment. It cannot "know" about the success of one of its experiments until at least one generation has lived its life, and it can achieve adaptation only to such environmental givens as are present, with a sufficient statistical constancy, over comparatively long periods of time. In the parlance of biocybernetics, the duration of one generation is the "dead time" that has to elapse before the mechanism under discussion even begins to register an input.

THE REGULATING FEEDBACK CYCLE

All mechanisms that *bridge* this dead time by acquiring and exploiting information at shorter notice are dependent on the functioning of structures programmed by the trial-and-success method of the genome. This is true of the simple regulating feedback cycle as well as of the highest processes of knowledge. We are faced with the hen-and-egg problem: how could a genome come to exist without a negative feedback cycle, and vice versa?

An organism's recovery of its inner equilibrium after a disturbance caused by a change in its environment indicates that information concerning the quality and the quantity of the change has been fed into the living system. If an organism accelerates its breathing rate in a medium of lowered oxygen concentration, if it discontinues ingesting food in an ambience in which food abounds, this means that the organic system possesses information, not only concerning its own present and specific demands, but concerning the supply that the environment is offering at the moment.

Regulating feedback cycles exist in all degrees of complication, ranging from simple homeostasis that functions on a "merely chemical" level up to the most complicated processes in which sensory and behavior functions play a part.

Like many other mechanisms by which the individual is enabled to get instant information about its environment, that of regulating cycles can function again and again without any change of its underlying genetically programmed machinery. In other words, the structural substratum of the function remains the same. The instant information is exploited at once *but not stored* in any way. In fact, it is essential to the survival value of these mechanisms that their function can be repeated an unlimited number of times, keeping the organism adapted to quick environmental changes that can be expected to be reversed almost at once.

IRRITABILITY

All higher processes by which instant information is fed into and acted upon by the organism are dependent on its ability to respond to stimuli. "Irritability," as it has been called, is closely associated with motility, at least in its primitive forms. It is only by the division of labor between the nerve cell and the muscle that, in higher metazoa, irritability and motility have become divorced. We do not know of any organism that is able to move and yet is devoid of irritability. In principle, this is not impossible, since locomotion alone, without any input of instant information, could well be able to increase the organism's chances of gaining energy. On the whole, however, the faculty to respond to stimuli is mostly combined with that of locomotion. One is tempted to think that the primary and still most important function of both is to let the organism run away from dangerous surroundings, unless we think of a motility still simpler than locomotion—that of the organism contracting to a minimum space, offering the smallest possible surface of thickened and corrugated skin to the external world. The third type of response to stimuli is, of course, secretion. In all these cases, some overt response of obvious survival value proves that the organism has received instant information about a relevant given in its environment. It is only in the case of organisms with a highly complex central nervous system that stimulation can be received and its information content exploited and stored, while no direct response is immediately observable.

Otto Rössler (73) has proposed to define as behavior any process in which the information about the biological success of an activity is fed back into the living system by any way other than the selective effect on the genome. In my opinion, this definition is too widely inclusive, as it would embrace all gaining of information and energy achieved, in the way just described, by simple cycles of negative feedback and also by modification, of which I shall speak later. I would propose to confine the term "behavior" to all those activities in which motility and irritability combine their functions in gaining information and thereby increase the probability of an immediate energy gain.

PSEUDOPOD RESPONSE

Curiously enough, the most primitive response to stimuli that we know, that of the amoeboid cell, is directed in space, either at the stimulus or away from it. A similar faculty to aim a response in one particular direction of three-dimensional space does not appear again in the realm of organisms until a much higher level is reached; functionally, the directional response of amoeboid cells is analogous to what Kühn (48) calls a topotaxis, which involves the functions of a central nervous system and complicated sense organs. Yet the response simply consists in the ectoplasm lowering its surface tension wherever a "beneficial" stimulus impinges and, conversely, tightening it wherever a noxious one does. Pressure then forces the protoplasm in the direction of lowest resistance, causing the extrusion of a pseudopod toward a localized positive stimulus or contracting and retracting the body surface away from a negative one. Both these processes have been successfully simulated in nonliving models. However, having familiarized myself with the behavior of an amoeba, I believe this explanation to be too simple. I think I can see in direct observation that the ectoplasm of an amoeba possesses the faculty of changing, at a moment's notice, from gel to sol and back again. Though I cannot find any reference,* I am sure that this is well known to cytologists. What appears on superficial observation to be a mere increase of surface tension really is a quick jelling immediately below the surface, which is always covered with a skin of gelated protoplasm except where it sticks to a solid body, such as food particles. In gelating, the plasm contracts slightly, thus producing effects similar to those of an increase in surface tension. Furthermore, I do not

---

* Herbert Fischer has kindly brought to my attention the chapter on amoeboid movement in L. V. Heilbrunn, *An Outline of General Physiology,* in which an article by Mast, *Journ. Morph. and Physiol.,* 41 (1926) 347, is cited. On the basis of thorough investigations, Mast arrives at identical conclusions.

believe that the streaming of protoplasm is wholly passive. Identical currents of plasm occur in plant cells that are enclosed in a cellulose capsule and in which no change of external pressure explains the movement.

When a comparatively simple motor pattern can be turned to many different uses, the main part of the innate information necessarily is residing in the releasing mechanism that determines where and when the pattern is used to the organism's advantage. The amoeboid cell's one motor pattern serves locomotion, feeding, and escaping and must, correspondingly, be releasable in many different ways, causing the organism to move into favorable conditions (in the case of free amoebae actually effecting habitat selection), making it retract and flee from noxious stimuli and "effusively" run toward promising ones. Whoever has watched an amoeba in near-natural surroundings will have been surprised at the seeming "intelligence" of its behavior—in other words, at the wealth of innate and environmental information on which it acts.

KINESIS

The Proteus-like ability of the amoeboid cell to sprout a functional front, in whatever direction of space the organism is required to move, makes it superfluous for the cell to possess any other spatial guiding mechanisms. The loss of this capability is the price to be paid by evolution for the differentiation of any solid body structure. Only a few radially symmetrical metazoa are able to move, at least in one plane, in whatever direction an impinging stimulus makes desirable. If the octopods seem to have conquered the limitations imposed by structure, their apparent freedom of moving, amoeba-like, in any direction they want to is based not on the absence of structure, but on a supreme mastery of it.

All organisms that developed, in the interest of locomotion, structures stiffening and streamlining the body along one longitudinal axis need mechanisms that collect instant information concerning the desirability of spatial directions and steer the animals accordingly. The acquisition of instant information is, in these cases too, the function of a phylogenetically evolved machinery that *does not undergo any modification* in the process. The reaction therefore remains the same after any number of repetitions. The simplest orienting mechanism of this type is what Fraenkel and Gunn (16) have termed a kinesis. It consists simply in speeding up a randomly moving organism whenever conditions are noxious and slowing it down when they are beneficial. The effect is comparable to that which, though in

Konrad Z. Lorenz

this case most undesirably, a bad stretch of road has on automobiles. The enforced slowing down causes the traveling cars to come close together, their distance being inversely proportional to their speed. Without influencing the direction of locomotion, kinesis thus causes the organisms to spend more time in circumstances promising a gain of energy than in those that do not. This effect is increased if the organisms, as many animals do, move not in a straight line but in a zig-zag and if, on reaching a favorable environment, they increase the angles of their wavering to and fro. This response, called "klino-kinesis" by Fraenkel and Gunn, is by no means confined to protozoa and lower invertebrates but occurs in higher animals as well, for instance in grazing mammals and in humans picking mushrooms. However, in the phylogeny of behavior, kinesis seems to have been the first mechanism by which a nonamoeboid organism became able to receive and exploit spatially orienting information.

PHOBIC RESPONSE

A further advance in the evolution of information-gaining organizations is represented by what Alfred Kühn (48) called the phobic response. It is characterized by its inability to take into account the direction in which the moving organism hits upon a noxious stimulus situation. If the organism moves along a gradient of "improving" environmental conditions, it shows no response—unless, as often happens, a kinesis is at work simultaneously. However, on meeting a gradient along which conditions deteriorate, or on running up against a strongly noxious stimulus, the animal stops, goes into reverse, and, after backing up a certain distance, resumes its forward movement in an altered direction. The alteration of its course is achieved by a turning behavior *that bears no direct relation to the direction from which the releasing stimulation impinged.* In some protozoa, on strong stimulation, the turn may chance to comprise exactly 360° so that the organism, on starting to move forward again, runs into the releasing stimulus a second time and has to repeat its performance. Thus, while imparting directional information lacking in the kineses, one phobic response can tell the organism only what direction *not* to take, leaving it to a process of elimination to determine which course is free of noxious stimuli. Of course, the information concerning which stimuli are noxious and which beneficial is phylogenetically acquired and may be coded in very simple terms. Some ciliates "prefer" a certain concentration of H-ions, giving a phobic response when getting out of it. Statistically, this acidity signals the presence of putrescent organic matter and bacteria on which the animals feed. These organisms do not possess any information that there are any acids other than CO_2 and get caught in a death trap if, for instance, a drop of oxalic acid is offered.

TAXES

On a much higher level, in respect to the amount of information gained as well as to the complication of physiological mechanisms involved, we find the type of orienting behavior that Kühn has termed *taxes,* or *tropic reactions.* Since the publication of his now classic book *Die Orientierung der Tiere im Raum* (48), a vast amount of research has been done on the subject, and the biocybernetical approach of H. Mittelstaedt (61, 37) and his school has helped us understand the mechanisms involved in the more subtle process of orientation in space. I need not attempt to give a survey of all this work; it is sufficient for my present purpose to say that all these mechanisms, from the simplest "tropotactic" response of a planarian that finds its prey by turning toward an olfactory stimulus until receptors on both sides of its head receive an equilibrated amount of stimulation, to the highly complicated feedback circles enabling a mantis to strike at a fly with great precision, one and all cause the organism to turn directly into that direction in space that promises the greatest probability of gaining and/or preserving energy. In other words, *the angle at which the animal turns is directly determined by the angle between the impinging stimulus and the longitudinal axis of the organism.* While the phobic response tells the organism only that one particular direction in space is "bad," the tropic response conveys the information as to which one, among all the innumerable directions in space that it could choose to take, is the most promising.

If one compares the efficiency of the three principles of spatial orientation—kinesis, phobic response, and taxis—not only direct observation, but also an assessment of the information imparted by each, reveals the fact that the phobic response conveys a multiple of the instant information furnished by kinesis and that taxes surpass both of these by another multiple.

RELEASING MECHANISMS AND FIXED MOTOR PATTERNS

In the preceding sections on the pseudopod response of the amoeboid cell, on kinesis, and on phobic responses, I have already emphasized the fact that a great amount of specific information concerning certain relevant conditions prevailing at the moment in the environment is

Konrad Z. Lorenz

fed into the organism by the *selective* function of the releasing mechanisms. It is the *afferent* part of what Ivan Pavlov (63) called an unconditioned reflex that acts like a filter, permitting only very specific kinds of stimulation to take effect. This function has also been likened to that of a lock that can be opened only by a specifically structured key—hence the term "key stimulus."

In protozoa and lower metazoa, in which the inventory of possible behavior patterns is limited and consists mainly of going away from danger and toward situations promising energy gain, no very high demands are made on the selectivity of the releasing mechanism. Though the faculty of the amoeba to know "good" from "bad" is remarkable, it is less so in some ciliates, as in paramecium, which works on the hypothesis that all acids of a certain concentration are "good," poisonous ones included. Also, it is to be supposed that all releasing mechanisms in protozoa act on a chemical basis rather than on the principle of stimulus conduction found in organisms with a centralized nervous system.

Organisms of the latter type, particularly those with an articulated skeleton—arthropods and vertebrates—invariably possess elaborate and complicated motor patterns whose coordination is entirely blueprinted in the genome. Their coordination is, in most cases, achieved without proprioceptors, as E. von Holst (32) has shown in his classic papers on central coordination, while their orientation in space is accomplished by an elaborate apparatus of multiple taxes. Quite lately, E. Taub and A. J. Berman (87) have shown that even in primates the coordination of fixed motor patterns is largely independent of proprioceptors. The guidance by afferent controls is not by any means an indispensable prerequisite for the performance of fixed motor patterns, as is proved by the occurrence of so-called vacuum activities, in which a whole pattern is performed without the object toward which it is normally oriented. A fixed motor pattern is, in many cases, an extremely specialized tool that can be applied to advantage only in one particular situation. The wonderful coordination with which a quelea weaver attaches the first grass fibers of its nest to a branch can be used for absolutely nothing except this function. Since a species may possess quite a number of equally specialized motor patterns, it is of the greatest importance that the organism possess rather detailed innate information determining which pattern ought to be performed in what situation. Furthermore, quite a number of behavior patterns of very different functions can be released by the same sense organs, and the performance of a pattern in the wrong place may be disastrous. If a baby apistogramma were to approach a fish other than its mother in its specific schooling-and-following behavior, this would spell destruction just as surely as if it should respond to its mother with an all-out escape response.

In such cases, the selective filtering of stimuli must obviously be done by the central nervous system. We have little information as yet as to how it is done, though the work of Letvin and others on the retina of frogs and fishes has given us some idea of the mechanisms achieving this function. (The retina, incidentally *is* part of the central nervous system in vertebrates.) All evidence agrees with the assumption that it is *configurations* of stimuli that are responded to selectively. What has been termed "key stimulus" in ethological literature is, in many cases, such a specifically effective configuration, and this not quite precise expression has led to misunderstandings with stimulus physiologists. Much experimental work has been done by ethologists in investigating the releasing mechanisms, and in many cases the innate information contained in them has been analyzed with all desirable precision—for instance, in the Kuenzers' study (47) of the young of apistogramma and nannacara. For a general survey of all these investigations I recommend W. Schleidt's review in the *Fortschritte Zoologie,* 1964 (76).

Observing the function of releasing mechanisms under natural conditions, one is tempted to overassess the amount and the specificity of innate information contained in them. If one observes a tame hand-reared young raven, which up to that moment has never paid any attention to living prey, make a determined dash at the one sick jackdaw among dozens of healthy ones and kill it skillfully with one well-aimed blow at the back of its skull, one is amazed at the amount of innate knowledge underlying this behavior. The bird seems to know that it could not prey on healthy jackdaws; it seems to recognize the symptoms of illness, to conclude that they promise success to an attack, and to know exactly how and where to launch the attack. On close examination, the innate information underlying all this complicated sequence of behavior boils down to very few and simple, if important, data. The raven, like many birds of prey and also many carnivores, possesses a mechanism that releases motor patterns of prey-catching and responds to irregularities in the prey's locomotor actions. A slight stumbling, an irregularity of wing-beat, or the like elicits a predatory attack with the mechanical predictability of a reflex, as trainers of big carnivores have learned to their cost. An analogous response in hawks and falcons is used by falconers in the construction of the "lure." Furthermore, the raven's fixed motor pattern of grasping with both feet and delivering a fearful blow of the bill exactly between them is supplemented by a built-in orienting mechanism that directs it at the back of the prey's head. It is characteristic of all releasing mechanisms that the innate information contained in them is coded in a surprisingly simple and, at the same time, most effective way. For example, the stinging response of the common tick, *Ixodes rhizinus,* is released by any object having a temperature of roughly 37°C and smelling of butyric acid. Simple though these key stimuli are, it is difficult to visualize a natural situation in which the response could be elicited by anything except the animal's adequate host, a mammal. Similarly, the baby apistogramma will follow any object that shows black and yellow markings roughly corresponding to that of the mother and that performs jerking movements of a certain frequency and amplitude; the male stickleback will fight any simple dummy that has a red undersurface; the jackdaw will attack any living creature carrying something black and dangling; and so on.

In spite of the simplicity of its coding, the instant information that the releasing mechanism conveys about a present, relevant given in the animal's environment is reliable enough to permit a rigid linking of the receptor and the effector patterns, even in those cases in which the pattern consists in a very specific fixed motor pattern that would be not only useless but even detrimental in any but the adequate situation for which it is phylogenetically programmed.

The combination of a releasing mechanism with a fixed motor pattern released by it must develop a very great survival value if one is to judge by the frequency with which it is found in higher animals. Indeed, it is so common that it was regarded as the prototype of instinctive activity by O. and M. Heinroth (28). They avoided definitions on principle, but all their examples of what they called *angeborene Triebhandlungen* are combinations of unlearned releasing mechanisms and fixed motor patterns. A tremendous amount of phylogenetically acquired information can be packed into this type of program, because a few selective mechanisms acquiring instant information guarantee the motor patterns being performed at the right time and at the right place.

The realization of the fact that at least three intrinsically different sorts of mechanisms—taxes, releasing mechanisms, and fixed motor patterns—worked together as subsystems in one *Triebhandlung* led to further analysis. I discovered independently what Wallace Craig (10) had known for many years—namely, that the threshold of key stimuli is dependent on the discharge of the fixed pattern, being lowered whenever it had not been realized for some time and raised after it had. Craig also had clearly realized what I had not—that the internal buildup of the motor pattern does, in this manner, affect not only the thresholds of key stimuli but the organism as a whole, causing a general state of unrest and making the animal move about, thus increasing the probability of its meeting the releasing stimulus situation. In its simplest form, this "appetitive behavior," as Craig called it, is essentially the same as a kinesis.

Tinbergen and Baerends were the first to show that the three elementary subsystems—appetitive behavior, releasing mechanism, and fixed motor pattern—are very often linked together in other and more complicated sequences. An initiating appetitive behavior achieves a stimulus situation that, instead of immediately releasing the terminating motor pattern, causes a switch of appetitive behavior that now is directed at another equally specific stimulus situation. Such links may follow each other in considerable number, and the chain of events may branch out, because, on reaching a certain situation, the animal develops an equal readiness for several subsequent activities, and which of them is released depends on further key stimuli. G. P. Baerends, in his classic work on the digger wasp *ammophila* (2), has achieved a deeply searching analysis of this hierarchical organization of instinctive behavior.

Hierarchically organized chains of appetitive behavior, releasing mechanisms, and fixed motor patterns are far more adaptable to present environmental circumstances than are simpler arrangements, for the obvious reason that every one of the multiple releasing mechanisms and of the built-in orienting mechanisms feeds its own instant information into the organism. The hierarchical organization permits an enormous amount of innate information to be packed into a program without incurring the disadvantage of the rigidity characteristic of any single, specialized fixed motor pattern. The studies of P. Leyhausen (50) have shown that in higher mammals such as cats, this type of organization can account for an enormous plasticity of behavior, and also that it persists unchanged even if it is modified, overlaid, or even completely hidden by learned forms of behavior.

Although, as I shall explain in the next chapter, the epoch-making new feedback of success or error that underlies all true learning very probably originated in rather complicated and highly integrated systems involving appetitive behavior, releasing mechanisms, and fixed motor patterns, it would be a grave error to assume that their function is dependent on any form of adaptive modification by learning. In fact, we know that it is not; there are many animals in which such systems function only once in the individual's life, so that no opportunity of learning by experience ever arises. The work of the Peckhams (64) and of Jocelyn Crane (11) on spiders, and that of Ernest Reese (69, 70) on hermit and coconut crabs, provides many convincing proofs of this fact. Even in higher animals, in which these systems are typically improved upon by experience, they must be able to function without this help at least enough so that the success essential to successful conditioning is reached after not too many unsuccessful attempts.

Chapter 4. Learning

All the procedures hitherto discussed, by which the organism acquires instant information about conditions prevailing in its environment, are the functions of physiological mechanisms that can repeat their performance any number of times *without undergoing any change, least of all any adaptive change, of their inner machinery.* The only way in which such a change can be wrought is the devious route of feeding back, to the genome of the species, whatever biological success a mutation or recombination of genes may have achieved by altering the machinery of behavior.

In spite of the fact that such machinery can be changed, as organs can, only by the procedures of evolution, its function can achieve an amazing adaptability to the circumstances prevailing, at the moment, in the organism's environment. A complicated behavior system consisting of several hierarchically organized appetences, releasing mechanisms, and fixed motor patterns (p. 32), guided in space by innumerable built-in orienting mechanisms including most complicated feedback organizations (p. 27), commands a wealth of cognitive processes that gather information and enable the organism to act on it instantaneously. As M. Konishi (44) has pointed out, it is a fundamental error to equate "unlearned" or "phylogenetically programmed" with "stereotyped." In fact, the fixed motor pattern is the only subsystem of phylogenetically programmed behavior to which the attribute "stereotyped" can be applied with any justification.

ADAPTIVE MODIFICATION

There is, however, one type of cognitive process that is entirely different, physiologically, from all those based on the repeatable function of phylogenetically programmed mechanisms and must, therefore, be strictly distinguished from the latter. This process is based on changes in the organism's structure caused, during its ontogeny, by environmental influences. Such a change is called a *modification.*

Modification in itself is a ubiquitous phenomenon; practically any permanent change in an organism's environment, provided it is not immediately lethal, will cause some modification or other, at least in young and growing individuals. But modifications of this kind are very far from being necessarily adaptive; indeed, their chance of being so is no greater than that of any random mutation or recombination of genes, and this, as geneticists assure us, is extremely small. If a modification is the regular response to a certain environmental change and is, at the same time, clearly *adaptive to* this particular influence, we are safe in assuming that this modifiability is "selected for"—in other words, that it is the function of a built-in mechanism, already programmed by the trial-and-success procedure of the genome. Such an "open program," as Ernst Mayr (60) called it, has for its prerequisite, not less, but much more genetically acquired information. This seeming paradox might well be illustrated by a parable. A prefabricated house can be erected only on a perfectly level and hard basis, such as the terrasses of "pa hoe hoe" lava in Hawaii, on which part of Hilo is built. The necessity to adapt an otherwise similar building to a site of irregular structure and composition demands, on the part of the architect, methods of acquiring much additional information concerning the ground, as well as the learned knowledge of how to deal with it adequately in adapting the understructure of the house to its substratum. Any form of regularly adaptive modifiability—like that of a plant stretching toward the light when there is too little of it, and thus obtaining sufficient illumination, or that of a mammal's fur growing longer in a cold climate—necessarily presupposes a genetical program so cleverly constructed by phylogeny that it can realize different adaptive possibilities according to different information coming from the environment. Thus, adaptive modification is a truly cognitive process.

This kind of open program, which is able to react adaptively to different environmental inputs, is familiar to the biologist from the results of experimental embryology. The embryo's ectoderm possesses the prospective potency (*prospektive Potenz,* Spemann) of forming a neural tube and a brain, or the lens of an eye, or simple skin; it possesses all the innate information necessary to build any of these very different structures. Which of them it realizes is dependent on the input it receives from its tissue environment. It builds a neural tube when there is a chorda dorsalis beneath it, a lens when there is an eye bladder, and simple skin when it is not thus specifically influenced. The process of calling forth, by a specific environmental influence, the realization of that part of an open program that is adaptive (or, in other words, phylogenetically constructed to fit that particular influence) is called *induction* by experimental embryologists. For our consideration of cognitive processes, it is immaterial whether the input determining the realization of such an adaptively modifiable open program comes from another subsystem pertaining to the same organism or from an environmental circumstance to whose regular occurrence the species is phylogenetically adapted. In other words, all adaptive modification is *essentially identical with induction*.

Adaptive modification is found in the lowest organisms. In some bacteria with organellae serving the intake of certain chemicals—for instance, phosphorus—are increased in number when the phosphorus concentration of the medium is lowered. It takes the cell some time to grow these contrivances; the compensatory response to the dearth of phosphorus is by no means instantaneous. Conversely, if the phosphorus content of the culture medium is suddenly brought back to normal, the organism will actually "overeat" until it has again dismantled the surplus organellae. The cognitive function of this adaptive modification in a low organism is closely akin to that of a simple feedback cycle, which, as I have explained (pp. 23–24), procures for the organism information about the availability (one might say the market situation) of certain substances.

In all adaptive modification, it is *the machinery* on which the organism's way of responding is dependent that is altered by what may be called loosely "individual experience." In respect to the time it requires to gather information, adaptive modification is intermediate between the cognitive procedure of the genome and all the processes gaining instant information. Unlike the latter, it is able to *store* knowledge over varying periods. Some processes of adaptive modifications, such as those of embryonic induction, are irreversible for the life span of the individual; some, such as those in our example of the bacterium, are reversible within a comparatively short time; some are between these two extremes. In any case, adaptive modification combines the extremely valuable faculties of *acquiring* information in a comparatively short time and of *storing* it during time lapses of varying size order. Neither the cognitive function of the genome, nor that of the mechanisms acquiring (but not storing!) instant information, is able to perform *both* of these functions!

The more complicated a biological system, the less likely it is that a random modification will effect anything but disintegration. In the whole world, there is hardly a system more complicated than the central nervous organization underlying the behavior of a higher animal. One of the greatest achievements of phylogeny is to have constructed systems of this sort in such a way that they are still adaptively modifiable by an input occurring during the individual's life. There never was a greater error in the history of science than the empiricist philosophers' belief that the human mind, before any experience, was a *tabula rasa,* a blank, unless it is the reciprocal, but intrinsically identical, assumption of nonbiological psychologists that "learning" must, as a matter of course, "enter into" any physiological behavior processes whatever. The worst aspect of both these reciprocal errors is that they obscure the central problem of learning—the question: how does learning come to be adaptive?

TYPES OF LEARNING OTHER THAN CONDITIONING

In *Evolution and Modification of Behavior* (55), I gave an intentionally all-embracing definition of learning, equating it with any adaptive modification of behavior. Also, I have tried to give a survey of many different types of modifiability of behavior, laying more stress on those that do not involve conditioning than on those that do. To avoid repetition as far as possible, I shall do the opposite here, discussing only three examples of learning other than conditioning.

Motor Facilitation by Exercise. The machinery of a new car is undoubtedly modified in an adaptive way by the process known as "breaking in." Something similar occurs with some motor patterns of young animals. Wells (97) has shown that in the young of the common squid, *Sepia officinalis,* the prey-catching patterns, though not formally different from those of the experienced animal, are noticeably slower and less sure of their aim. In young domestic chickens, E. Hess (30) has demonstrated a similar process in the development of food-pecking, which becomes considerably more exact with exercise. The pecking becomes surer of its aim, even if the aim is quite wrong. When Hess fitted newly hatched chicks with prism goggles shifting the image of the food particles sideways, the birds never learned to compensate for this misleading shift, but the straying of the hits round the point at which they erroneously aimed diminished rapidly with "exercise." This proves that actual success in the hitting and taking up of food plays no role in rendering this motor pattern more exact.

Habituation. It is an extremely common phenomenon that stimulus situations that release a response at their first occurrence gradually cease to do so after a number of repetitions. This waning of the response is *not* influenced by whether or not the stimulus situation, to which the animal gets habituated, is followed by a reinforcing stimulus. Though superficially similar to fatigue (and perhaps evolved out of fatigue of specific receptor mechanisms), habituation has its survival value in *preventing* fatigue on the motor side of the response. This is accomplished by the *specificity* of habituation to a certain stimulus only. A hydra primarily contracts in response to a great number of stimuli—to a touch, to being passively moved in the water, to a concussion of the substratum, and so on. A hydra sitting in running water gets habituated to being moved to and fro by the current, while its threshold to all other contraction-eliciting stimuli is *not* changed. In other words, the motor side of the response is not affected; habituation is *stimulus-specific desensitization.*

In higher animals, this specificity can be so elaborate and so selective that it is impossible to explain without resorting to gestalt perception as an explanation. Wildfowl normally react to anything furry moving along the bank of their lake by a combination of escape and cautious mobbing, which is obviously a good defense against foxes and similar predators. Our birds in Seewiesen became specifically habituated not to chow dogs, which primarily represent supernormal key stimulation for the response, but to our individual chows; they mobbed those of a chance visitor as intensely as they would a fox. It is only in the context of the complex gestalt perception of the well-known individual dog that the key stimuli furry, red, and moving along the water's edge lose their effectiveness. Even when the known dog appears in an unaccustomed corner of the lake, there may be a recrudescence of the reaction.

In the process of habituation, an innate releasing mechanism becomes associated with the individually acquired perception of a gestalt in such a manner that the primarily releasing key stimuli cease to be effective, provided that they are being received together with and in the context of the complex configuration of very many stimuli characteristic of that particular acquired gestalt. In contexts that are different from this, the key stimuli retain their original effectiveness. Very often a slight change in the situation, scarcely perceptible to the human observer, causes the habituation of an animal to break down completely, as in the example of the *Anatidae* mobbing the well-known dog when it appears in an unaccustomed place.

This very specific form of habituation confronts us with one great riddle. We know quite a number of innate responses that, in spite of their obvious survival value, wane rapidly if released a number of times in quick succession, as W. Schleidt (75) has shown in the escape reaction released in turkeys by flying predators and as R. Hinde (31) has demonstrated in the owl-mobbing response of the chaffinch. In the latter case, the response did not regain its original intensity even after a rest period of several months, nor did the strongest possible reinforcement—letting the subject be chased by a real owl—counteract the desensitization. It is hard to believe that mechanisms so elaborately adapted by phylogeny are made to function only once or twice, losing most of their efficacy after that. There must be something we miss in our experiments—perhaps only that we ruin the response by impatiently releasing it too often in too short a time, or that we do not change in our laboratory experiments the concomitant stimulus situation often enough.

Sensitization of Avoidance Responses.   There is a type of learning process generally subsumed under the conception of conditioning that I propose to treat as something entirely different, because it is not necessary to assume, for its explanation, the complicated feedback apparatus reporting success or failure of which I shall speak in Chapter 5.

A key stimulus eliciting escape reactions of the utmost intensity is associated, after very few repetitions (often after a single exposure), with the concomitant or immediately preceding stimulus situation. In low invertebrates, the effects of this process grade from mere sensitization by these "conditioned" stimuli to their complete releasing of the escape response without the help of the primarily eliciting unconditioned stimulus. All the "conditioning" hitherto demonstrated in animals not possessing an integrated central nervous system is of this type; to the best of my knowledge, no case of conditioning by reinforcement (which would involve the feedback cycle, to be discussed later) has been proved below the level of annelid worms.

In higher vertebrates, this kind of learned avoidance response involves the functioning of the most complicated perceptual mechanisms, much in the same way as habituation does, except that the effect is the very opposite of a desensitization. A dog that once had been squeezed in a revolving door retained the avoidance response thus acquired for years, possibly for its life, to the extent of insisting on crossing the street to pass, at a gallop and with its tail between its legs, the locality of the trauma on the opposite sidewalk. Horsemen know to their displeasure how stubborn analogous responses are in their mounts.

Konrad Z. Lorenz

Constancy Functions and Gestalt Perception. A very peculiar and, in the highest organisms, extremely important cognitive function, which involves an equally peculiar form of sensory learning, is performed by those of our brain mechanisms that process the multiplicity of incoming sensory data and organize them so as to make meaningful *perceptions*. Punctiform, isolated data are meaningless in principle; the organism does not react specifically to single, absolute stimuli, like a note of determined pitch, or to light of a certain wavelength, but to *patterns* that are characteristics of *objects* or *situations*. The response is never dependent on the sameness of the single, absolute sensory data that make up the pattern and is therefore independent of constant conditions of perception. Differences in color of illumination, in distance or direction, and in absolute pitch do not make any difference to the response. A bee, as Wilhelm Ostwald (62) put it very graphically, is not in the least interested in recognizing a certain wavelength of colored light; what it must be able to do is to recognize a certain flower by what we call "its" color—that is to say, by its property of reflecting certain colors in preference to others. Also, the bee must be able to do so independently of the color of the illumination in which it happens to see the flower at the moment. Erich von Holst (32) has shown in what a comparatively simple manner the special mechanism of color constancy computes, from the color prevailing in the visual field, the probable color of the impinging illumination and, by relating this to the color actually reflected by an object, the color-reflecting properties of the latter—in other words, "its" color.

Analogous mechanisms ascertain the size of an object independently of the distance at which it is seen and of the size of its retinal image, which varies with the square of this distance. Others make sure that we perceive an object as remaining stationary in a certain direction, though with the movements of our body and our sense organs the stimuli emanating from it impinge from altogether different angles. Again, it is Erich von Holst to whom most of our knowledge of these fascinating processes is due.

The most amazing of the constancy functions is the one that permits us to perceive an object of complicated structure as having a constant and rigid form, even when we view it from different sides. We are too familiar with this achievement to realize the tremendous stereometrical computations that it must indubitably perform. If I turn the spectacles I hold in my hand to and fro in front of my eyes, their retinal image assumes very different forms; yet a built-in apparatus functioning without my awareness interprets all these changes correctly as movements of a rigid body and not as changes of form. If the spectacles should contract or wriggle during the process, I should perceive it immediately. This interpretation functions without the help of stereoscopic vision: if I shut one eye, it still works and does so even when I see only the shadow of a thing, except that, in this case, the sense in which it turns is ambiguous.

It must not be forgotten that the original connotation of the German word "gestalt" is simply "external form." Indeed, the most important of the criteria postulated for a typical gestalt by Christian von Ehrenfels are clearly given even in the simpler constancy functions: the perception of the object remains the same, though it can be "transposed" into different colors, sizes, and aspects, and it is certainly something very different from the simple sum of sensory data that are integrated into it. Gestalt perception, even in its highest form, is nothing but a constancy function, though it contains, as integral parts, most other constancy functions known to science.

The functions of constancy perception are "objectifying" in the most literal sense of the word. It is they that make it possible for us to perceive an object as an entity that remains identical in the course of time. In essence, all these functions are based on a process of abstracting, from a chaos of accidental and ever varying sensory data, those few patterns that are constantly characteristic of an object. The operations by which they achieve this abstraction are so closely analogous to those of rational thought that a great man like Helmholtz could actually mistake them for "unconscious conclusions" (*unbewusste Schlüsse*). However, they are performed by neural organizations of a level altogether different from that of ratiocination, and they are altogether inaccessible to our self-observation. Egon Brunswik (7) coined for them the term "ratiomorphic."

Ratiomorphic perceptual processes first developed in phylogeny in the service of objectification, in what gestalt psychologists called *Ding-Konstanz*. Their survival value first lay exclusively in enabling the organism to recognize certain relevant objects as remaining identical through time, the variability of conditions under which they are perceived notwithstanding. A superlatively important change of cognitive function took place when the mechanism attuned to do just this proved to be able to achieve, by virtually the same operations, something that came close to conceptualization. An apparatus made to abstract, from varying accidental sensory data, those that are characteristic of one object is also able to abstract, from many objects, those regularly recurring configurations of data that they have in common. The same sort of built-in computer that enables me to recognize my own, individual dog, in all kinds of illuminations, in all possible body postures, viewed from nearby or from a distance and from all possible angles, is able just as well to perceive the gestalt quality of "dogginess" in a St. Bernard, a Pekinese, a Dachshund, and so on. A small child, just able to call all kinds of dogs "Bowwow," has not abstracted the zoological diagnosis of the species but responds to just this super-individual gestalt quality, which is *not* a concept but is certainly the prerequisite and precursor of all conceptualization.

It is my conviction that what many thinkers call "intuition," and what Einstein called *Einfühlung,* is the function of the same ratio-morphic mechanism. In my paper on "Gestalt perception as fundamental to scientific knowledge" (57), I pointed out that very probably all scientific discoveries of laws of nature are primarily guided by the discoverer's gestalt perception. The first sign that the perception of a lawfulness is beginning to stand out against the background of the "white noise" of chaotic accidental data is that the phenomena in which it prevails begin to assume a quite particular, if as yet quite undefinable, and intriguingly attractive quality. The potential discoverer finds himself irresistibly compelled to occupy himself with the phenomena in question and quite automatically to gather more and more information about them until, often quite suddenly, the gestalt of the suspected lawfulness stands out from the background of accidental data with such convincing clarity that one wonders how one could have overlooked it for such a long time.

Quite obviously, the highly complicated perceptual processes here under discussion imply something like an unconscious memory—in other words, a *storage* of information that is inaccessible to our self-observation. Equally obviously, the final "clicking" of perception takes place at the moment when redundancy of the information gathered is sufficiently great to compensate for the "noisiness" of the channel through which it is received. Judging from the time intervals that often lie between subsequent discoveries made by the same discoverer on the same object, a very retentive storage mechanism must be at work.

Deductively minded scientists tend to underrate the importance of the perceptual process just described, or even deny its existence. Its subconscious nature makes it very easy to overlook or to "displace" (in the psychoanalytical sense), at least for anybody who has an emotional bias against anything as "unscientific" as intuition or *Einfühlung.* Such people honestly believe that all their scientific work on a successful discovery consisted in verifying, by deductive procedures, randomly chosen hypotheses, while all the time it is their gestalt perception to which their choice of object and hypothesis—and, therewith, their success—is due.

Karl Popper (67, 68) has cast serious doubt on the validity of the logic of induction, which proceeds from many singular statements to a universal one. He points out the important asymmetry between verifiability and falsifiability: a universal statement can never be derived from a singular one, while conversely a singular statement, verified beyond reasonable doubt, can falsify a universal statement, irrespective of the number of singular data from which it has been inferred. Though seemingly irrefutable logically, this statement is none the less erroneous. For one thing, there does not exist, in practice, any theory that fits absolutely, covering all the facts. When we attempt to explain a tolerably complicated process by a hypothesis, there always remains quite a number of facts that refuse to fit in snugly. Donald Campbell (9) has shown, most convincingly I think, that the procedure in verifying a hypothesis is nothing but a special case of the process of *pattern matching,* which is the basis of all indirect, objectivating knowledge, which Egon Brunswik (7) has termed *distal* knowledge. "Science," as Campbell says, "is the most distal form of knowledge. . . . The processes and entities posited by science . . . are all very distal objects very mediately known via processes involving highly presumptive pattern matchings at many stages." The attempt to match theory and data is never *entirely* successful. In the practice of research, we do not abandon a theory on the finding of one datum that apparently contradicts it. We do not discard the laws of gravity when we see a toy balloon seemingly fall upward. What does cause us to reject a theory is the finding of an alternative one that fits the facts more exactly, though still by no means to perfection—which no theory ever achieves.

The second consideration is that real contradictions—not seeming ones, like the toy balloon falling upwards—very rarely do occur once a tolerable degree of certainty is reached. Our present-day cosmology may still undergo some radical changes, but I simply refuse to consider the possibility that facts will ever come to light that give the lie to the statements that the earth is revolving round the sun and that man is descended from animals.

The third reason is that gestalt perception proceeds inductively with such very satisfying results, its admitted well-known errors notwithstanding. Even if the long-term storing of information, of which I have spoken, should have no other function than that of compensating for the noisiness of accidental data by redundancy of relevant information, gestalt perception would still be a highly important cognitive

Konrad Z. Lorenz

process. However, I suspect that it is much more. Without it, the procedure of scientific induction would be impossible. The abstraction of a general lawfulness out of a mass of singular data would indeed be as impossible as Popper holds it to be, if those data were just randomly collected information in the sense of information theory. However, they are not, having been preselected and predigested by a procedure that involves Campbell's principle of pattern-matching, sifts the relevant from the irrelevant and accidental, and accumulates, not an amorphous mass of data, but organized knowledge. The ratiomorphic process of gestalt perception, aided by rational induction, is the sole means at our disposal by which we are able to *detect unsuspected* lawfulnesses. Gestalt perception does so directly; there *is* no other way for human beings to "see," for the first time, a new regularity in the chaos of impinging sensory data. Rational induction performs a similar function only by supplying gestalt perception with that redundant information we call the basis of induction.

The most important cognitive function of gestalt perception is that function which, on the ratiomorphic level, is analogous to rational abstraction and is, indubitably, the indispensable prerequisite of conceptualization. Wolfgang Köhler (42) does not hesitate to call the result of perceptual abstraction a concept. His term *anschaulicher Begriff* is not easy to translate into English. *Anschaulich* is something that can be imagined, visually or acoustically; it is doubtful whether gestalt perception occurs in the realm of any other senses.

Nonverbal Thought.   Cognitive functions closely akin to the formation of these perceptual concepts have been closely investigated by Otto Koehler and his pupils (41). Pigeons, shell parakeets, jackdaws, and ravens proved to be able to distinguish *simultaneously* presented quantities by the *number* of their parts, irrespective of the individual size of the latter. The stimulus objects were, in most cases, plasticine splotches, which were applied in different and widely varying forms and sizes (and differently in each of the experiments) to the covers of the little dishes containing the reward. The number is recognized as such, even if the objects to be "counted" change quite suddenly. A jackdaw trained to open the dish whose cover showed four plasticine spots and to leave alone one showing three was offered four and three mealworms lying openly on top of the dish covers. The bird at once ate the four mealworms and then turned away, ignoring the three others and not opening another dish.

Animals that had proved able to "see" numbers presented to them simultaneously could also be trained to *act* a number of times successively. Pigeons, magpies, and others could be trained without any punishment to open one dish after the other until they had obtained a number of rewards. Kinaesthesis and rhythm were excluded as clues by distributing the rewards in an ever varying way over a greater or smaller number of dishes, so that the bird one time got the prescribed number of rewards by opening one or two dishes, while another time it had to open a number of dishes—in some cases, many more than the learned number of rewards. In another series of experiments, pigeons were taught to take a certain number of grains falling out of a chute successively at quite irregular intervals. In one of Koehler's films, it is very impressive to see one of his birds peck up, in quick succession, six grains and then wait patiently for a period of more than 30 seconds (which is a long time for a delayed response in a bird) for the last grain "due" to it. Thus, the pigeons learned to "act to" seven rewards, irrespective of whether their distribution in ten identical dishes with unmarked covers was 2111110000, 4300000000, 0231010000, 0111400000, or 1111100020.

The most amazing feat achieved by this kind of perceptual conceptualization in animals was their choosing, by sample and by doing so, from a temporal sequence of "counted" events to a number of objects seen simultaneously and vice versa. A jackdaw learned to take as many of the mealworms arranged in a circle as was indicated by the number of plasticine spots shown in its center. A magpie was faced with the following arrangement: seven dishes, which the bird had learned to open one after the other, contained in random distribution a varying number of mealworms ranging from one to seven. Another row of seven dishes was marked one to seven by irregular plasticine spots on their covers. The bird learned to open that dish whose number corresponded to the number of mealworms it had found by opening the first row of seven dishes. An African grey parrot learned to take the number of hempseeds indicated by a number of whistles given in varying intervals and durations on a flute.

A different kind of perceptual abstraction was achieved by common domestic mice. The animals, which had been blinded, had mastered the task of learning a maze containing twenty T-shaped bifurcations at which they had to decide between a right and a left turn. All possible clues, such as olfactory traces on the path, orientation marks from outside the maze, and so on, had been carefully eliminated. After thorough training, the mice were confronted with new mazes differing from the original one in the following four points. In the first, the straight runs were of double length. In the second, the 90° angles were replaced by angles of 45°, and in the third by angles of

135°. The fourth represented a mirror image of the maze in which the mice had been trained. Surprisingly, all animals proved to be able to run through the new mazes without committing appreciably more errors than they had in the last stages of their training in the original maze.

Imprinting. A fixation of a response to a stimulus situation encountered only once or a very few times is effected by the process called "imprinting." If, at a particularly sensitive period in its ontogeny, the individual is exposed to a complex stimulus situation that contains certain key stimuli, a whole complicated system of behavior patterns may be fixated, in a more or less irreversible manner, on that complex situation. As Heinroth already knew and as E. Hess (29), F. Schutz (77, 78), M. Schein (74), C. Immelmann (35, 36), and others have conclusively demonstrated, all of the sexual behavior of a bird, for instance, may in hand-reared individuals thus be "imprinted" on humans or on another species used as foster parents in an experiment.

Imprinting differs from other learning processes in several important characteristics. It is confined to a particular, and often very short, sensitive period in the individual's life; it is never quite reversible; and so on. In all these respects it is closely akin to the embryogenetic process of inductive determination. What seems to distinguish it from true conditioning is that a strong positive response is fixated on a complex releasing stimulus situation without the function of those factors that usually act as reinforcements. In fact, the classic object of imprinting experiments, the sexual behavior of some birds, is fixated on its object at an ontogenetic phase at which the strongest reinforcement of this response, the consummatory act of copulation, is a long way from having matured. Nor can the effect of imprinting be undone in those cases in which the experimenter succeeds in the conclusive experiment of inducing his subjects to copulate with a species other than that on which their sexual responses had been imprinted. However, the fact that the usual reinforcements of sexual responses are not effective does not preclude the possibility that other reinforcements, as yet not recognized as such, are at work and that imprinting still may be a special case of true conditioning, though a very special one.

At a certain level of central nervous organization, an entirely new cognitive process has come into being, which derives information from the success as well as from the failure of a behavior pattern *just performed.* A temporal sequence of behavioral events becomes "circuited" in such a manner that a report on the biological success or failure of the physiological processes that terminate the chain is conducted back to its initiating links and effects their adaptive modification.

With the "fulguration" of this new feedback cycle, a new information-acquiring system has come into being, which conveys specific information about what to do and what not to do, not to the species' store of genetic information but directly to the physiological machinery that determines the individual's behavior and retains the message, if not with the pertinacity of the genome, nevertheless in the form of an adaptive modification that may last for an individual's life span. One single performance of a sequence of behavior patterns can thus bring, within minutes or even seconds, an adaptive change of behavior equal to that which the genome's primal method would need at least the time lapse of one generation to achieve. In fact, the gain is twice greater, because the genome gains information by its successes only, while the individual learns by its failures as well. These advantages are so obvious that it is easy to understand why the cognitive mechanism of conditioning has evolved in practically all metazoa possessing a sufficiently complicated and integrated central nervous system.

On the other hand, it is equally easy to understand why it could not develop in protozoa, or in metazoa with a more or less diffuse neural organization: obviously, a system able to feed back the success or failure of a behavior pattern into the machinery of another that has preceded it in time has, as a prerequisite of its function, a certain minimum number, as well as a considerable minimum complexity, of the subsystems integrated into it. The initiating mechanism, which sets the whole sequence of behavior going, must possess a special adaptive modifiability attuned to the message of success or failure coming from the activities terminating the whole action. The latter, on their side, must be furnished with proprio- and exteroceptor mechanisms that contain sufficient innate information to enable them to distinguish reliably between biological success and failure. *I do not see how one could construct a simpler thought model than this and yet be able to account for the biological function of true conditioning.*

The system of physiological mechanisms that undergoes an adaptive modification through conditioning never is "one reflex," as Pavlovian terminology implies. Even the classical salivating response is really only one part of a complicated system of feeding behavior, *all* of which is activated by the conditioned stimulus and which, in the experiment, is prevented from being performed only by the simple means of tying the dog to a frame. My late friend Howard Liddell told me about an unpublished experiment he did while working as a guest in Pavlov's laboratory (51). It consisted simply in freeing from its harness a dog that had been conditioned to salivate at the acceleration in the beat of a metronome. The dog at once ran to the machine, wagged its tail at it, tried to jump up to it, barked, and so on; in other words, it showed as clearly as possible the whole system of behavior patterns serving, in a number of *Canidae,* to beg food from a conspecific. It is, in fact, this whole system that is being conditioned in the classical experiment. It is very far from my mind to disparage the methods or the value of Pavlov's experiments. In order to make quantification possible, it is entirely legitimate to isolate, by artificial means, a response like salivation; my point is only that, while doing so, one must keep thoroughly aware of what he has done. What is completely forbidden by the laws of systems analysis is deceiving oneself into believing that the artificially isolated part is all that counts and is sufficient to explain the functional properties of the system.

If one surveys, from the viewpoint of a biologically minded systems theory, the essential facts known about conditioning by success and error, he is confirmed in the opinion that this type of adaptive modification occurs only in behavior systems with a rather elaborate genetical program. There is, in most cases, a releasing mechanism that gains in selectivity, and appetitive behavior that is modified, and even new motor patterns that are constructed on the basis of the individually gained, instant information furnished by the reports of success or failure. Practically all the simpler and phylogenetically older information-gaining mechanisms go, as integral parts, into the making of such an adaptively modifiable system, but they are not modified themselves.

Before I discuss the important question of where in such a system the innate information is situated that *teaches* the organism what to do and what not to do, I want to say a few words about the physiological nature of adaptive modifiability of behavior through conditioning, or through learning generally. The search for the engram, as Lashley (49) has called it, has not been too successful as far as its localization in the nervous system is concerned; nor do we know much about the changes in the single nerve cells or synapses, on which it is based. This state of affairs explains why, when the coding and storing of phylogenetically acquired information was discovered, many serious scientists tended to the hypothesis that learned information was also coded and stored in the form of chain molecules. This hypothesis, however, makes it necessary to postulate the function of two physiological mechanisms, the existence of which is, to say the least, improbable. One of them would be needed to transpose into the form of chain molecules, not only sequences, but configurations of neural impulses, much as a Morse apparatus writes a series of electrical impulses on a paper tape, but multidimensionally. A second mechanism would have to perform the reciprocal task of retranslating the information thus coded into series and configurations of nervous impulses causing well-coordinated behavior patterns. Furthermore, this hypothesis fails to explain in the least why the faculty of learning is as directly correlated to the size and complication of the central nervous system as it obviously is. Lately, an eminent biochemist, Gierer (20), has shown by convincing arguments that the theory of individual experience being coded in chain molecules is untenable. Furthermore, many of the experimental results that seemed to support it have been proved to be irreproducible under more critical conditions. In view of all of this, it still seems most probable that the adaptive change wrought by learning in the machinery of behavior is, like all modification, a process closely related to, if not identical with, induction (in the sense of experimental embryology) and that the locus at which it takes place is in the synapses.

INNATE TEACHING MECHANISMS

The open program furnished, ready made by phylogeny, to each individual of a species of higher animals is always elaborately constructed so that the "open" parts concern variable, unpredictable parts of the environment, while other parts, which are necessarily genetically programmed in a practically invariable form, contain the information telling the individual what to do and what not to do. As I said on page 46, and as I explained more explicitly in my book *Evolution and Modification of Behavior* (55), any physiological mechanism effecting reinforcement or the opposite must contain sufficient innate information not to confound biological success and failure in the report that it feeds back to the machinery of precedent behavior. The existence of "innate teaching mechanisms" must be postulated, unless one prefers to explain the obvious adaptive function of learning by the assumption of a prestabilized harmony between the organism and its environment. Paraphrasing Kant's definition of the a priori, one can say that the innate is what is there before all learning and must be there in order to make learning possible. In order to achieve its programmed modifying effect, it must be resistant to modification.

It is a fascinating endeavor to ascertain, in such a modifiable system of behavior patterns, which of its subsystems are being adaptively modified by learning and which are the ones that do the teaching. In the type of behavior system that was called an "aversion" by Wallace Craig (10) and an "appetite for quiescence" by Monika Meyer-Holzapfel (33), an appetitive behavior, which may be represented by all possible gradations from a simple kinesis to learned motor skills, is continued until the organism has reached a specific stimulus situation in which it comes to rest. The most frequent function of this simple system is to guide the organism in selecting habitat conditions favorable to its survival—optimal temperature, humidity, or illumination; the right kind of cover; and so forth. The innate information resides, in this case, exclusively in a receptor organization that "knows" the right conditions and reinforces all precedent behavior that has successfully led to establish them. As in many other instances, the immediate reinforcement here consists in a relief of tension. This is the classic case of Hullian conditioning.

In systems comprising specialized and complicated fixed motor patterns, the teaching information often is contained in the motor coordination itself. When performed in the adequate situation, and only then, the fixed motor pattern produces a specific extero- and proprioceptor feedback, which is wired back, as a report of biological success, to the physiological mechanisms initiating the activity. This feedback has the double function of bringing the activity to an end for the time being and of strongly reinforcing all behavior patterns precedent to the achievement of this end. A good example of a simple behavior system built on this principle is found in the nest-building behavior of the jackdaw and other corvides. Standing on the potential nest locality, with nesting material held in its beak, the bird performs a downward and sideward sweeping movement, which brings the material into forceful contact with the substratum or, later on in the process, with other nesting material already accumulated. The moment the twig or branch carried by the bird meets a resistance, the sideways shoving becomes stronger and, at the same time, saccaded into a series of quick, trembling thrusts, similar to those a man performs with a pipe-cleaner in order to get it through an obstructed part

Innate Bases of Learning **49**

of the pipe stem. When these thrusts succeed in wedging the twig in, so that it offers an increased resistance to the movement, the latter gains in intensity, to end in an orgiastic maximum once the twig really sticks fast. After this consummatory act the bird loses interest for the time being. Unlike many other songbirds, the jackdaw possesses no highly specified releasing mechanism containing innate information as to what the nesting material should be like. When, for the first time in its life, the naive bird is aroused to a nest-building mood, it will grab, carry, and tremble-shove practically all objects small enough to be handled, the most unlikely on my records being pieces of ice and settings of small electric bulbs. None of these things ever gets so firmly lodged by being tremble-shoved as to procure the drive-assuaging stimulus situation that spells biological success. This failure very quickly extinguishes the individual's response to inadequate objects, while an equally quick positive conditioning is effected to adequate ones. In fact, the birds become "connoisseurs" of that kind of twig that is just flexible enough to be shoved into crevices, just twisted enough to stick well, and so forth. Hence, very often most of the material used in all the nests of a jackdaw colony comes from one species of tree.

There are other and more complicated systems of behavior that make use of the extremely specific information forthcoming from the feedback of fixed motor patterns performed in their several adequate situations. The brown rat, as Eibl-Eibesfeldt (14) has shown, possesses three motor patterns achieving the collecting and general arrangement of nesting material. The first is running out (from a potential nest site that has to be determined by precedent learning), grabbing nest material, carrying it back, and dropping it at the point of departure. (Inexperienced rats, deprived of material, did exactly this with their own tails, so that the experiment had to be repeated with tail-less rats.) The second motor pattern consists in the rat sitting in the nest center, turning to and fro and heaping up, with its forepaws, a more or less circular wall of nesting material. The third is patting the inside of this wall with the forepaws so as to tamp down and smooth the inner surface of the nest cavity. A naive rat, offered paper strips or other soft material for the first time, will get into a frenzy of *all three* of these activities, each of which is performed to complete perfection, not differing even on analysis by slow motion pictures from those of an experienced rat. However, the naive rat does something the experienced one never does: after having carried two or three paper strips, which are lying flat on the ground, it will perform the heaping-up movements in the empty air above them and even do the patting movements, tamping down a nest wall not yet in existence. It is the failure to get the "rewarding" reaffirmation that teaches the rat not to do the heaping-up movements before enough material has been carried in, or the patting movements before a sufficiently high nest wall has been heaped up.

Fascinating illustrations of the necessity to ascertain the localization of innate information have come to light through the work of Mazakazu Konishi (43, 45). In songbirds, the sound utterances denoting simple signals—such as warning calls, flight calls, and the like —are inherited as simple fixed motor patterns, just as are the calls in gallinaceous birds, anatidae, and many others. The song of some passerines, however, is not based upon any inherited motor patterns, even in species in which a bird reared in the isolation of a sound proof room develops a recognizable species-specific song. Konishi demonstrated that birds that were deafened before a certain age developed nothing but an absolutely amorphous twittering, which was more like a noise than a note. The innate information about how the specific song ought to sound is situated in a template that lies *exclusively on the receptor side*. The young bird, which, in the so-called subsong, utters a wide range of sound combinations, much as the human baby does, matches fortuitously produced utterances with its auditory template and retains those that match best. In this respect, subsong plays the role of exploratory play.

Something similar is true of fixed motor patterns as well in all those cases in which they are not linked, in a closed program, to highly specific innate releasing mechanisms. The spontaneity of the fixed pattern then plays an important role in the teaching process. Progressive lowering of the threshold of the unreleased pattern urges its provisional discharge at substitute objects or in not quite adequate situations, and recurrent appetitive behavior forces the organisms to try again and again, even in spite of otherwise strongly extinguishing and discouraging experiences, until at last the fully rewarding consummatory situation is hit upon.

There are, of course, many other and very different "teaching mechanisms," of which I shall discuss only one more because its importance was recognized long ago when the actual problem, the nature of the innate information, was not fully realized. The widely accepted assertion that it is the fulfillment of tissue needs that acts as a reinforcement is certainly quite correct, as far as it goes; but there remains the question of how the modifiable parts of behavior—those that achieve the choice and intake of the necessary substances—get the information indispensable for doing so correctly. That this information is very detailed indeed is shown by Curt Richter's experiments (71, 72) in which rats successfully put together a perfectly balanced diet even when the nutriments furnished to them were split up into the simplest possible ingredients, the component amino acids of protein being offered in separate dishes. Since the rat as a species cannot possibly have innate information about these components of its food, much less about the correct proportions of the ingredients, the most economical explanation of this amazing feat seems to be that the organism has "feelers" (in the cybernetical sense), in all the homeostatic cycles of its metabolism, that report any deviation from the biologically correct values of reference. In agreement with this assumption, the rat eats tentatively very little of any foodstuff as yet unknown to it, thus gaining the opportunity to record "how it feels afterwards"—or, more objectively expressed, to let the food intake affect its metabolism. This kind of feedback, far from creating only avoidance responses, causes all the specific food preferences described by Richter, as the results of John Garcia and his colleagues (18) demonstrate quite conclusively.

These examples are sufficient to show two facts. First, the innate information underlying the adaptiveness of learning may be localized in quite unexpected parts of the behavior system that, as a whole, is modified in the process. Second, the learning process itself cannot, in principle, be understood without understanding the whole system that is being modified. This is true of all other teaching mechanisms as well, a discussion of which would lead us too far afield.

PROCESSES MODIFIABLE BY TEACHING

In *Evolution and Modification of Behavior* (55), I have shown, I hope conclusively, that, unless one believes, again, in the miracle of a prestabilized harmony, it is quite impossible to assume a general adaptive modifiability of *all* physiological mechanisms of behavior. All known observational and experimental facts support what common sense tells us anyway: the information relevant for one specifically adaptive process must be gathered by an equally specific cognitive mechanism, and there can be, in each species, only a limited number of such mechanisms.

If one surveys, from the obligatory viewpoint of systems analysis, the physiological mechanisms underlying the behavior of a species of higher animal, one encounters a limited number, not only of those physiological processes that are able to acquire and to feed back to precedent behavior mechanisms the information spelling success or

Konrad Z. Lorenz

failure, but also of those mechanisms that are adaptively modified by this report. To the best of my knowledge it was Otto Storch (86) who first called attention to the fact that an adaptive modification of receptor patterns, termed *Erwerbs-Rezeptorik* by him, occurs so much more frequently and at much lower levels of evolution than does *Erwerbs-Motorik*, the analogous improvement of motor patterns.

I need not enlarge on the fact that the most frequent form of learning consists in feeding new information into the releasing mechanism, making it more selective and, at the same time, susceptible to stimuli that regularly precede in time the unlearned key stimuli, thus enabling the organism to prepare for action. In vertebrates, there is hardly one releasing mechanism known that is not thus adaptively modified by conditioning, as shown by W. Schleidt (76), to whose paper I refer the reader for detailed facts.

As regards the adaptive modification of motor activities, the simplest and most primitive effect seems to be the coupling of two or more preexistent fixed motor patterns, as exemplified by Eibl-Eibesfeldt's rats. I doubt whether the way in which the acquisition of apparently new motor patterns of learned motor skills is achieved is physiologically different. As I have explained in more detail in *Evolution and Modification of Behavior,* that which is called a path habit in mice and many other small mammals can be regarded as "one" motor skill, because the motor units contained in it are welded into one coherent sequence. Each single unit, however, consists of a mechanism of fixed motor patterns and taxes that is also encountered in other combinations or sequences. In other words, the new skill is achieved by stringing, end to end, in a particular and specifically adapted sequence, single motor patterns that, as such, are phylogenetically ready-made possessions of the species. In man and in those mammals able to acquire highly differentiated new motor skills, this faculty is dependent on the existence of extremely small elementary motor patterns, each of which is independently releasable and at the disposal of the will—hence the term "voluntary movements." They can be welded together in practically any coordination, which, once established, functions with the expediency of a fixed motor pattern.

SELECTION PRESSURE EXERTED BY LEARNING

Once, somewhere back in the evolutionary process, the "fulguration" of the great feedback cycle of conditioning had integrated, into a new functional whole, a number of physiological mechanisms that previously had performed their species-preserving functions separately or in the framework of smaller, preexisting systems, each of them was allotted, in the context of the integrated organization, a function that was in some ways different from the one it had hitherto performed. By this change of function, a new selection pressure was brought to bear on the mechanisms of appetitive behavior, releasing mechanisms, fixed motor patterns, consummatory actions, and so on. All processes that had to perform the function of innate teaching mechanisms became specialized in the function of feeding back, into the initiating links of the chain, as unambiguous and energetic reports of success or failure as possible, while the initiating processes themselves evolved an ever growing degree of adaptive modifiability.

The structure and functional properties of the consummatory act, in particular, were never fully understood before their teaching function was realized. In a nonconditionable system of behavior patterns that functions only once in the individual's life, such as that of copulation in many arthropods, the only feedback emanating from the consummatory act is the one that switches off appetitive behavior as well as the receptiveness of the releasing mechanism. For obvious neurophysiological reasons, a much greater quantity of nervous impulses, as well as a much more complicated configuration of their message, is necessary to perform the new function of a conditioning feedback of success or failure. A comparison between the consummatory act in nonconditionable and conditionable systems seems to agree with this deduction. After one has observed the elaborate and excited courtship dance of a salticid spider, one is astonished to watch the quiet way in which it proceeds to copulate. Conversely, the enormous general excitation pervading the whole organism during the consummatory act of copulation in a mammal, for instance in a stallion, makes it very probable that these fireworks are not mere epiphenomena but are essential for creating sufficient nervous impulses to impress and modify the machinery of antecedent behavior, effecting a strong reinforcement.

The innate information underlying the function of all teaching mechanisms must, for obvious reasons, be shielded against any random change by individual modification. For this reason the terminating links of any conditionable chain of behavioral systems invariably are those that are most rigidly phylogenetically programmed: "the end of the chain is always instinctive," as Wallace Craig (10) put it. It is the initiating processes of a behavior system on which the selection pressure making for greater modifiability takes effect. Thus, appetitive behavior and releasing mechanisms have been selected for the greatest possible degree of adaptive modifiability.

It is in the framework of appetitive behavior that all motor learning, all of the *Erwerbs-Motorik,* has evolved. The random activity that, in the primitive and unconditionable forms of appetitive behavior, had been the only effect of the internal buildup of an unassuaged motor pattern—or, in the case of an appetite for quiescence, of a disturbing, biologically threatening stimulus situation—constituted the matrix that could be organized to form the open program of adaptively modifiable behavior. There are many examples of primitive unconditionable appetitive behavior, but the opposite is not true: there does not seem to exist any known case in which conditioning by reinforcement could be demonstrated in a behavioral system *not* including typical appetitive behavior.

The releasing mechanism, as the afferent part of a conditionable system of behavior, is under a selection pressure directly opposed to the one exerted upon it when learning does not enter into the picture. In the latter case, the releasing mechanism itself contains all the innate information concerning when and where the particular behavior is to be discharged with the best chances of gain, and therefore a maximum selectivity is of survival value. If, on the other hand, all or most of this information is obtained from a teaching apparatus that records success or failure at the ultimate end of a sequence of behavior patterns, high selectivity of the releasing mechanisms ceases to be an asset. Particularly if a well-developed appetitive behavior impels the animal to try repeatedly, so that repeated failure does not do serious damage by postponing ultimate success all too long, a rather sketchy, unselective releasing mechanism may increase the scope for trials, thus increasing the adaptability of the whole behavioral system. The method of trial and error really gains more essential information: in the case of the nest-building of the jackdaw, it really extracts from the object the information about those properties on which its use as nesting material really depends. As is to be expected, trial-and-error behavior is very definitely correlated with an "intentional" (that is, a "selected for") unselectivity of releasing mechanisms.

EXPLORATORY BEHAVIOR

Out of the extremely common trial-and-error behavior that practically all the young of higher vertebrates show to some degree, a new type of cognitive function has evolved. While all young and inexperienced animals "explore" to the extent of trying their several behavior patterns in this situation and that, typical exploratory behavior is characterized by a strong and autonomous appetitive motivation directed at stimulus situations *new* to the individual. A young corvide bird, confronted with an object it has never seen, runs through practically all the inventory of its behavior patterns, except social and sexual ones. It treats the object first as a predator to be mobbed, then as a dangerous prey to be killed, then as a dead prey to be pulled to pieces, then as food to be tasted and hidden, and finally as indifferent material that can be used to hide food under, to perch upon, and so on. All these behavior patterns, the initial cautious mobbing excepted, are identical with those serving the experienced bird to obtain food. However, it would be a great mistake to assume that hunger is the motivating force behind this behavior. Quite the contrary; if the bird were really hungry, it would not indulge in exploratory behavior but resort to a method it already knows as leading to satiation—for instance, begging from the human foster parent. Exploratory behavior can function only in what Gustav Bally (3), following Kurt Lewin, terms *das entspannte Feld*—"the field free of tension." In exploratory behavior, motor patterns that are clearly adapted to very definite functions are thus performed under a motivation entirely different from the one that activates them in the biological situation in which they are "seriously" applied to achieve the survival value under whose selection pressure they have evolved. In this respect, exploratory behavior is closely akin to what is generally described as *play*. The appetite for new situations, which we usually call curiosity, supplies a motivation as strong as that of any other appetitive behavior, and the only situation that assuages it is the ultimately established familiarity with the new object—in other words, new knowledge. The young raven experimenting with feeding behavior on a new object does not want to eat; he wants to know whether it is edible *in principle*. The information acquired by exploratory behavior is *objective* in the most literal sense of the word.

As I have discussed exploratory behavior more explicitly in other places, I need to say very little more here. Exploratory behavior furnishes an excellent example of how a new cognitive function—and an extremely efficient one—can come into existence by just "wiring" a number of common, preexistent subsystems in a slightly different way. Fundamentally, the new "invention" consists in connecting a strongly motivated appetitive behavior, not essentially different from that which brings about the stimulus situation releasing a consummatory act, with a stimulus situation in which a conditionable system of the type already described (p. 46) can acquire a maximum of new and relevant information. All the physiological mechanisms thus integrated into a new cognitive process are those we already know, but

Konrad Z. Lorenz

the new systemic properties coming into existence with this new "fulguration" make a tremendous difference. In fact, *most of the difference between man and all the other organisms is founded on the new possibilities of cognition that are opened by exploratory behavior.*

INSIGHT LEARNING

When the totally inexperienced young animal performs, for the first time, a conditionable sequence of behavior patterns, this trial is by no means as blindly random as one of the genome's experiments in mutation and recombination of genes. Even in animals in which, as I have explained, a maximum development of exploratory behavior makes it desirable for releasing mechanisms not to be too selective, they still supply the inexperienced animal with a tolerably good "hypothesis" concerning when and where first to try a certain behavior pattern. Furthermore, every one of these first trials is guided, in space and time, by all the wealth of instant information supplied by the phylogenetically adapted mechanisms described in Chapter 3 and by others that have not been mentioned.

What is generally termed "insight" is usually defined by negative attributes only. Behavior is regarded as intelligent or guided by insight when the organism confronted with a new situation proves able to cope with it at once, although there are neither any phylogenetically programmed releasing mechanisms or motor patterns nor any learned perceptual responses or motor skills fitting the requirements of this special problem. One is tempted to add to this negative definition the exclusion of all the phylogenetically adapted mechanisms acquiring instant information. On close examination, however, this proves to be impossible. If a fish succeeds in circumnavigating an obstacle by the simple means of two simultaneously effective taxes, one that directs it toward the prey behind a little semidiaphanous glass screen and another that causes it to avoid the screen, this appears, at first sight, to be similar to the movement of a projectile in the resultant of the two forces of inertia and gravity. Yet there are all possible gradations between this simplest way of solving a detour problem on one hand and the highest achievements of the human intellect on the other. In another paper (58) I have tried to show how the faculty of complex insight has evolved with the necessity of more and more detailed information about the spatial structure of an organism's environment and how tree-climbing animals with prehensile hands stand in particular need of such information. Man's intellectual faculties have evolved "hand in hand with the hand," and even our present terms for our highest cognitive activities, such as insight, method, concept, object, and so on, still bear all the earmarks of their provenience from processes of spatial orientation.

In the present context, it is sufficient to say that insight is nothing but the function of complex systems of phylogenetically programmed mechanisms gaining instant information. Among these, it is mainly a multiplicity of taxes and of perceptual functions ensuring object-constancy that are integrated in the complex intellectual function.

Though the physiological processes of insight and of learning are essentially different from each other, their functions are practically always united in a joint act of cognition. Even in the most primitive kind of trial-and-error learning, the animal does not run, scratch, or peck indiscriminately in all directions but, by virtue of some taxis or other, possesses a measure of "insight" that quite considerably improves the chances of success. From this, there are all gradations to a type of behavior in which an intelligent animal gains an almost complete insight into the problem with which it is confronted, so that it is able to find, with high probability, an immediate solution and to retain it, after one single reinforcement, well enough never to err again. Insight actually is contained, to some degree, in all trial-and-error learning; what we choose to call "insight learning" is a question of arbitrarily defined quantitative differences.

If it is correct to say that insight enters into most of the more highly differentiated learning processes, it is equally correct to state that learning enters into all of the more complex achievements of insight. Even in solving, by insight, a comparatively simple detour problem, the animal will look around, taking in the structural details of the obstacle one after the other; and, though each of the mechanisms supplying the instant information on which the ultimate solution is based belongs to the type discussed in Chapter 3, the animal must *remember,* having looked to the left and having perceived an opening in the wire fence, that this exit is more easily accessible than the one it discovers a second later on its right. In the classical insight experiments conducted by W. Köhler (42) on chimpanzees, the successive memorizing of all the single details of the problem situation was clearly observable. This learning very probably was of the perceptual type discussed on pages 43–45.

An important relation between insight and learning was found and duly emphasized by Köhler. A problem-solution that was demonstrably achieved by insight tends to degenerate, after very few repetitions, into a routine performance learned by heart, so that a subsequent slight change in the problem, which certainly would not have prevented the animal from finding the solution at the first attempt, does so now, because the silly beast persists in the once successful procedure. This "degeneration" of insight into rote procedure has both its advantages and its dangers. It relieves insight from unnecessary strain—as, for instance, when we use mathematical formulas or logarithms without consciously realizing what we are doing and what they really are. On the other hand, the process under discussion may prevent us from finding obvious solutions because we are blocked by procedures and thought habits that force us to miss them by a hair's breadth only, but miss them nevertheless.

SELF-EXPLORATION

Most of the cognitive mechanisms discussed here take part in the highest achievements of the human mind. Some of them, like the "objectivating" abstraction performed by constancy perception, like the equally objectivating function of exploratory learning, and like insight, have been erroneously regarded as being specifically human. So was tradition of which I shall speak in the next chapter.

There is only one cognitive function that came into existence with the origin of man or that, to be more exact, constituted humanity by coming into existence. Here, once again, the fulguration of an entirely new principle came about, joining into a circle what up to then had been a linear process. With the extreme differentiation of man as a "specialist for nonspecialization" and with the concomitant development of his urge to explore, it seems to have been unavoidable that he discovered himself as an object that is very rewarding to explore. Though as simple as a snake biting its own tail, this process has given to the human community new systemic properties that are entirely absent in the animal world.

In another place, I have recently (54) discussed the consequences that the discovery of the self had for human social behavior. This paper, whose title is "The Innate Bases of Culture," would indeed form a logical sequel to what has been said here. In order not to exceed the frame set by the title of this lecture, I shall confine myself to summarizing what is relevant from the viewpoint of cognitive processes.

Seeing, for the first time, one's own reflection in the mirror of self-exploration need not necessarily have been accompanied by that wonderment at that which was hitherto treated as a matter of course, with that amazement that is the birth of philosophy. The simple matter-of-fact knowledge that the own subjective self is inhabiting a creature essentially similar to any fellow member of the species is sufficient to set off a new feedback cycle of knowledge processes that is epoch-making. Very probably the reflection by which the subject becomes aware of its own subjectivity has been the origin of all specifically human achievements and first of all of conceptual thinking, the prerequisite of verbal language, without which cultural tradition could never have come into being; it is the basis of conscience, which is primarily the simple consciousness of being one member of a society and which is the basis of rational morality. Of course, there are functions analogous to all these in animals. There is phylogenetically programmed social behavior that is analogous to rational morality—and is often confounded with it by anthropomorphically minded observers. There is true tradition in some social animals, of which I shall speak anon. There is something akin to the asking of questions and to the understanding of answers; there is true insight in the faculty of solving spatial problems in apes and some other mammals; there is a function closely resembling conceptualization in the objectivating abstraction achieved by constancy perception; and there are, last though not least, the phenomena of preverbal thinking described by O. Koehler (41) and discussed on pages 43–45. None of these functions has become unimportant, for all of them represent integral parts of conceptual thought, but this unique cognitive faculty did not come into being until the crucial moment when man perceived simultaneously, in the world he was exploring, not only the object he grasped, but his own grasping hand and his own act of grasping. It was then that the whole sensory and nervous process of "grasping" blossomed into conceptualization and that the central nervous image of whatever was being grasped became a concept.

If one observes a bored chimpanzee playing with his own hand, bending and extending the fingers slowly while intensely watching the process, one is tempted to believe that self-exploration of this kind may be at the root of reflection, and also that the action of the hand right in the center of the ape's visual field may have played an important role. On the other hand, a very social creature with an extremely strong urge to explore might well have directed its exploratory behavior at a fellow member of the species rather than at its own body. The play of asking questions and receiving answers, typical of all exploration, may have been played mutually by two individuals. The first mirror in which each of them saw himself may well have been the other. The close relationship between conceptual thinking and verbal communication make it probable that both can have evolved only in a species with a well-developed social organization. The relationship between these two faculties is so close that the question of which came first is yet another hen-egg problem. True, conceptual thinking can demonstrably function independently of verbalization, but it never would have reached the heights it did had it not been the indispensable prerequisite of verbal speech, thus developing under the selection pressure of the necessity to communicate. No system of concepts that are common to the members of a social group and communicable between them could ever have developed without verbal speech.

I do not overrate the function of speech as a help to truly cognitive functions. Formulating a thought in verbal speech has a function similar to that of jotting down on paper a sequence of mathematical operations—in other words, it is not much more than a memory aid. This function of storing knowledge becomes of superlative importance only when tradition develops to the point at which it is able to pass on, from one generation to the next, knowledge coded in the symbols of the spoken and the written word.

Chapter 5. Tradition

TRADITION IN ANIMALS

To the best of my knowledge, I was the first to demonstrate the existence of true tradition in an animal species. When, in 1927, I tried to settle a jackdaw colony, I discovered at my expense that hand-reared jackdaws are absolutely fearless of cats, dogs, and other predators, and consequently my birds were killed in quantities. There are two ways in which a jackdaw can become conditioned to fear—and mob —a predator. Any living creature carrying something black and dangling immediately releases in any jackdaw that is more than about three months old an all-out attack accompanied by a raucous rattling call. In my first unforgettable experience of this response, I released it myself by carrying a pair of black bathing trunks in my hand. This mobbing rapidly becomes conditioned to the predator that has been seen a few times carrying a dead jackdaw. The rattling call releases the whole mobbing response in every jackdaw within hearing distance just as surely as the sight of the predator carrying something black and dangling. The conditioning effect of a socially induced rattling attack seems to be even greater than that of the sight of a dead conspecific being carried away. In fact, I very much doubt whether any of the jackdaws living at my home at present has ever seen this sight, nor do I think that for many years any of these well-advised birds has been caught by a cat. Yet they mob cats violently and will continue to do so.

Steiniger (85) has shown experimentally that in a clan of rats the knowledge of a specific danger, such as a certain poison, can be preserved over several generations, long after the individuals that could have had experience of it must have died of old age. In Japanese macaques, Kawai and Kawamura (39, 40) demonstrated true tradition, which conveyed not only the knowledge of objects but—which is much more—that of certain motor skills, such as that of washing and at the same time seasoning potatoes in sea water or, in another instance, a very clever method of separating grain and sand by a procedure similar to gold-washing.

In all these cases, the act of passing on knowledge from one individual to the other is dependent on the presence of the object that the information concerns. The jackdaw can teach its young that cats are dangerous only when there is a cat at its disposal to mob; the rat must be able to demonstrate to its inexperienced conspecific how it urinates and defecates on the dangerous foodstuff to be avoided; and so on. To convey knowledge about a certain thing in its absence, true symbols are needed, and the only infrahuman creatures known that possess the faculty to use symbols and whose communication, therefore, most merits the term "speech" are the honey bee and, to a lesser extent, some of its closest zoological relations. In the darkness of the hive, one bee can tell another not only in what direction a new source of food is to be found, but also how rewarding it is and how far away. All this information is conveyed by a true symbol, a "dance" that, as Karl von Frisch (17) has shown, can also be interpreted correctly by the human observer familiar with its intricacies. It almost seems a pity that this beautiful symbolic language is concerned only with information about quickly changing environmental circumstances and that the information conveyed by it is stored for so short a time that no traditional knowledge can be built up on this basis.

Among nonhuman animals, there does not seem to be a case in which traditional knowledge is accumulated, from generation to generation, in the way it is in our species. We do not know why this is so; in principle, tradition could very well accumulate in any of the social higher animals.

Even in subhuman primates, as yet lacking conceptual thought and symbolic language, there are a number of properties contributing to render tradition particularly effective. There is a very closely knit society, in which parents and progeny stay in contact for a very long time; there is a lot of exploratory curiosity; and there is, most important of all, a strong tendency to learn motor skills by imitation. The behavioral norms laid down by tradition may be so characteristic of one particular social group of macaques that anthropologists are, in my opinion, quite justified in speaking of "subcultures."

However, it is only with verbal language and with teaching by word of mouth that tradition really began to accumulate and to store great hoards of information. As scientists, we are so much accustomed to associating a biological connotation with the terms "inherit," "inheritance," and the like, that we are apt to forget the sociological, juridic meaning that these words had long before the science of genetics was originated. If a man invents a bow and arrow or learns from a neighboring tribe how to make them, not only he and his progeny, but all the society to which he belongs, will henceforward be in possession of these important tools—nor will these be more likely to be forgotten again than a bodily organ of comparable survival value is likely to become rudimentary. What comes into existence with the human form of tradition is neither more nor less than the famous inheritance of acquired characters. Instant information, a flash of insight, or an unforeseen success of exploratory behavior is retained with a tenacity almost equal to that of the genome.

In conjunction with this new storing of information, all the great human cognitive functions have embarked on an entirely new and extremely venturesome way of evolution. The fundamental procedure of the twin feedback cycle gathering energy and knowledge has remained the same, and even all the old primal mechanisms are still functioning as indispensable, integral parts in a new system. In this system, however, human cognition and tradition, immensely more effective than any previously existing process of gaining and of storing information, have established a feedback cycle of their own, which drives our evolution forward at an ever increasing dizzy speed. It is easy to overlook the fact that, beneath this vertiginous process, genetic evolution is still proceeding at its own slow and cautious pace. The great dangers arising from the very rapidity of man's psychosocial evolution will be discussed at the end of this paper.

In the speeded-up psychosocial evolution of human society, a very particular form of habit formation played an important part in determining norms of behavior whose function is strictly analogous to that kind of fixed motor pattern that, following Julian Huxley (34), we call ritualized. In animal societies, communication is largely dependent on behavior patterns that, to a naive observer, immediately make the impression of being *symbols*. By comparative studies, we are well informed about the phylogenetical processes by which a motor pattern—for instance, one of nest-building—is transformed into one that *releases* the same behavior—for example, nest-building by a conspecific or some behavior of simple locomotion changed into one that induces fellow members of the species to follow the individual in performing it. In two papers (55, 56) I have explained how the effect of these signals is enhanced by "mimic exaggeration" of the optically or acoustically effective parts of the movement, by a strictly determined frequency and amplitude and redundant repetition, all of which serve to increase the unambiguity of the information imparted by them. Also, I have shown the amazing formal and functional analogy existing between phylogenetically evolved ritualized behavior and the social norms and rites developed in the history of human culture. The main functions of both kinds of ritualized behavior are, first, communication; second, holding together a social group; and, third, channeling aggression into more or less innocuous directions.

Phylogenetically ritualized behavior consists of true, autonomous fixed motor patterns, whose endogenous generating of stimuli brooks no repression and thus constitutes a strongly driving, motivating force. Social norms and rites originating by cultural ritualization derive an equally strong motivating force from altogether different psychophysiological mechanisms. Even simple, individually acquired habits tend to become so firmly ingrained that any deviation creates anxiety. In animals, it is of obvious survival value to adhere, as strictly as possible, to a chain of actions, once it has proved to be devoid of danger and, at the same time, successful. A creature not possessing any insight into the causality of its actions cannot possibly know which of them are essential for the safety as well as for the success of the whole performance. Even in human beings this tendency is still a demonstrably strong influence on behavior and, though absolutely sound in itself, is occasionally subject to that very tormenting hypertrophy that we know as compulsory neurosis.

Habits that have become ritualized in the course of cultural development are enforced by a second important factor, in addition to the compulsive anxiety that punishes every infraction: the love and reverence we feel for culturally ritualized rites and norms of social behavior contribute strongly to the continuity of their tradition. At the same time, the emotional tie by which any member is bound to the ritualized behavior of its own society is one of the most important factors on which group cohesion is dependent in all social units exceeding the number of individuals that can be held together by the bond of personal love and friendship.

Pseudo-speciation. It is hard to exaggerate the ubiquity of ritualization in the behavior of civilized man. Even if we ignore the fact that verbal language is, of course, a product of cultural ritualization, practically everything we do in the presence of other members of our society obeys the strictly prescribed rules of "manners." Certain manners are the characteristic of even the smallest cultural subgroups, such as schools or small military units. "Good" manners are, by definition, those of one's group, and the slight deviations found in a comparable other group are looked down upon.

In groups developing independently of one another, the difference in rites and social norms of behavior increases with the lapse of time. There are all possible gradations from the hardly discernible differences between small and closely related groups to the great gaps separating old independent cultures. In other words, the culturally developed social norms and rites are characteristic of ethnic groups of different age and size in very much the same manner as phylogenetically evolved structures or behavior patterns are of subspecies, species, genera, and higher taxonomic groups. Their history can be investigated by the same method of comparative study. Their divergence during historical development erects barriers between cultural groups much as divergent evolution does between species. Like species, cultures that are too different from one another cannot be "hybridized"; even if they are still close enough to one another, their mixing usually is detrimental to both of them. For these and other reasons, Erik Erikson (15) has spoken of cultural *pseudo-speciation.*

In itself, pseudo-speciation is a normal and altogether desirable evolutionary process. Very probably, a certain degree of being shielded from the influence of neighboring groups is advantageous to cultural development, much as geographical isolation accelerates and facilitates the evolution of a species. The negative side of pseudo-speciation, however, is that it causes the members of one cultural pseudo-species to regard those of another not only as inferior but, when the cultural differences are sufficiently great, as definitely not quite human. In many primitive tribes, the name of the own tribe is synonymous with "man," and from this viewpoint it is not really cannibalism if one eats people of other pseudo-species. What makes pseudo-speciation particularly dangerous is that it suppresses all psychophysiological mechanisms normally inhibiting the killing of a conspecific, while, on the other hand, not obstructing intraspecific aggression in the least. The members of other pseudo-species are hated as only human beings can be hated, while they can be killed with no more compunction than animals.

The culturally ritualized norms of social behavior that represent the bonds by which a large cultural group is held together play, in the individual group member's emotional life, very much the same role as its individually known and loved friends or close relations. They are loved in a similar way, and if they are threatened, or seem to be threatened, they evoke the same kind of collective defense reactions. As far as these norms and rites can be regarded as "institutional"—which they are insofar as they are dependent on tradition —*war is institutional. The underlying, phylogenetically programmed behavior patterns of collective defense-attack are not,* but the object-situations releasing them in so dangerous a manner *are.* This fact is the silver lining in a very dark cloud threatening humanity.

COGNITIVE FUNCTIONS OF CULTURE

This short review of what I have written in other papers about the processes of cultural ritualization and pseudo-speciation is indispensable in understanding that which is essential to the viewpoint of this paper: the cognitive function of culture.

The immensely quick and effective new mechanism of acquiring and storing new knowledge—which, as I have said, achieves a true inheritance of acquired characteristics—endows cultures with a strange life of their own. The hoard of super-individual knowledge, wisdom, and skills that constitutes man's spiritual existence, *"das geistige Sein"* in the philosophy of Nicolai Hartmann (25), has just as physically real a base as does its great counterpart, the information store of the genome. Among all the elementary physiological processes that serve the gathering and retaining of information, there is hardly one that is not, as a functional and indispensable part, built into the great, integrated cognitive process of human culture. Of all the genetic blueprints existing on our planet, that upon which the brain of man himself is built is the most complicated and contains more phylogenetically ac-

Konrad Z. Lorenz

quired information than any other. It is nothing but such brains that, by forming a community continuous in time and coherent in space, have built up, on a next-higher level of integration, something very like a super-individual collective brain of society. Again, the new system, possessing entirely unprecedented systemic properties, originates by a process of integration. A few words must be said about the properties of this new cognitive mechanism.

The single norms of social behavior that are firmly structured by ritualization, and are handed down as cherished possessions from one generation to the next, form in any culture a sort of skeleton, a supporting structure. In this respect, their function is closely analogous to that of phylogenetically programmed patterns of social behavior in the social life of an animal species. Like these, they also form a system whose adaptedness presupposes an enormous amount of information. As I have explained, very complicated cognitive mechanisms, exploratory learning, insight, and even self-exploration have taken part in the acquisition of this enormous hoard of knowledge.

In view of this fact, it is somewhat surprising that the individual member of a culture does *not* possess any insight into or conscious knowledge of the functions performed by the several rites and social norms of his own culture. In other words, this conscious knowledge or insight has been *lost* in the course of ritualization. Patterns of behavior that indubitably originated on the basis of purposeful exploration and real understanding of their function, and which, at their origin, must have been completely plastic and adaptable, have congealed into rigid sequences of behavior in whose mechanical performance insight takes no part. In its ultimate form, such a custom often is not essentially different from one that took its origin from a purely magical superstition.

This "calcification" of originally intelligent behavior is well known in the formation of individual habits of many animals. W. Köhler (42), as I have already mentioned in the discussion of insight learning, has given many instances in which a problem solution unquestionably achieved by insight degenerated rapidly into a habit and was then applied blindly as a "method" in situations in which it could not possibly be successful. In the development of individual behavior, this solidification of originally intelligent patterns has a positive side to it, insofar as it relieves the highest brain functions of the necessity to repeat, again and again, a difficult performance in exactly the same way—as, for instance, by knowing mathematical formulas by heart we are saved from having to deduce them intelligently every time we use them.

In cultural life, the solidification of a once plastic behavior has still another survival value: rules of behavior whose necessity and survival value may be intelligible, though perhaps only barely, to the most intelligent members of society must unconditionally be obeyed by all, including the most stupid. This makes it desirable to bring to bear all the factors that enforce the strict observance of traditional norms: love of the "cherished" custom, magical fear at its infraction, actual fear of a superego and of discrimination by fellow members of the society, and, at the highest level, even the sense of social responsibility.

Without the support given by the "skeleton" of these rigid structures, no culture could ever develop and live. In fact, it could never even have acquired and stored the information that *makes* it a culture. It has often been said that cultures "grow naturally." The information that underlies the social order of any cultural society, though acquired for the largest part by insight and intelligent exploration, is paradoxically stored in a manner that makes it not directly accessible to the insight and intelligence of the individual. The most direct way to exploit the wisdom contained in traditional rites and norms of social behavior is to live by them. Otherwise, only a very thorough and complicated analysis can tell us about the function of the single rites and norms, for even those that seem unadaptive and useless *may* have an indispensable function, which could cause their abolition to have the most unexpected and disastrous repercussions for the functioning of the whole.

For this reason, there is an indubitable survival value in the seemingly most inadaptive reluctance of all cultures to permit their sacred customs and habits of thought to be changed by insights. Men stubbornly refuse to accept any new information that is apt to cast any doubt on the accepted truths and values of their own culture. It is the die-hard fighters for cultural tradition who burn a Giordano Bruno and do their worst in trying to silence a Charles Darwin.

The full realization of this definitely stultifying effect of the extreme conservatism characteristic of all cultural ritualization is apt to arouse strong doubts in the value of culture as a cognitive mechanism. These doubts, of course, are unjustified. One might, by the same reasoning, doubt the survival value and the indispensability of the information contained in the genome, just because a phylogenetically programmed behavior pattern miscarries or proves inaccessible to adaptive change by insight. The support of solid structure is indispensable to any living organism, and it is an inescapable fact that this support must be paid for by the heavy price of giving up certain important degrees of free-

Konrad Z. Lorenz

dom. A worm can bend in any place of its body, an arthropod or a vertebrate only where joints are built in.

ONTOGENY OF CULTURED MAN

As Arnold Gehlen (19) has aptly put it, man is by nature a creature of culture. It would be a grave error to assume that human ontogeny can take its normal course without cultural tradition. By its specific phylogeny, our species is so programmed that very many of the neural structures determining our behavior are quite unable to function without the input of culturally ritualized information. The best example for this is the speech center in the right *gyrus supramarginalis* of the human brain, whose function presupposes the existence of a highly complicated system of verbal symbols originated by cultural ritualization and passed on by tradition. Were it possible (which it is not) to rear a human being in complete deprivation of cultural tradition, the result would be, not a "reconstruction" of a precultural ancestor of humanity, but a grievously crippled creature with great parts of its brain out of commission.

The process by which an adolescent comes into possession of the rites and social norms characteristic of his culture contains some peculiar psychophysiological mechanisms whose function may well be that of a phylogenetically programmed, built-in "joint" in the otherwise very rigid cultural tradition. At and shortly after puberty, young people normally seem to loosen their allegiance to traditional norms. which they had unconditionally accepted during their childhood. They begin to regard traditional ideals rather skeptically and to cast about for new causes to embrace. Obviously, old solidified structures have to be dissolved in order to make room for new ones. Just as a crustacean must shed its skin in order to grow, and must live through a rather dangerous period until the new exoskeleton has solidified, every new generation of cultured humanity must undergo a period of "moulting" its ideals, in order to endow culture with even a limited degree of plasticity and adaptability.

As the psychiatrist knows only too well, this is a truly critical period in human ontogeny, and it is so in exactly the same sense as a moult is dangerous to a crustacean.

Chapter 6. Science

If I dedicate a particular chapter, however short, to modern natural science, it is to emphasize my conviction that it is an entirely new cognitive mechanism, which, contrary to public opinion, simply did not exist until before the last few centuries. Science presupposes culture, but it rebels, at the same time, against the rigidity of cultural tradition. It is also super-cultural, much in the same manner as culture is super-individual. It has the faculty of integrating, into one collective cognitive process, the knowledge acquired by many independent cultures. If the psychosocial evolution achieved by culture, and mainly by the cultural inheritance of acquired characteristics, progresses faster, by a few powers of ten, than normal phylogenetical evolution does, the same relation prevails between the speeds of scientific and cultural development.

This discrepancy of pace could not fail to generate dangers. In fact, an immediate consequence of scientific knowledge, the all-too-rapid development of technology, is sufficient in itself to threaten humanity with extinction. In one particular way, science is apt to increase the danger of a break in tradition, as I shall explain in the final chapter.

Chapter 7. Pathology of Knowledge

DYSFUNCTION AS A SOURCE OF KNOWLEDGE

I have endeavored to show, as clearly as I could, in what relation learning stands to other cognitive processes and, in particular, how it is dependent on them. This has led us to an extensive, if necessarily cursory, survey of what we know about the comparative physiology of cognition. I cannot refrain from discussing, in this last chapter, some thoroughly disquieting pathological phenomena afflicting some specifically human cognitive mechanisms. Pathology is the legitimate field of application of all physiology, the physiology of human social behavior not excepted. In fact, the social behavior of modern Western cultures is so thoroughly infiltrated with pathological disturbances that the approach of the medical man, of the pathologist, is the only one that can give us any hope at all of ever arriving at a true understanding of it.

On superficial consideration, even that hope seems slim indeed. It would seem that the attempt to analyze a system that is extremely complicated anyway is rendered next to impossible by the further complication of its being disturbed by pathological influences. However, this is not so. A mechanism's malfunction may in itself be a clue to the understanding of it. In fact, a great part of physiological research relies on intentionally *creating* malfunctions in order to deduce from them the normal function and the survival value of the mechanism in question. Similarly, some of the basic facts that started off ethology as a new branch of research were discovered only by the study of the malfunctions of certain physiological mechanisms underlying behavior. The nature of the fixed motor pattern would never even have been noticed, let alone understood, had it not been for its miscarriage in the abnormal circumstances under which the captive animal lives. The motor pattern being discharged at inadequate substitute objects or even *in vacuo* called C. O. Whitman's (99) and the Heinroths' (28) attention to its spontaneity and to its independence of external coordinating stimuli. As long as we are able to recognize, beyond reasonable doubt, the survival function in whose service a mechanism has evolved, its malfunction tells us *more* about its physiological causality than its performance under circumstances in which it achieves its full survival value. Watching a wolf bury some prey in the wild woods does not teach us much; watching a six-week-old puppy going through the identical sequence of movements on the parqueted floor of our best room tells us quite a lot indeed. In one of his last letters to me, my late friend Ronald Hargreaves wrote that he had come to ask, as the first question of a biologically minded psychiatrist approaching the problems of any mental illness: "What is the survival function of the mechanism which is here miscarrying, and what deviations of its normal functioning can explain the pathological phenomena here found?" There is a relationship of reciprocal elucidation between the approaches of the evolutionistic, teleonomically minded physiologist and that of the medically minded pathologist, and it is my quarrel with the majority of modern sociologists that they do not see the necessity of applying this "principle of reciprocal elucidation" in the attempt to disentangle the Gordian knot of human social behavior. Nobody will ever succeed in this who is not gifted, simultaneously, with the biologist's flair for the teleonomy of physiological functions *and* with the "clinical eye" to perceive the tenuous borderline between that which is still physiological and that which is clearly pathological.

A knowledge process is just as constitutive of life as is a dynamic process that gains and stores energy. Loss of one must ultimately spell death just as surely as loss of the other. Our emotional appreciation, as already mentioned, inescapably attributes *values* both to gains of knowledge and to gains of energy. Correspondingly, we value living systems according to the amount of relevant, organized information (in other words, knowledge) they possess and also according to the capital of potential energy at their disposal. It is by the same standard that we apply the attributes of "lower" and "higher" to species of animals or plants and to human cultures. We are swayed in this value judgment much more by the amount of knowledge than by the size of the energy-capital a living system possesses, and justly so. Even a great loss of capital does not necessarily jeopardize the survival of a living system. A species can lose an enormous percentage of its individuals and still survive, as the rabbit did after myxomatosis; even a human individual can be starved to less than half his normal weight and suffer no permanent damage.

On the other hand, the loss of teleonomically acquired, organized, and organizing information causes a much more dangerous decrease of the living system's chances of survival, as it unavoidably implies a loss of specific adaptedness. From this rule there is only one exception, which concerns one of the partners in a symbiosis: domestic animals and plants, for instance, can afford to lose quite a lot of their genome-bound knowledge, because man, as their symbiont, makes up for the deficit. This is not true, of course, of the host of a parasite. The crustacean *Sacculina carcini,* which grows like a shapeless tumor on the abdomen of crabs and which, having lost its eyes, brain, legs, and body structure, looks pretty "low" and "degenerate," really possesses just as much adaptive genetic knowledge as any average crustacean.

Sudden loss of genetic knowledge invariably results in pathological phenomena. If details are dropped out of the genetic blueprint of the general, large-scale structure of an organism and its organs, the consequence is a malformation; if the loss concerns the small structure of tissues, the result is all too often a regression to an ontogenetically or phylogenetically more primitive type of structure. Between the two, all intermediates are possible. The beautiful cultivated rose, sung by so many poets, owes the beauty of its corona to so-called doubling, which consists in stamens being malformed, regressing to the simpler form of petals. For me, even the beauty of the "queen of flowers" has

Konrad Z. Lorenz

a flavor of the satanic and bears a chilling reminder of malformation, tumor, and cancer—the difference is only one of degree. The greater the loss of knowledge and the deeper, consequently, the regression, the more devastating becomes the disintegration of the whole. If the stamens forget that they ought to produce pollen and content themselves with being simple petals, there is a loss of fertility, but the rose still lives to enchant its symbiont, the gardener who has bred it. If the loss of knowledge goes so far that, in the body of a metazoan, some cells altogether forget that they are parts of an adult, multicellular organism, they will naturally revert to the behavior of a unicellular animal or of an embryonic cell, which means that they will start uninhibitedly to multiply by division. For obvious reasons, the malignity of any tumor is in direct proportion to the "immaturity" of its tissue.

Genetic knowledge is not easily lost; species of wild animals and plants are under the constant influence of natural selection, which does not easily let them forget what they have already learned. A human culture has a complicated and finely adapted structure, which makes human beings behave as members of a supra-individual system, of a society. The information underlying it can be forgotten much more easily than the knowledge stored in the genome—it can be snuffed out in one generation or two. Individuals and groups of individuals can then behave, in relation to the living system we call a culture, in exactly the same manner as a malignant tumor does within the smaller system of an individual. Again, the ruthlessness of destruction is proportional to the loss of knowledge.

DEHUMANIZATION

It cannot be my task here to convince the reader of the fact that our culture is in imminent danger of extinction. In that respect, I can refer to the work of Max Born (6), Kurt Hahn (22, 23), John Eccles (13), and others. My problem is how to explain some of these phenomena of disintegration on the basis of pathological malfunctions of certain cognitive mechanisms discussed in this paper. What is so intensely alarming about this destruction is that, of all the values created by human culture, those that must be regarded as the highest and most constitutive possessions of our species are the ones that are most susceptible to the affliction. It is, therefore, quite correct to subsume the processes here under discussion under the concept of *dehumanization.*

There are nonscientific humanists who sincerely believe that science as such is inhuman in principle and guilty of present-day phenomena of dehumanization. There is one grain of truth in this otherwise vastly unjust accusation: as Max Born has pointed out, an attitude of skepticism, which is entirely justified in science, can become disastrous when applied to traditional norms of social behavior. In science, it is legitimate and even necessary not to believe anything that cannot be demonstrated to be true by scientific verification. A culture, with all its immensely complicated systems of social norms of behavior, possesses an enormous treasure of wisdom and knowledge that has not been acquired by scientific research, nor even by exploratory behavior and insight, but that has grown organically, much as the knowledge in the genome has grown. Just as we can attain insight into the knowledge contained in the genome only by the detour of research, we do not possess immediate knowledge about the functions of the single norms of social behavior prescribed by the tradition of our own culture. Therefore, if the angry young man asks us why he should comply with a certain taboo or norm of social behavior, the only scientifically correct answer we can give him is: "I do not know, but nobody can predict what dangerous repercussions the abolition of this particular part of a highly complicated system of interactions may produce." Whereupon the angry young man, having a high regard for "exact" natural sciences and a low one for biology, let alone psychology and sociology, goes away deeply dissatisfied.

However, I believe it is an error to assume that science, in a process of one-way causation, exerts a dehumanizing effect on present-day culture. On the contrary, I am convinced that the roots of the dangerous decline lie much deeper and that, if science threatens to become less and less humane, it is because scientists, being only human and being no less typical representatives of their time than nonscientific people, are not by any means immune to the general illness of our culture. Practically all the phenomena we encounter—and deplore —in present-day science have their close parallels in nonscientific culture: a utilitaristic blindness to ultimate values; a short-sighted tendency to lose sight of ultimate goals and to mistake for the latter that which is of no intrinsic value in itself, but valuable only as a means to reach a goal; a devout belief in the superlative importance of amassing great quantities of something or other, accompanied by a complete neglect of the quality of whatever is being amassed; and a ruthless readiness to debunk, regardless of losses, any amount of important knowledge in order to simplify and make more convincing some ideological dogma of the day.

However, there exists, not only a more or less neutral disregard of knowledge handed down by tradition, but in many cases an active

Konrad Z. Lorenz

hostility against it. In nonscientific culture it is all too obvious that there is a noticeable negative correlation between the values attributed to certain norms of social behavior by one generation and the next. The same phenomenon indubitably occurs in science, too. In biology, for instance, descriptive morphology and systematics were considered to be superlatively important by our elders, while they are not only negelected but despised and even regarded as unscientific by a deplorably great part of today's scientific youth.

Another process of dehumanization, equally affecting scientific and nonscientific life, is the isolation that affects individuals as well as small family groups and is, paradoxically, caused by too great a population density. Crowding causes an alarming lack of interest in the fellow member of the species and even of the community. There are unbelievable but sure records of cases in which rape and murder have been committed by daylight in crowded streets, while hosts of people walked by and did not interfere, being afraid of "getting involved." In science, the very number of coscientists has a similar effect. It is becoming more and more difficult to keep abreast of the literature in even one's own small branch of science, let alone science in general. Division of labor and specialization proceed apace, and with them the stultification of the specialist, of which I have already spoken (p. 19). Modern scientists, great specialists in their own fields, are quite often astoundingly uneducated people. This, of course, misleads them into overestimating the importance of their own branch of research, with the consequences of explanatory monism and reductionism. In a similar way, most of the reduction phenomena in current nonscientific attitudes have their corollaries in science. Although they are basically unscientific, they are sufficiently widely spread and fashionable among scientists as to mislead many nonscientific custodians of culture to think that science in itself is inhuman.

Of these tendencies, two particularly dangerous ones have received the names of *scientism* and *reductionism*. I reject the term "scientism" because it implies that too much devotion to science can become an addiction and a vice, which I do not think it can. The fallacy thus described is the one already discussed—the erroneous belief that scientific research is the only legitimate source of knowledge. "Reductionism" is not so easily defined. One factor entering into it is what Donald Griffin (21), in a paper recently read at the International Ethological Conference in Stockholm, described as the "simplicity filter." It consists in the all too widespread belief that a scientific investigation can be made more "exact" by limiting the research to measuring a few arbitrarily chosen parameters, thus willfully shutting our eyes to any possible information concerning the real complication of the investigated system. This procedure is, of course, just as stupid as the one erroneously ascribed to the ostrich.

Closely allied to the fallacy of the simplicity filter are those of explanatory monism and reductionism. These have in common the endeavor to explain, on the basis of one or two relatively simple explanatory principles, the functions of a very complicated system. Explanatory monism is characteristic of most great discoverers of a new explanatory principle. Jacques Loeb sincerely believed that he could explain all the behavior on the basis of tropisms; Pavlov thought the same of reflexes and conditioned reflexes. Much can be said in extenuation of the discovering genius who, in the comprehensible euphoria of his achievement, oversteps the limits of scientific thought. However, it must be remembered that the damage done by this transgression is all the greater, the greater the discovery. Very many people, scientists included, are taken in when the justly admired genius commits the sin of pretending fraudulently, as Eccles said, to be able to explain phenomena that are beyond the range of the newly found principle.

Quite often, simplicity filters and reductionism are camouflaged under the mask of purposefully distorted operationalism. The distortion lies in confining definitions to possible experimental results, while altogether neglecting the investigation of structure. In my opinion this fallacy arises from two motives. One is the attempt to ape as closely as possible the methods of modern atomic physics, in which *there are no structures to describe*. For a critique of this blindness to structure —and to the necessity of *descriptive* science—I need only refer to the papers on this subject by George Gaylord Simpson. One consequence of this superstition is that any *single* experience or observation, however important, is considered scientifically negligible. If this were true, all that part of medical science that is built up on case histories would have to be condemned as "anecdotal."

The second motivation, closely linked with the one just discussed, is the veneration for great numbers that is so fashionable nowadays, in science as well as in nonscientific civilization. It can enter into a devastating union with the misunderstood "operationalism" just described. If the operation chosen is sufficiently simple, it is easy to pass through it, like different kinds of food through a mincing machine, great numbers of objects so as to obtain results on which an impressive lot of mathematical operations can be performed.

Another grave error, which is closely allied to those just described, consists in confounding information (in the information theory sense) with knowledge. P. Weiss (94, 96) has pointed out the pernicious consequences of this confusion. Information theorists have, with a certain highhandedness and disregard for biological considerations, divested the concept of information of its semantic connotation. In common parlance, the word "information" in itself implies the sending and receiving of a message, the understanding of which is of survival value both to the sender and to the receiver. These need not necessarily be symbionts—the threatening of a big moose against a wolf is of survival value to both species. The concept of information theory, on the other hand, is a very abstract one. What the creators of information theory really had in mind was to analyze the sending and the correct understanding of messages by human communication techniques. They could presuppose a system of symbiotic senders and receivers, as well as the fact that the transmitted messages made sense. Therefore, they could afford to strip the concept of information of all these properties, which to the biologist seem constitutive of what is commonly called information and which, in common parlance, mean organized, relevant information—in other words, knowledge.

It is extremely easy to confound two conceptions associated with the same term, and, for research workers infected by the fashionable adoration of numbers, it is apparently a matter of course to equate the two conceptions associated with the term "information." They greedily collect data, which certainly means accumulating information in the sense of information theory. But they commit the great error of thinking that they gain knowledge. The sheer accumulation of data is at best the humble soil on which the tree of knowledge can grow, and even then so-called intuition, which really is the function of gestalt perception, must be at work if the soil is to be fertile. Not even the oldest and most primitive mechanisms of cognition, such as those discussed in this paper, ever function on the basis of an indiscriminate collecting of data. Not even the random procedure of the genome ever acquires or retains irrelevant information; in fact, it is quite unable to do so, because it is always natural selection that guides the tree of knowledge in its orderly, well-organized teleonomic growth. A really random procedure seems to be the sad prerogative of some branches of present-day science, which, to put it bluntly, collect information instead of knowledge. This leads to extreme specialization, because the research worker, losing sight of the great context in which knowledge is valuable, becomes isolated in his mechanical rote performance, which appears to him, if to nobody else, of extreme importance. This kind of science can stray so far from everything that is of human interest as to further the erroneous belief of some non-scientific humanists that science as such is inhuman.

The fallacy that Ernst Mayr, George Gaylord Simpson, and other biologists, including myself, are calling reductionism and are trying hard to fight does *not* consist in the belief that all processes of animal and human life (barring subjective experience and circumventing the mind-body problem) can be explained, at least in principle and in the case of a utopian ultimate success of research, on the basis of the elementary physical and chemical processes and structures. Even if it should be entirely wrong, this belief is a safe working hypothesis that can never become an impediment to science; before we hit the borderline of knowledge, we shall become aware of the inexplicable! However, we are convinced that an *explanation* of all the phenomena found in a living system can never be based solely on the understanding of the elementary processes *alone* or on the laws of physics and chemistry prevailing in them. Such an explanation has another, equally indispensable prerequisite. We know that very different structures can be built of identical elements in which identical physical and chemical laws are prevailing. As I have already explained (p. 20), the functional properties of the whole *cannot be deduced* if one knows only these elements and these laws, however exhaustive this knowledge may be. One has to know the very particular *structure* in which these elements are put together, and, in order to understand that, one has to know the historical process in which they have, in actual fact, been assembled in the history of evolution; that which we call the "explanation" of, or the "full insight" into, the workings of a living whole or system has, for its indispensable prerequisite, *all* of these different sorts of knowledge, each of them obtained from a different source and by a different kind of approach. Investigation may start at any chosen level, and it is not, as some reductionists believe, "inexact" to start at the highest possible level, with the ambitious endeavor to understand ourselves. From what has been said about systems (p. 20), it is clear that the "wholes" of one level of integration are parts of the next higher one and that one may hope, in principle, as Crick says, "to have the whole of biology 'explained' in terms of the level below it, and so right down to the atomic level" (12). Thus far, the most emphatically antireductionistic biologists—let us say Paul Weiss (95), Ernst Mayr, and George Gaylord Simpson—will go along with Francis Crick. Antireductionism is *not* to be confounded with neovitalism!

However, the reductionistic trend, of which John Eccles has accused Crick's book *Of Molecules and Men,* is certainly there. Though he says, with great insight, "I think that this distinction—between the behavior of an organism and its evolution—is of crucial importance" and, in the preceding sentence, that chance may produce effects on evolution "which basically alter the historical process," he somehow does not seem to appreciate the fact that insight into the historical process and its consequences to structure are both indispensable in order to have the whole of biology "explained" in terms of the level below it, and so on right down to the atomic level. However, Crick does not regard history as a science, as he clearly asserts, while speaking of the actual process of evolution, that "it may be history *rather than science*" (italics mine).

It is a fundamental error to believe that history is not a science and is, therefore, dispensable to biology. History and historical events that happened but once are real *causes* that have influenced the course of phylogeny. If we ask *why* we have, on both sides of our head, ears to hear with, one of the causally explaining, indispensable answers to the question is: *because* we are descended from water-breathing verte-brates that happened to have gill openings in that place, which were later used as sound-conducting canals. Even if we should ever attain full insight into the causality of all the interacting systems constituting a living organism as it is today, and even if we should do so to the utopian point of being able to *make* it, we still should not know why it is as it is and not quite otherwise as long as we do not know about its history.

The same discrepancy becomes more apparent when we consider a man-made machine. As far as its present composition and function is concerned, it is quite easy to understand and to make. The moment, however, that we ask about why its design is exactly as it is, we postulate an answer that embraces all the teleonomy of the construc-tion, the survival value it has to the constructor, and the whole history of technology and that of mankind which enabled it to construct machines. Reductionists and neovitalists alike tend to forget that automobiles and locomotives do not, like Przewalski horses, roam the wilds independently of man, but are cuticular organs of *Homo sapiens,* just as the beautiful paper shell is one of *Argonauta argo.*

I wonder whether it is on these points that Michael Polanyi will disagree with me; should he do so, it will be in the opposite direction from that in which Francis Crick would. My opinion is that all life processes can ultimately be accounted for by the laws of inanimate nature *and* by the working of the organically evolved *structures* in which these laws do not suffer any infraction, but in which other laws, too, are prevailing—laws that are not deducible from the elementary laws of physics and chemistry but can be understood only on the basis of the additional knowledge of structure. Mendel's law, for instance, became easily explainable once the structure of the nucleus and the behavior of chromosomes during the process of fertilization became known.

One important point that may be a consolation to neovitalists is that even in the utopian event of a complete reduction of all biological laws, right down to the basis of more elementary laws and of structure, there will always remain a remnant that cannot be rationalized, because it is practically impossible to follow up all the innumerable causal chains influencing history. The "nonrationalizable" or historical remnant (*der nicht rationalisierbare oder historische Rest,* as Max Hartmann calls it) will always obviate the complete "reducibility" of biological phenomena.

After what has been said about systems and about the way in which new systemic properties come into existence, it ought to be self-evident that, with new systemic properties, *new laws* come into existence. The Mendelian laws, the Weber-Fechner law, and others that prevail only in living systems are laws of nature by the same token as the lawfulness of a planet's orbit. The lawfulnesses prevailing in a living system govern orbits within orbits; their sum total, within a higher organism, is of an immense and, at the present stage of our knowledge, quite unpredictable complication. Francis Crick's assertion that all biology "can be explained in terms of the ordinary concepts of physics and chemistry, or rather simple extensions of them" is, in my opinion, a very monster of an understatement.

I am as much out of sympathy with any form of vitalism as Crick is. I think that the assumption of any factors, such as a *force vitale,* a whole-producing power, biotonic laws, and so on, is strictly illegitimate, as it arbitrarily draws a line prohibiting further progress of natural explanations. However, it is an unforgivable error to underrate the complexity that the natural explanation of the functions of a highly differentiated central nervous system necessarily must attain. Nor is the historical remnant that can never be explained completely negligible. To give a natural explanation of a living system, it is necessary to understand the morphology and the function of all its parts or subsystems, to understand the survival value of each detail, to know its whole phyletic history and its causes, including all the manifold selection pressures that directed its course and made the organism what it is at present. It is also necessary to know the whole process of morphogeny in which the genetical code is decoded by each individual. When we know all that, we have arrived at the level at which biochemistry can dig still deeper and achieve the ultimate explanation on the basis of chemical and physical laws. I should hardly call all that indispensable knowledge, stemming from quite a number of independent sciences, "a rather simple extension" of physics and chemistry.

I fully agree with Michael Polanyi (65) when he asserts that man-made machines are not more reducible to physical and chemical laws than their maker himself is. I also agree that, even without drawing into consideration the irreducibility of the historical remnant, there is one all-important phenomenon that will always defy an explanation by natural science, and that is our subjective experience. The body-mind problem is, in my teacher Max Hartmann's opinion (which I fully share), insoluble in principle. However, everything concerned with physiological causation, including the demonstrable effect of natural selection in evolutionary history, *can* be explained in a perfectly natural way, at least in principle. If this assumption should be erroneous, it still does no damage as a working hypothesis: none of us will be disappointed if, in the final success of scientific research, he should run up against God. The arbitrary erection of dogmatic, vitalistic barriers, on the other hand, can do damage and has done so, particularly in my own field, in the study of instinctive behavior.

I do not believe that Francis Crick really thinks that all other sciences are rather simple extensions of physics. In *Molecules and Men* he says so, angrily arguing against neo-vitalists, and in the same book he gives a perfectly correct description of how, in science, the research on every level of integration drives its analysis downwards, to the next lower one. I believe we should wrong him if we read into his assertion the belief that these higher and more complicated levels of biological phenomena do not have their own laws, which are laws of nature quite as much as are those of physics.

However, the sentence of "rather simple extensions" of physics, uttered by a Nobel Prize laureate, will of course be pounced upon and greedily misinterpreted by hosts of young scientists. There are superlatively strong motivations to do so. The pernicious belief that the patient and laborious study of morphology, comparative anatomy, and phylogeny, that the whole historical aspect of life can simply be skipped, offers an irresistibly seductive fool's paradise to the young, the cocksure, and the impatient. Inability to wait is one of the serious defects of present-day youth, in nonscientific life as well as in science, and so it is welcome news to many that great things can be achieved in biology without having to study all those tiresome, old-fashioned subjects.

Another superlatively strong motivation to which otherwise highly intelligent young scientists succumb without resistance is the command of *fashion*. Again, the urge to be a typical representative of the fashionable and uniform group is the same in everyday life and in science. In biology, all description, whether of morphological detail or of behavior, is regarded as obsolete and even as unscientific. Few professors of zoology would nowadays accept a doctor's thesis that contains neither experiments nor diagrams or statistics; still less would students dream of submitting one. Among my own young people I am again and again surprised at the extent to which they are swayed by fashion. It is incredible what simple things, which can be much better said in a few sentences, they try to express in innumerable diagrammatic curves and mathematical expressions. I need not say more; George Gaylord Simpson, with wonderful satire, has already said what is necessary.

ETHOLOGICAL CAUSES

What is common to all these different phenomena of reductionism is a *loss of knowledge,* a dropping out of great portions of relevant, organized information. Such a loss, as I have already explained, inescapably causes *pathological* symptoms of disintegration in the system concerned. Reductionism is quite literally a disease of science, and I have already professed my belief that the underlying disturbance is one that primarily afflicts the everyday life of our culture. If it produces even more alarming results in science, it is because scientists can afford to lose their minds even less than other people.

It is often very difficult to see the obvious. *"Das ist das Schwerste von allem, was dich am leichtesten dünket, mit den Augen zu sehn, was vor den Augen dir liegt,"** as our greatest German poet says. I sincerely believe that, looking at the common everyday life of my contemporaries and particularly that of my family and my friends, and comparing my own generation with the next, I can see some of the causes of dehumanization. Most of them are directly or indirectly linked with overpopulation.

A direct consequence of crowding is the frightening decline of the interest we take in "our neighbor." Not only the incredible callousness already mentioned, but also the less reprehensible indifference of which all of us are guilty, is caused by the excessive demands constantly made on our social response by the unceasing presence of comparative strangers. We are literally being milked dry of the milk

* "The hardest of all is that which seems the easiest—to see what is right in front of your eyes."

Konrad Z. Lorenz

of human kindness. If one comes to a thinly populated country in which everybody has a 20-mile drive over bad roads to his next neighbor, one is struck by the warmth and the sincerity of human kindness that one meets in everybody.

The second, and probably much more dangerous, source of dehumanization lies in the breakdown of the mechanisms handing down tradition from one generation to the next. Indirectly, this most disrupting phenomenon is itself a consequence of overpopulation. It begins with inconspicuous but lasting damage done to the relationship between the generations during the first months of infancy. Mothering a child is a *full-time job* and the fact that it is absolutely impossible for most modern mothers to dedicate sufficient time to their baby definitely impairs the latter's education. Education begins by very simple childish games. I do not know the English equivalent of *Bocki-Bocki stoß* and *Hoppe, hoppe Reiter, wenn er fällt so schreit er,* but I am sure they exist. One must have seen the lighting up of a baby's face when it first grasps the idea of this kind of primitive joke. Many modern and, worse, scientifically oriented young mothers not only have no time for such apparently silly baby games, but additionally feel self-conscious about indulging in them. I believe they are ashamed of treating a small baby so anthropomorphically!

This very early education surprisingly seems to be quite indispensable. It is the child's primary introduction to *communicative rites* as such, and it seems that if this is not effected at the correct sensitive phase of development, the baby's readiness to communicate at all suffers. In other words, the slight damage that present-day babies suffer by their mother's lack of time and skepticism is of the same sort as the severe impairment caused by hospitalization, which, as René Spitz's work (82, 83, 84) has conclusively shown, produces a syndrome indistinguishable from that of psychotic autism. If our babies are made autistic even to the very slightest degree, a most dangerous first step to dehumanization will have been taken.

It has been my experience that young mothers flatly disbelieve me when I tell them what feats of education were achieved about forty years ago with very young babies. I simply do not dare to tell them the age at which my children were toilet-trained. Today, the diaper-distorted behinds of quite big children can be seen in the best families, including my own. Older medical men will bear me out that forty years ago, most children, when ordered to bed because they were running a temperature, really obeyed this order. Today, it seems to be impossible to enforce it, rare cases excepted. The word "uneducated" is the correct one to attribute to most modern children; they literally "do not know the first things"—and how should they, since nobody tells them?

The curse of present-day childhood and adolescence is lack of personal contact, first with the mother, later with the father, and still later with teachers. I remarked in Chapter 5 that adolescents undergo a sort of moult in their allegiance to traditional ideals and that this process is of obvious survival value, devised by evolution to prevent the "calcification" of the social norms and rites that constitute the behavioral "skeleton" of a culture. I have also explained what social relationships must exist between two generations in order to make acceptable to adolescents the traditions of their elders. In a past that was happier at least in this one respect, the critical period was not too dangerous, either for the individual undergoing it or for the culture in which it wrought necessary but slight adaptive changes. Until quite recently, all the sociological conditions under which tradition becomes acceptable to the adolescent were fulfilled; today it is a rare and a lucky family of which this can be said. When the son was still learning his craft from his father and was ambitious about it, very little disciplining was necessary to make him acknowledge the old man's superiority. There was not too much trouble about the rank order relationship between the two. In many professions, as in European peasantry, the son's taking over was a strictly ritualized procedure that generated as little hostility as possible. Also, the close contact between the generations and their cooperation in aiming at common goals contributed to engender, in the young generation, a warm love and friendship for the older people, altogether compatible with respect.

Today, few children ever see their father at work (and if mine observed me staring into an aquarium, they could not possibly understand that this was work); most of them meet him only in his exhausted state coming back from his shop or office. Having suffered enough anger and irritation during the day, the last thing he wants to do is to talk about his work. He wants nothing but peace; he is in no mood to discipline a naughty child, and he may even snarl at Mom, should she have to do so for good reasons. There is nothing to admire in Dad and still less in Mom, even if she is the better disciplinarian: she is the lowest-ranking creature in the child's social group, because she has to do all the really dirty work and because she is, in most cases, obviously rank-inferior to the charlady, whose favor she is currying for fear that this superior woman might give notice.

Things are even worse if the parents have been in touch with a certain type of child psychology and have absorbed, if not digested, the environmentalist theory that it is only frustration that makes mice and

Konrad Z. Lorenz

men aggressive. An exaggerated fear of losing their children's love, should they punish them, enforces some parents' tendency to believe this nonsense. The results are intolerably aggressive children who, in every case I myself had occasion to observe for a sufficient time, end up by becoming neurotic. Putting oneself in such an unfortunate child's place, it is easy to imagine what a superlatively disconcerting experience it must be to find oneself unable to evoke the natural response of anger in one's social partner, and, instead of the instinctively expected, ardently desired, and well-deserved slap, to elicit nothing but restrained, impersonal reproof and glib, pseudo-reasonable explanations. It must have the nightmare quality of inanely beating against a rubber wall enclosing one on all sides.

An additional factor, which rarely seems to be considered by the nonfrustration theorists, is the *insecurity* that the child very probably feels, because, according to a child's obvious logic, such despicable weaklings, who allow themselves to be bullied and snarled at by a two-year-old, cannot possibly afford any protection against strangers. Moreover, these strangers must appear dangerously hostile to a nonfrustration child whose fond parents do not realize the effect their insufferable offspring has on other people. These do not enjoy watching their furniture broken, their dogs beaten with heavy instruments, and their assiduously reared goslings' necks wrung—all personal experiences of my own. Even if the long-suffering host bears these trials with fortitude and politeness, the child intuitively senses the clenched fist in his pocket. Children have a very fine perception of involuntary nonverbal communication, much as dogs and horses have. Small wonder that they go crazy, living, as they must feel they do, in a hostile world insufficiently protected by servile and cowardly underlings. Small wonder that they altogether reject the traditions of their parents' generation: one does not submit to the precepts or imitate the norms of social behavior of one's despised slave.

While, for the reasons mentioned—and probably for many others as yet unknown—the effectiveness of the mechanism that hands down tradition from one generation to the next is rapidly waning, the *demands* made on it are progressively increasing. The rapid change forced on human social life both by the explosive increase of population and by the doubtful blessings of advancing technology necessitates correspondingly fast adaptive changes in the norms of social behavior of our culture. As both processes accelerate, the adaptive changes demanded of our culture from one generation to the next increase apace. In other words, the amount of traditional norms and rites that *have* to be jettisoned *and replaced by others* becomes greater from generation to generation. The gap between the old and the young was never as great as it is today, but it is predictable with great certitude that the differences to be bridged between our children and our grandchildren will be even greater.

Even today there is a distinct threat of a *complete* break in the continuity of our culture. Continuity as such is being disparaged. There is an increasing incapability of pursuing long-term projects. The inability to postpone immediate satisfactions for the sake of later and greater gains is one of the most striking characteristics of present-day youth. The capability to form permanent attachments, be they to objects, to localities, or to persons, seems to be rapidly disappearing. Some people leave their home and friends with less difficulty than I experience in selling an old car. Particularly in the United States, people often do not take their furniture with them when they move to another city; they sell it and buy new. This lack of attachment to old associations is, of course, furthered by the producers, whose interest lies in making fashions in clothes, cars, TV sets, and so on change as fast as possible, as Vance Packard correctly describes in his book *The Waste Makers*. Travel agencies try to attract customers by the prospect of "making new friends," while real friendships, lasting a lifetime, seem to become rarer and rarer.

A positive avidity for new stimulus-situations goes hand in hand with the rapid sensory adaptation to old ones, which thus become ineffective and "boring." Boredom is so much a characteristic of modern youth that it actually influences the cast of features, particularly in girls. It has become positively unfashionable to look lively and amused! Kurt Hahn has made a special study of this modern boredom and its more special causes, and he has even found some remedies that offer the hope of combating it successfully. Boredom is, of course, also one of the causes of increasing drug addiction, though probably not the most important one, which, I suspect, lies in the overpowering urge to identify with a group of some sort, of whatever sort.

When young people, for the reasons mentioned, find themselves quite unable to accept the traditions of their parents, they cast around for other ideals, for a new cause to embrace. Not finding an adequate object in a community striving for real ideals, they will accept substitute objects of amazing inadequacy. As Craig, Seitz, Lissmann, myself, and many others have demonstrated, the withholding of the adequate object of an instinctive response causes a progressive lowering of all the "key-stimuli" that emanate from it and are responded to selectively by the organism. After long deprivation, Craig's pigeons copulated with rags (10), Seitz's (79, 80) and Lissmann's (52) fish fought the crudest dummies, and Kruijt's Bankiva cocks, deprived of any object whatsoever, tried to attack their own tails (46). Young people, being human and endowed with fantasy, will *make* themselves a substitute object, by creating some sort of a group whose cause they can embrace. The "rockers" and "mods," for instance, constituted themselves, or to be more precise, each other, for no other aim than to vent their unassuaged militant group enthusiasm, and the same is true for many other kinds of gang formation. The film *West Side Story* is an ethologically exact and extremely moving illustration of this phenomenon. To belong to the poorest possible community seems to be better than not to "belong" at all, and authorities like Kurt Hahn and Aristide Esser think that this is one of the motives for joining the wretched brotherhood of drug addicts.

Militant enthusiasm needs something to fight for, and it needs somebody to fight against. Unluckily, the second is much easier to find nowadays than the first. Wise men are cudgeling their brains in trying to abstract the concepts of real values that are worth fighting for and to formulate them in such a manner that they become intelligible to everybody and able to awaken enthusiasm for the causes "all humanity ought to be fighting for." It is a difficult task.

On the other hand, any tolerably intelligent young man in the skeptical phase of his ontogeny cannot fail to find lots and lots of things that are amiss in our culture and really worth fighting against. I am all for protesting, to cite one instance, against the competitive rat race of modern commercialism, which consists in a number of cycles of positive feedback and which, therefore, cannot fail to snowball into disastrous effects. Everybody in his right senses must agree with the young people protesting against this unnatural nonsense, but for the life of me I cannot understand how anyone could conceive the idea that an effective counter-measure might consist in abstaining from washing and cutting one's hair. I am out of patience with the languid, bored, boring, unwashed, unsexed, unavailing reefer-smokers. It is said by people who have some sympathy for them that they are at least harmless. They *may* be, but the sociopathological state of affairs of which they are a symptom is *not:* unrequited yearning for a cause to embrace, with the concomitant threshold-lowering that facilitates the eager acceptance of false ideals, all go together to form the fertile soil on which the dangerous seeds sown by demagogues thrive best. The veneration that some present-day German students avow for Mao Tse-tung is a blatant example. These things are dynamite.

CONCLUSION

Everything I have said about the probable ethological causes of the dehumanizing loss of knowledge is based on observations that were not made with scientific purpose but that, in my opinion, any tolerably biologically minded man of my age, who has children and grandchildren, cannot fail to make. I may claim, however, that two men who are scientific world authorities, one on small children and the other on adolescents, will support what I have said about the innately programmed prerequisites for the acceptance of tradition: René Spitz, psychiatrist and psychoanalyst, who knows more about small babies and their needs than anybody else in the world, and Kurt Hahn, the pedagogue, who possesses unequaled insight into the processes of adolescence. None of us is being assertive, and none of us believes that we can suggest all the necessary preventive measures against progressive dehumanization, but we *are* agreed on some unavoidable conclusions. The problem is one of education, and the problems are different concerning each of the two critical periods in human ontogeny: the baby *would* gladly and even greedily soak in the education offered to it, but does not get enough of it. The adolescent *could* get any amount of education—more is offered to him and on easier terms than ever before in the course of history—but he refuses to accept it.

In the case of the baby, it is easy to *prescribe* an unfailing remedy, although it is easier said than done that the young mother should spend most of her time playing, with her baby, games that may seem silly to silly persons but are the adequate education of babyhood.

In the case of the adolescent, the problem is how to create, or recreate, the circumstances under which he is ready to accept knowledge. It is not a question of the subject-matter to be taught, nor one concerning the learning process itself. What we have to know, in order to accomplish our purpose, is the phylogentic programming of that particular kind of learning by which traditional knowledge is passed on from one generation to the next. The problems we have to solve, if we are to save our culture, concern the innate bases of learning.

REFERENCES

1. Adler, M. J. *The difference of man and the difference it makes.* New York: Holt, Rinehart and Winston, 1967.
2. Baerends, G. P. "Fortpflanzungsverhalten und Orientierung der Grabwespe, *Ammophila campestris.*" *Tijdsch. Ent.,* 84 (1941) 68–275.

Konrad Z. Lorenz

3. Bally, G. *Vom Ursprung und von den Grenzen der Freiheit: eine Deutung des Spieles bei Tier und Mensch.* Basel: Birkhäuser, 1945.

4. Bennett, J. G. *The dramatic universe.* Mystic, Conn.: Verry, 1967.

5. Bertalanffy, L. von. *Theoretische Biologie.* Berlin: Bornträger, 1933.

6. Born, M. *Von der Verantwortung des Naturwissenschaftlers.* München: Nymphenburger Verlagshandlung, 1965.

7. Brunswik, E. "Scope and aspects of the cognitive problem," in Bruner, J. S., et al. (eds.), *Contemporary approaches to cognition.* Cambridge: Harvard Univ. Press, 1957.

8. Campbell, D. T. "Evolutionary epistemology," in Schilpp, P. A., *The philosophy of Karl R. Popper.* La Salle: Open Court Publishing Co., 1966.

9. Campbell, D. T. "Pattern matching as an essential in distal knowing," in Hammond, K. R. (ed.), *The psychology of Egon Brunswik.* New York: Holt, Rinehart and Winston, 1966.

10. Craig, W. "Appetites and aversions as constituents of instincts." *Biol. Bull.,* 34 (1918) 91–107.

11. Crane, J. "Comparative biology of salticid spiders at Rancho Grande, Venezuela, IV: An analysis of display." *Zoologica,* 34 (1949) 159–214.

12. Crick, F. *Of molecules and men.* Seattle: Univ. of Washington Press, 1966.

13. Eccles, J. C. Contributions at the Van Leer conferences in Frensham Pond and Villa Serbelloni, 1967, 1968.

14. Eibl-Eibesfeldt, I. "Angeborenes und Erworbenes im Verhalten einiger Säuger." *Z. Tierpsychol.,* 20 (1963) 705–54.

15. Erikson, E. H. "Ontogeny of ritualisation in man." *Philos. Trans. Royal Soc. London B,* 251 (1966) 337–49.

16. Fraenkel, G. S., and Gunn, S. D. *The orientation of animals.* Oxford: Clarendon Press, 1961.

17. Frisch, K. von *Tanzsprache und Orientierung der Biene.* Berlin: Springer, 1965.

18. Garcia, J., and Ervin, F. R. "Gustatory-visceral and telereceptor-cutaneous conditioning: Adaptation in internal and external milieus." *Comm. in Beh. Biol.* In press.

19. Gehlen, A. *Der Mensch, seine Natur und seine Stellung in der Welt.* Bonn: Athenaeum, 1958.

20. Gierer, A. "Uber die Funktion von Desoxyribonukleinsäuren und die Theorie der Regulation der Genwirkung." *Naturwiss.,* 54 (1967) 389–96.

21. Griffin, D. R. Lecture delivered at the 10th International Ethological Conference in Stockholm, 1967.

22. Hahn, K. "Die List des Gewissens," in *Erziehung und Politik, Minna Specht zu ihrem 80. Geburtstag.* Frankfurt: Verlag Öffentliches Leben, 1960.

23. Hahn, K. "Gedanken über Erziehung." *Die Antike,* 4 (1928).

24. Hartmann, N. *Die philosophischen Grundlagen der Naturwissenschaften.* Jena: Fischer, 1948.

25. Hartmann, N. *Der Aufbau der realen Welt.* Berlin: W. de Gruyter, 1964.

26. Hartmann, N. *Grundzüge einer Metaphysik der Erkenntnis.* Berlin: W. de Gruyter, 1949.
27. Hassenstein, B. *Kybernetik und biologische Forschung.* Frankfurt: Akademie Verlagsgesellschaft Athenaion, 1966.
28. Heinroth, O., and Heinroth, M. *Die Vögel Mitteleuropas.* Berlin: Behrmühler, 1924–28.
29. Hess, E. H. "Imprinting, an effect of early experience." *Science,* 130 (1959) 133–41.
30. Hess, E. H. "Space perception in the chick." *Sci. Am.,* 195, I (1956) 71–80.
31. Hinde, R. A. "Factors governing the changes in strength of a partially inborn response, as shown by the mobbing behavior of the chaffinch (*Fringilla coelebs*)." *Proc. Royal Soc. B,* 753 (1960) 398–420.
32. Holst, E. von. "Regelvorgänge in der optischen Wahrnehmung." *Pflüg. Arch.,* 236 (1935) 149–58.
33. Holzapfel, M. "Triebbedingte Ruhezustände als Ziel von Appetenzhandlungen." *Naturwiss.,* 28 (1940) 273–80.
34. Huxley, J. S. "The courtship of the great crested grebe." *Proc. Zool. Soc. London,* 25 (1914) 253–91.
35. Immelmann, K. "Prägungserscheinungen in der Gesangsentwicklung junger Zebrafinken." *Naturwiss.,* 52 (1965) 169–70.
36. Immelmann, K. "Zur Irreversibilität der Prägung." *Naturwiss.,* 53 (1966) 209.
37. Jander, R. "Die optische Richtungsorientierung der roten Waldameisen (*Formica rufa L.*)." *Z. vergl. Physiol.,* 40 (1957) 162–238.
38. Jepsen, G. L., Mayr, E., and Simpson, G. G. *Genetics, paleontology, and evolution.* Princeton: Princeton Univ. Press, 1949.
39. Kawai, M. "Newly acquired pre-cultural behaviour of the natural troop of Japanese monkeys on Koshima Island." *Primates,* 6 (1965) 1–30.
40. Kawamura, S. "The process of sub-cultural propagation among Japanese macaques," in Southwick, C. H. (ed.), *Primate social behaviour.* New York: Van Nostrand, 1963, pp. 82–90.
41. Koehler, O. "Vom unbenannten Denken," in Friedrich, H. (ed.), *Lebendiges Wissen 99.* Wiesbaden: Dietrich, 1953, pp. 271–79.
42. Köhler, W. *Intelligenzprüfungen an Menschenaffen.* Berlin: Springer, 1964.
43. Konishi, M. "Effects of deafening on song development in two species of juncos." *Condor,* 66 (1964) 85–102.
44. Konishi, M. "The attributes of instinct." *Behaviour,* 27 (1966) 316–28.
45. Konishi, M. "The role of auditory feedback in the control of vocalisation in the white-crowned sparrow." *Z. Tierpsychol.,* 22 (1965) 770–83.
46. Kruijt, J. "Ontogeny of social behaviour on Burmese red jungle fowl (*Gallus gallus spadiceus*)." *Behaviour Suppl.,* 12 (1964).
47. Kuenzer, E., and Kuenzer, P. "Untersuchungen zur Brutpflege der Zwergcichliden Apistogramma reitzigi und A. borelli." *Z. Tierpsychol.,* 19 (1962) 56–83.

48. Kühn, A. *Die Orientierung der Tiere im Raum.* Jena: Fischer, 1919.
49. Lashley, K. S. *In search of the engram. Symposia of the society for experimental biology 4: Physiological mechanisms in animal behaviour.* London: Cambridge Univ. Press, 1950.
50. Leyhausen, P. "Uber die Funktion der relativen Stimmungshierarchie." *Z. Tierpsychol.,* 22 (1965) 412–94.
51. Liddell, H. Personal communication (1951).
52. Lissmann, H. "Die Umwelt des Kampffisches *Betta splendens Regan.*" *Z. vergl. Physiol.,* 18 (1932) 65.
53. Lorenz, K. "Der Kumpan in der Umwelt des Vögels." *J. f. Ornithol.,* 83 (1935) 137–215 and 289–413. Reprinted in *Über tierisches und menschliches Verhalten.* München: Piper, 1965.
54. Lorenz, K. "Die instinktiven Grundlagen menschlicher Kultur." *Naturwiss.,* 54 (1967) 377–88.
55. Lorenz, K. *Evolution and modification of behavior.* Chicago: Univ. of Chicago Press, 1965.
56. Lorenz, K. "Evolution of ritualization in the biological and cultural spheres." *Philos. Trans. Royal Soc. London B,* 251 (1966) 273–84.
57. Lorenz, K. "Gestaltwahrnehmung als Quelle wissenschaftlicher Erkenntnis." *Z. f. experimentl. u. angewandte Psychol.,* 6 (1959) 118–65. Reprinted in *Über tierisches und menschliches Verhalten.* München: Piper, 1965.
58. Lorenz, K. "Psychologie und Stammesgeschichte," in Heberer, G. (ed.), *Die Evolution der Organismen,* 2nd ed. Jena: Fisher, 1954, pp. 131–72.
59. Maturana, H. R., Lettvin, J. Y., McCulloch, W. S., and Pitts, W. H. "Anatomy and physiology of vision in the frog *(Rana pipens).*" *J. General Physiol.,* 43, Suppl. 6 (1960) 129–75.
60. Mayr, E. *Animal species and evolution.* Cambridge: Harvard Univ. Press, 1963.
61. Mittelstaedt, H. "Die Regelungstheorie als methodisches Werkzeug der Verhaltensanalyse." *Naturwiss.,* 8 (1961) 246–54.
62. Ostwald, W. *Mathetische Farbenlehre.* Leipzig: Unesma, 1930.
63. Pavlov, I. P. *Conditioned reflexes.* New York: Oxford Univ. Press, 1927.
64. Peckham, G. W., and Peckham, E. G. "Observations on sexual selection in spiders of the family *Attidae.*" Milwaukee: Occasional papers of the National History Society of Wisconsin, 1889.
65. Polanyi, M. "Life transcending physics and chemistry." *Chemical and Engineering News* (1967).
66. Polanyi, M. *Personal knowledge towards a post-critical philosophy.* Chicago: Univ. of Chicago Press, 1958.
67. Popper, K. R. *The open society and its enemies.* New York: Harper & Row, 1962.
68. Popper, K. R. *The logic of scientific discovery.* New York: Harper & Row, 1962.
69. Reese, E. S. "A mechanism underlying selection or choice behavior which is not based on previous experience." *Am. Zool.,* 3 (1963) 508.

70. Reese, E. S. "The behavioral mechanisms underlying shell selection by hermit crabs." *Behaviour,* 21 (1963) 78–126.
71. Richter, C. P. "The self-selection of diets." *Essays in biology.* Berkeley, Calif.: Univ. of California Press, 1943.
72. Richter, C. P. "Total self-regulatory functions in animals and human beings." *Harvey Lectures,* 38 (1942–43) 63–103.
73. Rössler, O. E. "Theoretische Biologie." Lecture delivered at Max-Planck-Institut für Verhaltensphysiologie, 1966.
74. Schein, W. M. "On the irreversibility of imprinting." *Z. Tierpsychol.,* 20 (1963) 462–67.
75. Schleidt, W. M. "Reaktionen von Truthühnern auf fliegende Raubvögel und Versuche zur Analyse ihrer AAM's." *Z. Tierpsychol.,* 18 (1961) 534–60.
76. Schleidt, W. M. "Wirkungen äußerer Faktoren auf das Verhalten." *Fortschr. Zool.,* 16 (1964) 469–99.
77. Schutz, F. "Homosexualität bei Tieren." *Stud. Gen.,* 5 (1966) 273–85.
78. Schutz, F. "Sexuelle Prägung bei Anatiden." *Z. Tierpsychol.,* 22 (1965) 50–103.
79. Seitz, A. "Die Paarbildung bei einigen Cichliden, I." *Z. Tierpsychol.,* 4 (1940) 40–84.
80. Seitz, A. "Die Paarbildung bei einigen Cichliden, II." *Z. Tierpsychol.,* 5 (1941) 74–101.
81. Simpson, G. G. "The crisis in biology." *The American Scholar,* 36 (1967) 363–77.
82. Spitz, R. A. *Hospitalism. The psychoanalytic study of the child,* I. New York: International Universities Press, 1945, pp. 53–74.
83. Spitz, R. A., and Wolf, K. M. *Die Entstehung der ersten Objektbeziehungen.* Stuttgart: Klett, 1957.
84. Spitz, R. A., and Wolf, K. M. *The first year of life.* New York: International Universities Press, 1965.
85. Steiniger, F. "Zur Soziologie und sonstigen Biologie der Wanderratte." *Z. Tierpsychol.,* 7 (1950) 356–79.
86. Storch, O. "Erbmotorik und Erwerbmotorik." *Anz. Mat. Nat. Kl. Österr. Akad. Wiss.,* 1 (1949) 1–23.
87. Taub, E., and Berman, A. J. "Movement and learning in the absence of sensory feedback," in Freedman, S. J. (ed.), *The neurophysiology of spatially oriented behavior.* Homewood, Ill.: Dorsey, 1968.
88. Teilhard de Chardin, P. *La vision du passé.* Paris: Editions du Seuil, 1957.
89. Tinbergen, N. *Instinktlehre.* Berlin: Parey, 1952.
90. Tinbergen, N. "On aims and methods of ethology." *Z. Tierpsychol.,* 20 (1963) 404–33.
91. Tinbergen, N. "Some aspects of ethology, the biological study of animal behaviour." *Advan. Sci.,* 12 (1955) 17–27.
92. Thorpe, W. H. *Science, man and morals.* London: Methuen, 1965.
93. Weidel, W. *Virus, die Geschichte vom geborgten Leben.* Berlin: Springer, 1957.
94. Weiss, P. "Science in the university." *Daedalus,* 93 (1964) 1184–1218.

95. Weiss, P. "Renewable resources." *Nat. Acad. Sci. Public.* 1000-A (1962) 1–17.
96. Weiss, P. "Science looks at itself." *The Graduate Journal,* 5 (1962) 43–59.
97. Wells, M. J. *Brain and behaviour in cephalopods.* London: Heinemann, 1962.
98. Wertheimer, M. *Produktives Denken.* Frankfurt: Kramer, 1957.
99. Whitman, C. O. *Animal behavior.* New York: Atheneum, 1899.

—

Biochemical Aspects
of Learning and Memory

by Holger Hydén

Introduction

As a philosophical question, the mechanism of learning and memory in relation to man's nature was treated early in the literature (58). In his discourse *Meno* (77), Plato describes for us Socrates' plea for the view that problem solving occurs when a man remembers knowledge resident in the soul for generations. To learn is to remember. In today's language, we could formulate this view in speaking of a mechanism of *selection* for memory. John Locke was of an opposite opinion—that the mind of man is like a blank tablet on which experience will chisel the writing (64). Today, one would speak of a mechanism of *instruction* for memory in rephrasing the words of Locke.

The experimental approach to learning mechanisms has been a hard field to cultivate when the aim has been to trace anatomical, physiological, or biochemical correlates. Would-be discoveries have often turned out to be delusions. It may be appropriate to quote Polanyi (78) about the content of empirical statements: "it relies on clues which are largely unspecificable, integrates them by principles which are undefinable and speaks of a reality which is inexhaustible."

Learning means the capacity of a system to react in a new or modified way as a result of experience. Memory is the capacity to store information that can later be retrieved with high distinction to steer the function which is correlated with new information.

In discussing trends within the field, it is important to consider ethology, the study of an organism's behavior in its environment. Molecular neurobiology, with its methods and approach, can be expected to increase its gain greatly if applied to that genetically programmed activity of organisms that is not affected by experience.

The Electrophysiological Approach

Beginning in 1930, studies were undertaken to discover whether learning could be correlated with lasting changes in the electrical activity of the nervous system. Positive results were few, although discussion of the problem was furthered by the formulation of several hypotheses (60, 65). Interest was—and still is—focused on processes in the synapse. It could be shown, however, that long-term memory is not dependent on the maintenance of electrical activity circulating over certain neural nets. Recently, insects, especially cockroaches, have been used for the electrophysiological study of learning. Thus, Luco (65) has presented evidence of the opening of previously closed synapses at the establishment of new motor behavior. Adey (2, 3), using electrodes permanently implanted in the brains of cats, found, at attentive learning, a regularization of slow electrical activity in the hippocampus and a decrease of the impedance. These phenomena spread from the ventral to the dorsal portion of the hippocampus. Adey has ascribed these changes in the impulse activity to the neuroglial cells around the pyramidal nerve cells.

Short-term and long-term memory, with an interposed period for fixation, are terms of especial significance. It is assumed that a short-term memory can be ascribed to transitory changes in synapses mainly of an "electrical nature." During the first hour(s) after training, animals are highly sensitive to interference. But once a fixation of learning has occurred (10 seconds to several minutes), the stored information can withstand interference by electrical shock, extreme temperature changes, and poisoning by chemicals. Long-term memory has, therefore, generally been assumed to have its basis in long-lasting anatomical or molecular changes. It may be assumed, however, that as we accumulate information about primary processes in the brain, the gap will be bridged between electrical and molecular events in brain cells.

The Biochemical Approach

During recent years, an increasing number of studies on biochemical processes in the brain and their relation to learning and memory have been published. Their number is already too great to be included in a discussion of this kind, so we will restrict our scope mainly to the ques-

Holger Hydén

tion: do macromolecular changes in brain cells occur specifically for learning and not at physiological stimuli that sustain only an increased neural function?

Among probable molecular candidates that could serve learning and memory, small molecules with a short lifetime can be excluded. For various reasons carbohydrates and lipids enter only in secondary roles. The most likely candidates are the information-rich proteins and RNA. The following considerations may be noted: Any molecular mechanism for memory that can also serve instinct behavior and experiential learning for a life cycle must have an easy access to the genome. At the expression of gene function, the different types of RNA act as vehicles for phenotypic expression. Brain cells have an abundance of RNA—in fact, no somatic cell type can compete with the big neurons as a producer of RNA.

Such considerations raise the question of the extent of gene activities in such highly differentiated cells as brain cells. It is now known that only a limited number of gene areas are active in differentiated cells (20 percent is probably a high number) (63). In adult cells, genes can be activated, for instance, by external factors such as hormones, which can penetrate to the genes and exert their effect via RNA on specialized target cells. Hormones seem to be able to influence only certain cells, however (82). A pertinent question is, therefore, whether factors in the environment or internal factors may be able to activate gene areas in brain cells.

Highly informative proteins are more likely than RNA to act rapidly, on a trigger mechanism, as executive molecules in millions of brain cells. In such molecules, the biological function is one of conformation, which is given by sequence. At the acquisition of memory, an external stimulus causes an internal transition in brain cells from one state to another by a small energy expenditure, and the new state of mechanism persists. At retrieval, the stored information is matched with information incoming from the environment.

At this point, I would like to stress that *there is no evidence for the presence of mechanistically taping "memory molecules" in brain cells.* As will be shown below, the data instead indicate a synthesis at learning of proteins and small amounts of RNA of a unique composition. Katchalsky and Oplatka (57) have raised the question of whether the products of a changed synthesis of macromolecules can be transmitted to a structure with higher permanence, for example membranes.

It is interesting to consider time constants for macromolecular synthesis in relation to memory function. At nucleic-acid synthesis, 1,000 nucleotides are synthesized per second. One hundred amino acids are made per second, and it takes one second to form a protein. By contrast, the nervous system operates with higher time constants at retrieval and processing of information. An estimate is 10^{-8} to 10^{-9} seconds. This means time factors for weak bonds; hydrogen, hydrophobic, and ionic bonds; and conformational changes.

Interference with Synthesis of Macromolecules in Brain Cells and Its Effect on Memory

Different lines of approach can be discerned in experimental research on learning and memory. Flexner (25, 26) and Agranoff (4, 15) and their colleagues have inhibited synthesis of macromolecules in the brain and observed the effect on animal behavior. Flexner (25) found that inhibition of protein synthesis by puromycin injected in the temporal cortex and in the hippocampus destroys memory (maze learning) in mice. In analyzing the mechanism of this phenomenon, they used an antibiotic (acetoxycycloheximide), which inhibited protein synthesis by inhibiting transfer of amino acid from s-RNA to the polypeptide but did not interfere with the messenger RNA. The heximide was without effect on both short- and long-term memory, and, furthermore, it protected memory against the destructive effect of puromycin. From these experiments it seemed that the initial macromolecular change underlying maintenance of memory involved a change in the quantity of one or more species of messenger RNA.

In further experiments on rats given acetoxycycloheximide, Flexner and colleagues (26) observed an initial period of memory consolidation that was independent of protein synthesis. During an intermediate period, memory could not be expressed when protein synthesis was inhibited more than 90 percent. Memory returned, however, at least 20 hours after protein synthesis had been restored to normal rates. The conclusion of Flexner and colleagues is that the protein concentration of the brain can fall to low levels with only temporary loss of memory, provided certain species of RNA are conserved to direct the resumed protein synthesis when inhibition disappears.

Agranoff and colleagues used puromycin injected intracranially into goldfish in behavioral experiments. When puromycin suppressed protein synthesis 50 to 80 percent in the brain, memory fixation was temporarily suppressed (4, 15). The *formation* of long-term memory required protein synthesis in the brain, but the *maintenance* of long-term memory did not appear to depend on protein synthesis.

The attempts made at our laboratory follow another line. We have established a new behavior in animals and analyzed macromolecules in isolated brain cells to study whether some specific biochemical changes occur that can be correlated with the learning process. This has required analysis of RNA and proteins in isolated neurons and glia with microchemical methods. These are unconventional methods, aiming at the determination and characterization of RNA and protein of the order of magnitude of 10^{-8} to 10^{-10} g. It seems justifiable, therefore, to give a short account of the methods used before describing the experiments. But first some information about the formation of RNA in the brain.

Biosynthesis of RNA in Brain Cells

The medium-sized and big neurons and also the glia are rich in RNA. As a matter of fact, the neurons have no competitors as RNA producers among somatic cells. They contain 20. to 2,000 $\mu\mu$g of RNA per cell (i.e., 5 to 10 percent of their dry weight), of which the main part is cytoplasmic RNA and has the characteristics of ribosomal RNA (see below). The guanine and cytosine values are high. The nucleolar RNA of neurons has the same characteristics.

The nuclei of nerve cells are usually small in comparison with the bulk of the cytoplasm. In Deiters' nerve cells from rats, for example, they contain 30 $\mu\mu$g of RNA compared to the 650 $\mu\mu$g of cytoplasmic RNA. This nuclear RNA has the following base ratios: A 21.4, G 26.2, C 31.9, U 20.5 (42). The explanation is presumably that the nuclear ribosomes and the nucleolar RNA, which is of ribosomal-RNA type, dominate.

There is very little RNA present in the dendrites, and no RNA has been found with certainty in the axons of mammalian nerves. Miani and colleagues (71) have tried electively to label axonal RNA of the hypoglossal nerve. They have described the presence of RNA with sedimentation characteristics of ribosomal RNA in the nerve. The possibility has not been excluded that this RNA originates from the myelin sheath or the Schwann cells, although the evidence points to the RNA being axonal in origin.

In Mauthner neurons from goldfish, Edström and colleagues have found axonal RNA in small concentrations (16, 19). Considering the volume of this large neuron, it turned out that the axon contains four times more RNA than does the cell body. Also, the axon of the lobster sensory stretch receptor was found to contain RNA (28). The RNA of the glia constitutes around 10 percent of the neuronal RNA (53, 54).

Biosynthesis of Nuclear and Cytoplasmic RNA from the Brain

The first example is taken from a study in our institute (22). Rabbits were given ^{3}H-labeled orotic acid, 150 μC, through permanent cannulae inserted into the fourth ventricle, in pulses from 15 to 180 minutes. At the end of this time, 0.2 to 0.4 g of the vestibular area of the brain stem was removed and homogenized. The RNA was extracted and subjected to sucrose-density gradient centrifugation, and the specific activity was determined as cpm/μg of RNA. As carrier, RNA from E. coli was used. After a 15-minute pulse, the nuclear RNA mainly shows low-molecular labeled RNA up to 16 S. After a 30-minute pulse, the sedimentation profile showed larger species of RNA molecules, labeled, 12 S to 30 S. The specific activity had increased from 27 to 123 cpm/μg RNA. This shift toward larger, heterogeneous species of RNA had proceeded in the RNA found after a 60-minute pulse, and the specific activity had increased to 335 cpm/$\mu\mu$g RNA. There is good reason to believe that the 8 to 12 S labeled RNA is a messenger RNA. A proof, however, requires template-activity studies and hybridization with DNA.

The sedimentation study of cytoplasmic RNA showed the presence of 8 to 12 S labeled RNA only after a 30-minute pulse. Thus, the same type of highly labeled RNA as in the sedimentation of nuclear RNA was found after a phase shift of 15 minutes in the cytoplasmic RNA. This agrees with what has been found and deduced from studies of different types of mammalian cells. It is taken to indicate a flow of nuclear RNA into the cytoplasm, although this question is not yet completely resolved. These data agree with those of Jacob and colleagues (53, 54), who found a high amount of radioactivity in the 10 to 45 S of the nuclear RNA from rat brains, 30 minutes after intracisternal injections of nucleotides. Examples of whole-brain RNA analyses from adult rats are given by Mahler, Moore, and Thompson (67), and by Yamagami and colleagues (86). The first-mentioned authors separated 4 S, 17 S, and 28 S RNA fractions and found small but significant differences in the base composition.

In the following presentation, it will be shown that an increase of RNA content of 30 percent can occur in neurons within one hour, with concomitant changes in guanine and cytosine values. One would like to assume that this is due to an excessive biosynthesis of nuclear RNA flooding the cytoplasm, because there is no evidence so far that there exists a mechanism for RNA synthesis in the cytoplasm. The possibility cannot, however, be excluded.

RNA Changes in the Brain with Age

Let us proceed to the question of RNA changes in neurons during a life cycle in rats. As has been pointed out, the rat—which has been the animal of choice for such studies—is immature at birth. The greatest changes in the chemical composition of the brain occur about two weeks after birth (see, e.g., Oja [74]), at which time the mature pattern of the electrical activity appears (80). The anaerobic part of the metabolism begins to decrease in relation to the aerobic part, and the animals begin to be more sensitive to anoxia (34). At two weeks of age their eyes open, the thermoregulation becomes stabilized and the motor activities coordinated. The total amount of RNA increases sharply between the first and second weeks. In the adult rat of 200 g weight, the ribosomal RNA content of the cortex decreases somewhat compared to the content at three weeks of age (1, 84). All these data are interesting, but it is clear that they are applicable only to the rat brain.

Adams (1) has shown a difference in the rate of RNA synthesis between newborn rats and adults. Incorporation of RNA precursors into nuclear RNA proceeded at a similar rate in both cases, but in the newborn animal there was very little incorporation in the ribosomal RNA during the first hour, then an increase. In the adult, the incorporation proceeded linearly from the very beginning. Adams is of the opinion that it is more likely that the ribosomal RNA in the adult brain has become self-replicating than that precursors are flowing from the nucleus to the cytoplasm at a greatly increased rate. During the first half-year, base-ratio changes that involve adenine and guanine also occur in the rat brain RNA (6).

During the maturation period of the first two weeks and of the first eight months, the rat brain differentiates morphologically and biochemically. A pertinent problem is whether gene areas successively become activated and available for transcription according to the program. Can key factors in the environment act as triggers, causing the system to react in new ways also as a result of experiences? As was pointed out above, in highly differentiated neurons and glia, as in other somatic cells that are highly differentiated, the percentage of active DNA can be expected to be low—around 10 to 20 percent.

If experience can modify species of RNA in brain cells, this should be reflected in changes in the RNA composition of individual neurons. Ringborg (79), in our laboratory, has chosen the pyramidal nerve cells of the hippocampus to test this possibility. It is known that the hippocampus is of great importance in learning. He used rats living among the other members of the litter. There is a steep increase in the amount of RNA content/cell from birth to adult age, while in old rats the RNA content/cell has decreased significantly. During maturation, a significant change in the RNA base ratios occurs.

A cyclic change in the RNA content of neurons of man also occurs during the lifetime. Samples were taken from neurologically sound persons, from three to more than eighty years of age, who died in traffic accidents (36). The RNA content increases up to the age of forty, when it reaches a certain average level that is maintained over two decades. After sixty, the RNA content falls quite rapidly. This life-cycle change in RNA is superimposed upon the short-term reversible fluctuations in RNA content that may be seen as a result of increased functional demands.

Some Microchemical Methods Used for Brain-Cell Analysis

It may seem strange that efforts have been made to develop and apply micromethods for the analysis of 10^{-10} g of RNA and proteins, especially in the case of brain cells. Why should not ordinary biochemical methods be successful, as in the case of the liver? The answer, after 15 years of experience with such methods, seems simple: it is because of the complicated structure of the brain. Micromethods are a prerequisite for the analysis of a small number of a defined category of neurons—perhaps 500 neurons, which, including their processes, constitute only 10 percent of the area in question. Furthermore, neurons and glia can react with inverse biochemical changes, as will be exemplified below. An analysis of the whole area, even if it constitutes only half an mg, will give average results; any differences will be leveled out. The straightforward solution is to separate glia, mechanically, from neurons—not any glia within the area, but the glia immediately surrounding the nerve-cell bodies to be analyzed. Their dry weight per sample has to be determined for the sake of comparison with the results of neurons. These neuronal glia are of a special significance to their neurons as compared to the glia situated around capillaries, perhaps at a 200 μ distance.

Sampling of Cells by Microdissection

As was pointed out above, the mechanical separation of neurons and glia has proven to be the method of choice if the purity of the sample is of importance. Nerve cells, including the first part of the dendrites and defined samples of glia, are removed from fresh brain sections. Free-hand dissection is preferred, using microtools made from stainless steel and a stereomicroscope with a magnification of 80 to 160 times (37).

How vital are such isolated neurons? By inserting microelectrodes into such nerve cells under visual inspection, we found that they maintained membrane potentials of between 40 and 70 mV. In nitrogen atmosphere the potential dropped, but it increased again to around 40 mV when oxygen atmosphere was reintroduced (33). One must therefore assume that the cell surface has closed at the points where it was damaged during the isolation of the cell, at the end of the broken dendrite processes, for example. Furthermore, the isolated neurons phosphorylated (13, 32). A study of the endogenous respiration revealed that when the oxygen consumption of the isolated neuron had decreased to zero levels after 180 minutes in a medium without substrate, and when glucose was then added, the oxygen consumption rose to high values (48). Isolated neurons have also been found to grow processes at cultivation (31). For biochemical analyses, therefore, fresh isolated neurons are satisfactory as material.

For precipitated, embedded, and sectioned brain material, the dissection is carried out with a De Fonbrune micromanipulator, under a phase contrast microscope. In some cases only nerve-cell nuclei were used for RNA analysis. For each analysis 25 to 30 nuclei were isolated by microdissection. The technique is briefly as follows: the isolated nerve cells, placed on a glass slide, were treated with cold phenol-saturated water for 15 minutes, followed by treatment with cold absolute ethanol for 10 minutes, and then were covered by paraffin oil. The effect of this treatment is to cause the nuclei to contract slightly, which is hardly noticeable at a magnification of 600 X. The nucleus from each nerve cell can then easily be removed with the aid of the micromanipulator. Twenty-five nuclei were used for each RNA analysis, and it was checked carefully that the cold phenol treatment precipitated all RNA in nerve cells.

Quantitative and Qualitative RNA Analysis

For the quantitative and qualitative analysis of RNA, the micro-methods developed at this laboratory were used. (A detailed technical paper describing the *microelectrophoretic* procedure has recently been published [16].) For each analysis, 500 to 700 $\mu\mu$g of RNA were used. The random error in the determination of the RNA in single nerve cells was found to be 4 percent. The average coefficient of variation of the microelectrophoresis of the analytical results was 5 percent for nerve-cell RNA and 7 percent for yeast RNA. In one case, it has been possible to compare the result of the microelectrophoretic separation of hydrolyzed RNA from biological material with that obtained by conventional macrochemical electrophoretic separations: the analysis of nucleolar and ribosomal RNA of mature starfish oocytes gave the same results with both methods (20). In model experiments on purified samples of RNA, the correspondence between macro- and microelectrophoresis is clear (16).

The advantage of microelectrophoresis over macroelectrophoresis is the possibility of analyzing samples at the cellular level. This has proved to be a *sine qua non* for nerve tissue, since its two cellular components, neurons and glia, differ in amount and composition of RNA.

The neuronal and glial RNA were determined on the same dry-weight basis determined by quantitative X-ray microspectrography (8), using a scanning and computing densitometer (49, 50).

RNA metabolism at the cellular level has been determined by a new micromethod (14, 59)—total, labeled RNA extracted from nerve cells or glia, or the individual bases obtained after electrophoresis on a microscopic cellulose strip, are combusted at 650°C in a single step in glass capillaries. These contain $KClO_4$ and Zn particles, and the organically bound tritium is transformed into hydrogen gas. The activity is determined in a modified Geiger-Muller tube (59). This method combines the high efficiency in tritium direction (>70 percent) and a low background (<5 cpm) and permits an accurate assay of low levels of radioactivity. The RNA metabolism of nerve cells and glia has been compared by means of these micromethods after electrophoretic separation of bases (14). The conversion relations

Holger Hydén

between the RNA purine precursor pools and between the pyrimidine precursor pools were the same in nerve cells and glia, although the labeled RNA in the two types of cells differed in composition. The synthesis of RNA was twice as rapid in the glia as in the nerve cells.

Egyhazi (21) has devised an RNA fractionation method at the cellular level with special regard to isolated neurons and glia. Nerve cells are extracted with phenol at 3°C, which leaves 50 percent of the RNA. Subsequent extraction with phenol at 45°C removes an RNA fraction with high adenine and uracil values. A similar treatment of the glia gave a ribonuclease-resistant RNA with a $(G + C)/(A + U)$ ratio of 0.77. This microfractionating method was combined with incubation of neurons and glia in low concentrations of ribonuclease (22). The material was taken from animals that had received ^{3}H-orotic acid through cannulae permanently inserted into brain ventricles. A small RNA fraction was obtained with a very high specific activity, more than 10,000 cpm/μg of RNA. The base ratios were characterized by relatively high adenine and uracil values.

Protein Separation and Incorporation Studies at the Cellular Level

Recently, a new micromethod has been devised for analysis of proteins from isolated brain cells (38). Since an ultimate task is to characterize also end products of the activity of the mechanism for macromolecular synthesis in brain cells, and a few results have been obtained, a short description will be given below.

Soluble proteins, extracted from fresh, isolated neurons or glia, are analyzed by disc electrophoresis on polyacrylamide gel in capillaries whose diameters are 200–300 μ (38). The manipulations necessary are carried out free hand. The sample contains around 10^{-8} g of protein. Homogenization of the cells is performed in a capillary with a twisted loop of 28-μ-diameter steel wire driven at 12,000 rpm. Separation current is 1.5 μA for 3 to 4 hours. The protein pattern is obtained by amido-black staining and scanned with a microdensitometer. The biosynthesis of proteins is studied on material from animals that received ^{3}H-labeled amino acids. The individual bands in the 200 μ diameter gel are cut out under a microscope, combusted in capillaries, and counted as described above.

For the localization of the acidic protein to the various types of brain cells, single diffusion agar precipitation was performed in 300-μ-diameter glass capillaries using antiserum against the acidic protein.

To localize this protein to intracellular details, the multiple-layer method of Coons was applied (12). This technique requires cryostat sections of the tissue, and the antigens are identified by fluorescence.

All these methods have been used over a number of years to study the effect on neurons and glia of increased motor activity (35), sensory stimulation (29, 30, 45, 52, 56), hormonal stimulation (18, 20), sleep (46, 47), and chemicals (23). In all these cases a significant increase of the amount of RNA and protein per neuron was found correlated with the change in neural equilibrium. In the cases tested, a concomitant RNA decrease was found per comparable dry weight of glia surrounding the neuron. Evidence, including base-ratio changes of RNA, has been presented to indicate that RNA was transferred from glia to neurons (44). Using other types of micromethods, Pevzner (76) has obtained similar results and come to similar conclusions. Increase of RNA synthesis in neurons under the above-stated conditions seems, however, to be an unspecific process reflecting maintenance of an increased neural activity.

The Emergence of Small Amounts of Adenine-Uracil-Rich RNA in Neurons and Glia During Learning Experiments

From our laboratory I would like to present two types of experiments performed on rats. In the first, neurons were sampled randomly from layers 5 and 6 in a small area of the sensory-motor cortex that has been shown to constitute a control area for the transfer of handedness (75).

The advantage of this experiment is that a paired t-test can be performed on the analytical values, since control cell material is present contralaterally in the cortex of the same rat. Furthermore, the sampling at random of cells from a defined cortical area will statistically include the variation between animals.

In the first experiment, right-handed rats were induced to use the left hand in retrieving food from far down a narrow glass tube (39). Training periods of 2×25 minutes per day were given. The neurons from both sides of the cortex, and from those areas whose destruction prohibited transfer of handedness, were analyzed. These control centers are situated bilaterally in the sensory motor cortex and comprise around 1 mm^3 of the cortex. Layers 5 and 6 are the most important. These neurons have a large nucleus in comparison with the cytoplasm. Therefore, the analytical result will mainly reflect nuclear RNA.

Holger Hydén

Eighty-eight rats were used for the analysis of 14,000 cortical neurons. As was stated above, the advantage of this learning experiment is that the controls are present in the same brain. Therefore, a paired *t*-analysis could be performed on the results from the neurons of both sides. Other control experiments were also performed.

A significant increase occurred in the amount of RNA per cell from the learning side of the cortex. In an extension of the work published (43), the amount of RNA was found to have increased from 220 $\mu\mu$g of RNA per ten nerve cells to 310 $\mu\mu$g. When the base ratios of the neuronal RNA of the control side were compared with those of the learning side, the ratio $(G + C)/(A + U)$ was found to have decreased significantly from 1.72 to 1.51 (39). (See Table 1.)

TABLE 1 Changes in the RNA base composition of cortical neurons from the control (left) side and from the learning (right) side.

	Controls (mean)	Learning (mean)	Change in percentage	P
Adenine	18.4 ± 0.48	20.1 ± 0.11	+9.2	0.02
Guanine	26.5 ± 0.64	28.7 ± 0.90	+8.3	0.01
Cytosine	36.8 ± 0.97	31.5 ± 0.75	−14.4	0.01
Uracil	18.3 ± 0.48	19.6 ± 0.56	+7.1	0.05
$\dfrac{A + G}{C + U}$	0.81 ± 0.27	0.95 ± 0.035	+17.3	0.01
$\dfrac{G + C}{A + U}$	1.72 ± 0.054	1.51 ± 0.026	−12.2	0.02

SOURCE: H. Hydén and E. Egyhayi, "Changes in RNA Content and Base Composition in Cortical Neurons of Rats in a Learning Experiment Involving Transfer of Handedness." *Proc. Nat. Acad. Sci.*, 52 (1964) 1034.

In Table 2, the data are divided into two groups (44). The cell material from the cortex of animals 1 and 2 was taken on the rising part of the learning curve on the 3rd to the 5th day—i.e., during an early part of the learning period. The material from the other two rats was taken on the asymptotic part of the curve on the 9th to the 10th day. In this case, the animals had reached the maximal number of successful performances per training period already on the 6th to 7th day. The increase of the RNA content per neuron of the 3-to-5-

TABLE 2 Characteristics of the RNA formed per neuron during transfer of handedness correlated to training periods and performance of the animals.

Animal	Days (training periods 2 × 25 min/day)	Total number of successful reaches	Relative increase of total RNA per neuron (percent)	Δ RNA composition
1	3	107	33	A 25.5 G 36.1 C 9.7 U 28.7
2	5	163	23	A 24.5 G 35.7 C 11.7 U 28.1
3	8	625	63	A 26.2 G 34.9 C 16.1 U 22.8
4	9	1,041	105	A 21.0 G 35.2 C 24.0 U 19.8

SOURCE: H. Hydén and P. Lange, "A Genic Simulation with Production of Adenine-Uracil-Rich RNA in Neurons and Glia in Learning." *Naturwiss.*, 53 (1966) 67.

day animals lies at 25 to 30 percent. Qualitatively, the RNA formed in the neurons is characterized by a DNA-like base-ratio composition, with adenine and uracil values around 26. (Rat DNA has the following base composition: A 28.6, G 21.4, C 21.5, U 28.4.) The cytosine values were remarkably low. The results were statistically significant. The situation was far different for the animals that had trained for 8 to 9 days and performed with a maximal number of reaches—i.e., seventy to eighty reaches per period of 25 minutes. The RNA result deviated both quantitatively and qualitatively from those of group one. The relative RNA increase per neuron in the learning cortex was 60 to 100 percent, and the base-ratio composition of the RNA formed was similar to that of ribosomal RNA.

Holger Hydén

To conclude this discussion, we should remark that when the nerve cells within the learning part of the cortex were taken during the early and acute part of the learning process, the relative RNA increase per neuron was small. The nuclear RNA formed, however, had a DNA-like base-ratio composition. Thus, *a stimulation of the genome seems to occur early in a learning situation that the animal has not encountered before.* A differentiated formation of RNA occurs during a learning period in the neurons involved, and, to judge by the character of the RNA formed, the beginning seems to be characterized by a genic stimulation.

In the second learning experiment young rats, in order to feed, had to learn how to balance on a thin, 1-m-long steel wire strung at a 45° angle between the floor and a small platform with food (40, 42). Seventy-eight rats, given training periods of 45 minutes per day, were used for the analysis of 12,000 nerve cells. Vestibular Deiters' nerve cells clearly involved in this balance experiment were analyzed. These nerve cells have a large cytoplasm in comparison with a small nucleus (the ratio of nuclear to cytoplasmic RNA is 1:50), so if a whole cell is analyzed, the characteristics of nuclear RNA will drown in the bulk of the cytoplasmic RNA. Moreover, no base-ratio changes were detected during learning in the cytoplasmic RNA, although an increase from 680 to 750 $\mu\mu g$ of RNA was determined. Therefore, the nuclei were isolated and the base ratios of the nuclear RNA investigated. Then a clear increase in the ratio A/U of the nuclear RNA was found (1.06 to 1.32), but no significant change of the ratio $(G + C)/(A + U)$.

Since no control neurons can be obtained from the same brain in such an experiment, four different types of control experiments were performed with physiological stimulation and stress involving the vestibular pathways. No significant changes of the A/U ratio were found in these controls, although a significant increase of RNA per neuron could be determined. This result signifies that the increase in adenine and the decrease in uracil was specific for the learning experiment. What may be the significance of the synthesis of such a nuclear RNA fraction with such high adenine values? In defined parts of chromosomes from *Chironomus,* RNA has been extracted and found to have an asymmetric composition with high adenine values (17). This type of nuclear RNA stimulating amino-acid incorporation has been found in *Euglena* (9) and also in starfish oocytes (20). The conclusion is, therefore, that the nuclear RNA with a high A/U ratio found in the second type of learning experiment in rats was chromosomal RNA.

A conclusion of both these experiments is that factors in the environment (i.e., the new learning situation not encountered before by the animal) bring forth a stimulation of the genome of the glia and the neurons engaged and that this response can be characterized in biochemical terms. The analysis of the RNA in two learning situations has furthermore shown that the response of neurons and glia engaged in the behavior to be established differs from the response in physiological and chemical stimulation with respect to two important parameters. First, the content of RNA increases during learning in both neurons and glia. In physiological and chemical stimulation, the RNA changes 'were inverse. Secondly, adenine-uracil-rich asymmetric RNA is formed in both glia and neurons during learning. In the cases of stimulation, the RNA being formed had ribosomal RNA characteristics with respect to base ratios. By inference, the adenine-uracil-rich asymmetric RNA formed in learning is assumed to be of chromosomal type.

A preliminary study of the duration of the RNA in the neurons with the high A/U value gave the following result (42). Twenty-four hours after stopping the experiment and returning the animals to their home cages, no such RNA fraction could be found. When the training was resumed for 45 minutes and the nuclei analyzed, the RNA fraction with high A/U ratio was found again. The disappearance of the RNA fraction does not mean that the fraction ceased to be synthesized. It probably means that it is present in such small amounts as to be inaccessible with the present methods of analysis. Similar results on RNA changes in brain cells in a learning situation have been obtained by Shashoua (81).

These are current experiments, and I will briefly report a significant and reproducible result with the consent of Dr. Shashoua. He has used goldfish and challenged the entire CNS in a learning experiment, as simple as it was effective. He attached 0.5 g polystyrene foam below the jaw region of the fish, which turns the ventral side up and lifts the head above the water. In one hour the fish had learned how to swim dorsal side up, but at a 45° angle. The behavior was further adjusted in 3 to 4 hours to normal posture and swimming. The fish were injected with ³H-orotic acid above tectum, and the whole brain was homogenized after the experiment. RNA was extracted, and the uracil/cytosine ratio of the newly synthesized RNA was determined after alkaline hydrolysis.

The significant and reproducible result was an increase of the uracil/cytosine ratio from 3:1 in the control brain RNA to 6:1 in the trained fish. This agrees well with the base-ratio changes of cortical nerve cells that we found in learning experiments in rats (39). In that case, the uracil/cytosine ratio changed even more, around 5 times. In both types of experiments, the protein coded by such an RNA can be assumed to be an unusual and highly specific protein.

The Occurrence of Proteins Unique for the Brain

Brain proteins have been the subject of much interest. Proteins in general have a high information content and can react rapidly with high specificity. Brain proteins have a varying half-life time, but the majority seem to turn over within 10 to 20 days (62). It is interesting that soluble proteins unique for the brain have only recently been found and characterized (72). They are highly acidic, with a glutamic-acid content of 30 percent. Immunologically, these proteins gave a cross-reaction from homo to fish. The acidic proteins, localized mainly to the cell bodies of the glia and to a small extent to the nuclei of neurons, were not found in their cytoplasms (51). It was possible to separate the proteins into fractions with different turnover rates (70). The function of these proteins is unknown, but studies are under way to test whether they vary as a function of stimulation. If one calculates the composition of the messenger RNA that would code for a protein with the amino-acid composition of the acidic brain protein, it turns out, interestingly enough, that the basc ratios of this RNA agree with those found in the newly synthesized RNA in the cortex of rats at the transfer of handedness. The problem of protein synthesis in relation to storage of neural information is as challenging as the data are scarce at the present time.

Protein Synthesis in Brain Cells Stimulated by Extraneous Brain DNA

As was discussed above, a cyclic change in the amount of RNA per nerve cell was found over the life span of man and of rats. No explanatory comments can be offered at the present time.

It is clear, though, that the neuron represents one of the few cases where orderliness is not added to the organ during the life cycle by mitosis. An increase of the frequency of errors in transcription and translation at protein synthesis in brain cells can certainly be expected to have serious consequences for function with increasing age. We have, therefore, posed the question: can extraneous DNA, if taken up by brain cells, serve as a direct template for *in vivo* protein synthesis or otherwise stimulate the cells in a meaningful way? This is a complex problem, which can be elucidated only by steps. As a first practical step, we have studied whether extraneous brain DNA, if introduced into a recipient's brain, will stimulate the *in vivo* protein synthesis of brain cells (24, 41).

DNA of varying degrees of purity from brains of rabbits was prepared and injected into the brains of other rabbits with cannulae permanently implanted in the fourth ventricle. The first DNA preparation was precipitated from a chloroform-isoamylalcohol extracted brain homogenate. It contained RNA and proteins and will be called *crude DNA*. This was purified, the RNA removed, and a *double-stranded DNA* obtained. This DNA was denatured with solium-hydroxide to *single-stranded DNA*. The DNA, preceded by neomycin, was injected through the cannulae into the fourth ventricle in four portions during 2 hours. Then 200 μg of ^{3}H-leucine was injected during 2 hours.

The specific activity was determined as dpm/γ protein in the hypoglossal nucleus and the vestibular nucleus of the brain stem. The hypoglossal nucleus was directly flooded by the injected solution; the vestibular nuclei are more distant from the site of injection. This difference in localization is reflected in the results and demonstrates how far an effect will spread during the conditions used.

The samples were homogenized in acid and the precipitate dissolved in sodium hydroxide, which also breaks down RNA. We corrected for quenching by calibration curves.

The results shown in Table 3 demonstrate that *crude DNA* increased the *in vivo* protein synthesis in brain cells by 120 percent. *Double-stranded DNA* and *single-stranded DNA* also had a considerable effect (Tables 4 and 5). It can be seen that the effect of DNA on the brain cells in the region of Deiters' nucleus causes only a trend toward increase in protein synthesis but no significant differences. This reflects the fact that Deiters' nucleus is around 10 mm laterally located in relation to the hypoglossal nucleus and away from the point of application of DNA.

Thus, *extraneous double-stranded and single-stranded DNA* introduced in the brain induced an increase in the protein synthesis of brain cells *in vivo*. But RNA did not.

In *in vivo,* cell-free ribosomal systems, the addition of DNA has been found to stimulate amino-acid incorporation. McCarthy and Holland (68) and Naora (73) found that only denatured DNA stim-

Holger Hydén

TABLE 3 Effect of crude DNA on incorporation of ^{3}H-leucine into brain-cell protein as dpm/γ protein. Neomycin added, 2 × 30 μg.

	Crude DNA	Control	P	Percentage increase
Nucleus, Deiters'	268 ± 37 (5)^x	199 ± 30 (5)^x	0.1	
Nucleus, hypoglossus	852 ± 67 (5)^x	389 ± 46 (5)^x	< 0.001	+120

x = number of animals

SOURCE: *Biological and Clinical Aspects of the Central Nervous System.* Symposium held on October 16, 1967, to commemorate the 50th anniversary of the pharmaceutical department of Sandoz Ltd., Basel, pp. 43–45.

TABLE 4 Effect of double-stranded DNA on incorporation of ^{3}H-leucine into brain-cell protein as dpm/γ protein. No neomycin added.

	Double-stranded DNA	Control	P	Percentage increase
Nucleus, hypoglossus	510 ± 45 (4)^x	298 ± 12 (3)^x	< 0.01	+75

x = number of animals

SOURCE: *Biological and Clinical Aspects of the Central Nervous System.* Symposium held on October 16, 1967, to commemorate the 50th anniversary of the pharmaceutical department of Sandoz Ltd., Basel, pp. 43–45.

ulated protein synthesis, and antibiotics potentiated the effect. They found the effect to be relatively insensitive to actinomycin D, and they concluded therefore that no RNA synthesis was involved in the protein synthesis. They varied the base composition of the DNA that had been exposed to antibiotics and found a specificity of the amino-acid incorporation that was consistent with the code triplet data. McCarthy and Holland concluded that the single-stranded DNA had attached to ribosomes in the cell-free system and served a direct template at the polypeptide formation. By contrast, Wang (85) used a thymus ribosomal system but found that double-stranded DNA had a much

TABLE 5 Effect of single-stranded DNA on incorporation of
^{3}H-leucine into brain-cell protein as dpm/γ protein. NaOH
denaturation. Neomycin added, 2 × 30 μg.

	Single-stranded DNA	Control	P	Percentage increase
Nucleus, Deiters'	255 ± 29 (3)^x	199 ± 30 (5)^x	0.2	
Nucleus, hypoglossus	635 ± 22 (3)^x	389 ± 46 (5)^x	< 0.01	+65

x = number of animals

SOURCE: *Biological and Clinical Aspects of the Central Nervous System.* Symposium held on October 16, 1967, to commemorate the 50th anniversary of the pharmaceutical department of Sandoz Ltd., Basel, pp. 43–45.

stronger stimulatory effect on protein synthesis than denatured DNA. This effect was inhibited by actinomycin. It seemed necessary, therefore, to study some factors of importance to judge the *in vivo* mechanism in our experiments.

Actinomycin D inhibited the RNA formation by 95 percent when it was injected into the fourth ventricle. The normal pattern (Figure 1a) of the sucrose gradient profile of newly synthesized RNA disappeared (Figure 1b). It is not probable that the high incorporation around 4 S represents terminal incorporation.

The next question is whether actinomycin will inhibit normal protein synthesis if injected into the fourth ventricle of a control animal. It did not. (See Table 6.) If actinomycin had no effect also on the

TABLE 6 Effect of actinomycin D, 4 × 50 μg, on incorporation of
^{3}H-leucine into brain-cell protein as dpm/γ protein.

	Actinomycin	Control
Nucleus, Deiters'	192 ± 23 (4)^x	199 ± 30 (5)^x
Nucleus, hypoglossus	329 ± 38 (4)^x	389 ± 46 (5)^x

x = number of animals

SOURCE: *Biological and Clinical Aspects of the Central Nervous System.* Symposium held on October 16, 1967, to commemorate the 50th anniversary of the pharmaceutical department of Sandoz Ltd., Basel, pp. 43–45.

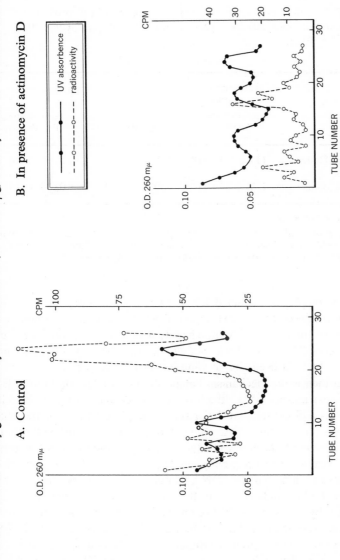

FIGURE 1 Sucrose density gradient analysis of brain RNA (about 300 μg) after injection of ³H-uridine into fourth ventricle.

A. Control

B. In presence of actinomycin D

UV absorbence
radioactivity

SOURCE: *Biological and Clinical Aspects of the Central Nervous System.* Symposium held on October 16, 1967, to commemorate the 50th anniversary of the pharmaceutical department of Sandoz Ltd., Basel, pp. 43–45.

117

DNA-stimulated protein synthesis, then one would assume that the injected DNA had served as a direct template. There was, however, a clear inhibition of the stimulatory effect of double-stranded DNA (Table 7). Surprisingly enough, the RNA residue after degradation

TABLE 7 Effect of double-stranded DNA on brain-cell protein as dpm/γ protein, inhibited by actinomycin D, 4×50 μg. Neomycin added, 2×30 μg.

	Actinomycin, double-stranded DNA	Control	P	Percentage decrease
Nucleus, Deiters'	111 ± 13 $(4)^x$	199 ± 30 $(5)^x$	$< 0,05$	44
Nucleus, hypoglossus	257 ± 35 $(4)^x$	389 ± 46 $(5)^x$	$\sim 0,05$	34

$x =$ number of animals

SOURCE: *Biological and Clinical Aspects of the Central Nervous System.* Symposium held on October 16, 1967, to commemorate the 50th anniversary of the pharmaceutical department of Sandoz Ltd., Basel, pp. 43–45.

of DNA, or phenol-extracted RNA, had no stimulatory effect on the protein synthesis. Phenol extraction of RNA was used to exclude the possibilities that the RNA attached to DNA as a hybrid had been made accessible to nuclease activity at the DNA–RNA split and therefore had not been able to stimulate protein synthesis.

What then is the mechanism behind the DNA effect on brain cells? Did the extraneous DNA attach itself to ribosomes in the brain cells and act as a direct template? *For* this assumption speaks the fact that the DNA, free from RNA, stimulated *in vivo* protein synthesis in brain cells, while the RNA residue after degradation of DNA had no effect. Against the direct-template hypothesis speaks the fact that actinomycin inhibited the DNA-stimulated protein synthesis. This negative finding indicates that the increased protein synthesis was mediated by RNA. It might be, on the other hand, that actinomycin could interfere with the binding between the ribosome and the DNA, which would block a protein synthesis on a DNA-ribosome basis.

The mechanism will take some time to analyze. The main problem related to the phenomenon is whether the protein synthesized through the extraneous DNA in the brain cells is a functionally meaningful protein. To test this possibility, behavioral studies and RNA and protein analyses are presently being carried out at our laboratory.

Transfer of Behavior by Brain Extracts

The third line of approach has involved the extraction of brain macromolecules from trained animals and the injection of these substances in naive animals during learning experiments. The idea was to shorten the time of learning and increase the retention by means of this procedure. Thus, Fjerdingstad and colleagues (27) extracted RNA from the brain of trained rats and injected the extract intracisternally in naive rats. The learning of the same task was facilitated in these rats in comparison with rats that received RNA from untrained animals or from rats that had not been injected. They also showed that brain RNA from animals trained differently had a differentiated effect on rats at intracisternal injection. Jacobson and colleagues (55) have obtained similar results in their experiments with injections of brain RNA. A lively debate arose about these experiments in various journals. In a 1966 issue of *Science* (10), seven laboratories reported negative results in their attempts to duplicate the experiments with "memory transfer." However, in a later number of *Science,* one of these laboratories (11) reported that, in a carefully planned study, brain extracts from trained rats, injected intraperitoneally into naive rats, shortened the time needed for learning. It therefore seems that the observation is correct and the phenomenon exists. As to the mechanism, most questions are still unanswered. How far is the RNA injected into a mammal broken down? How pure has been the brain RNA used for injections? In one study (66), it was not possible to recover from the brain labeled RNA that had been injected intraperitoneally. In this connection, the opinion has also been expressed that transfer of conditioned responses by brain extracts is an effect of peptides, not of RNA (83).

The Planaria Experiments

By now, an extensive literature exists on conditioning experiments on flatworms. McConnell reported in 1962 (69) that conditioned behavior in planaria could be transferred to naive flatworms by cannibalism. The discussion first dealt with the question of whether planaria on the whole could learn and involved such questions as habituation, classical conditioning, and avoidance learning, to name a few. In 1964, Bennett and Calvin (5) criticized severely the planaria experiments and their reproducibility and doubted that worms could be conditioned. This problem has now been settled insofar as several studies, also on interfering pseudo-conditioning, have shown convincingly that flatworms can learn. Even transfer of conditioned behaviors has been accepted by some as a reality. It has been suggested that the responsible mechanism is pinocytosis in the digestive canal, by which process unbroken molecules are incorporated into the organism.

A considerable activity is thus going on in many laboratories to search for a molecular correlate to learning and memory. Presumably, concepts within molecular biology will influence brain research for many years to come. In most fields, new concepts and ideas create a crisis-like uncertainty in some scientists, to quote Kuhn (61). Eventually, the new concepts will be assimilated and will serve productive activity—in those who still have the capacity to reorganize older, usually firmly established concepts.

Reference was made in the introduction to the ideas of Plato and Locke, illustrating that few theories prove to be new when seen in historical retrospect. Sir Lawrence Bragg (7) once said that the essence of science lies not in discovering facts but in discovering new ways of thinking about them.

REFERENCES

1. Adams, D. H. "The relationship between cellular nucleic acids in the developing cerebral rat cortex." *Biochem. J.,* 98 (1966) 636–40.
2. Adey, W. R., Kado, R. T., Didio, J., and Schindler, W. J. "Impedance changes in cerebral tissue accompanying a learned discriminative performance in the cat." *Exp. Neurol.,* 7 (1963) 259–81.
3. Adey, W. R., Kado, R. T., and Walker, D. O. "Impedance characteristics of cortical and subcortical structures: evaluation of regional specificity in hypercapnea and hypothermia." *Exp. Neurol.,* 11 (1965) 190–216.
4. Agranoff, B. W., Davis, R. E., and Brink, J. J. "Memory fixation in the goldfish." *Proc. Nat. Acad. Sci.,* 54 (1965) 788–93.
5. Bennett, E. L., and Calvin, M. "Failure to train planarians reliably." *Neurosci. Res. Progr. Bull.,* 2 (1964) 4–24.
6. Bernsohn, J., and Norgello, H. "Base composition of ribosomal RNA in newborn and adult rat brain." *Proc. Soc. Exp. Med.,* 122 (1966) 22–24.

7. Bragg, Sir Lawrence. *The history of science.* London: Cohen and West, 1951.
8. Brattgard, S.-O., and Hydén, H. *Acta. radiol. Supl.,* 94 (1952).
9. Brawerman, G. "A procedure for the isolation of RNA fractions resembling DNA with respect to nucleotide composition." *Biochim. biophys. acta.,* 76 (1963) 322–24.
10. Byrne, W. L., Egyhazi, E., and Hydén, H. "Memory transfer." *Science,* 153 (1966) 658–59.
11. Byrne, W. L., and Samuel, D. "Behavioral modification by injection of brain extract prepared from a trained donor." *Science,* 154 (1966) 418.
12. Coons, A. H. "The application of fluorescent antibodies to the study of naturally occurring antibodies." *Ann. N.Y. Acad. Sci.,* 69 (1957) 548–662.
13. Cummins, J., and Hydén, H. "ATP levels and ATP-ases in neurons, glia and neuronal membranes of the vestibular nucleus." *Biochim. biophys. acta.,* 60 (1962) 271–83.
14. Daneholt, B., and Brattgard, S.-O. "A comparison between RNA metabolism of nerve cells and glia in the hypoglossal nucleus of the rabbit." *J. Neurochem.,* 13 (1966) 913–21.
15. Davis, E., and Agranoff, B. W. "Stages of memory formation in goldfish: evidence for an environment trigger." *Proc. Nat. Acad. Sci.,* 55 (1966) 555–59.
16. Edström, J. E. "Microextraction and microelectrophoresis for determination and analysis of nucleic acids in isolated cellular units," in Prescott, D. M. (ed.), *Methods in cell physiology,* Vol. 1. New York: Academic Press, 1964, pp. 417–47.
17. Edström, J. E., and Beermann, W. "The base composition of nucleic acids in chromosomes, puffs, nucleoli, and cytoplasm of *Chironomus* salivary gland cells." *J. Cell Biol.,* 14 (1962) 371–79.
18. Edström, J. E., and Eichner, D. "Quantitative RNA-Unterschungen an den Gangliezellen des Nucleus supraopticus der Albino-Ratte unter experimentellen Bedingungen (Kochsalz-Belastung)." *Z. Zellforsch.,* 48 (1958) 187–200.
19. Edström, J. E., Eichner, D., and Edström, A. "RNA of axons and myelin sheaths from Mauthner neurons." *Biochim. biophys. acta.,* 61 (1962) 178–84.
20. Edström, J. E., Grampp, W., and Schor, N. "The intracellular distribution and heterogeneity of RNA in starfish oocytes." *J. biophys. biochem. Cytol.,* 11 (1961) 549–57.
21. Egyhazi, E. "Microchemical fractionation of neuronal and glial RNA." *Biochim. biophys. acta.,* 114 (1966) 516–26.
22. Egyhazi, E., and Hydén, H. "Biosynthesis of rapidly labeled RNA in brain cells." *Life Sci.,* 5 (1966) 1215–23.
23. Egyhazi, E., and Hydén, H. "Experimentally induced changes in the base composition of the RNA of isolated nerve cells and their oligodendroglial cells." *J. biophys. biochem. Cytol.,* 10 (1961) 403–10.
24. Egyhazi, E., and Hydén, H. "Factors affecting extraneous DNA-dependent protein synthesis in brain cells," in Lodin, Z., and Rose,

S. P. R. (eds.), *Macromolecules and the function of the neuron.* Amsterdam: Excerpta Medica Foundation, 1968, pp. 275–81.

25. Flexner, L. B., and Flexner, J. B. "Effect of acetocycloheximide and acetocycloheximide-puromycin mixture on cerebral protein synthesis and memory in mice." *Proc. Nat. Acad. Sci.,* 55 (1966) 369–74.

26. Flexner, L. B., Flexner, J. B., and Roberts, R. B. "Stages of memory in mice treated with acetocycloheximide before or immediately after learning." *Proc. Nat. Acad. Sci.,* 56 (1966) 730–35.

27. Fjerdingstad, E. J., Nissen, T., and Røgaard-Petersen, H. H. "Effect of RNA extracted from the brain of trained animals on learning in rats." *Scand. J. Psychol.,* 6 (1965) 1–6.

28. Grampp, W., and Edström, J. E. "The effect of nervous activity on RNA of the crustacean receptor neuron." *J. Neurochem.,* 10 (1963) 725–31.

29. Hamberger, A. *Acta physiol. Scand. Suppl.,* 203 (1963).

30. Hamberger, A., and Hydén, H. "Inverse enzymatic changes in neurons and glia during increased function and hypoxia." *J. Cell Biol.,* 16 (1963) 521–25.

31. Hillman, H. "Growth of processes from single isolated dorsal root ganglion cells of young rats." *Nature,* 209 (1966) 102–03.

32. Hillman, H., and Hydén, H. "Characteristics of the ATP-ase activity of isolated neurons of rabbit." *Histochemie,* 5 (1965) 446–50.

33. Hillman, H., and Hydén, H. "Membrane potentials in isolated neurones *in vitro* from Deiters' nucleus of rabbit." *J. Physiol.,* 177 (1965) 398–410.

34. Himwich, H. E., Bernstein, A. O., Herrlich, H., Chesler, A., and Fazekas, J. F. "Mechanisms for the maintenance of life in the newborn during anoxia." *Amer. J. Physiol.,* 135 (1942) 387–91.

35. Hydén, H. "Biochemical and functional interplay between neuron and glia," in Wortis, J. (ed.), *Recent advances in biological psychiatry,* Vol. 6. New York: Plenum Press, 1964, pp. 31–54.

36. Hydén, H. "The neuron and its glia—a biochemical and functional unit." *Endeavour,* 21 (1962) 83–84.

37. Hydén, H. "Quantitative assay of compounds in isolated, fresh nerve cells and glial cells from control and stimulated animals." *Nature,* 184 (1959) 433–35.

38. Hydén, H. Bjurstam, K., and McEwen, B. S. "Protein separation at the cellular level by micro-discelectrophoresis." *Analyt. Biochem.,* 17 (1966) 1–15.

39. Hydén H., and Egyhazi, E. "Changes in RNA content and base composition in cortical neurons of rats in a learning experiment involving transfer of handedness." *Proc. Nat. Acad. Sci.,* 52 (1964) 1030–35.

40. Hydén, H., and Egyhazi, E. "Glial RNA changes during a learning experiment in rats." *Proc. Nat. Acad. Sci.,* 49 (1963) 618–24.

41. Hydén, H., and Egyhazi, E. "Stimulation of protein synthesis in brain cells by extraneous DNA," in Lodin, Z., and Rose, S. P. R. (eds.), *Macromolecules and the function of the neuron.* Amsterdam: Excerpta Medica Foundation, 1968, pp. 269–74.

Holger Hydén

42. Hydén, H., and Egyhazi, E. "Nuclear RNA changes of nerve cells during a learning experiment in rats." *Proc. Nat. Acad. Sci.*, 48 (1962) 1366–73.

43. Hydén, H., and Lange, P. W. "A differentiation of RNA response in neurons early and late during learning." *Proc. Nat. Acad. Sci.*, 53 (1965) 946–52.

44. Hydén, H., and Lange, P. W. "A genic stimulation with production of adenine-uracil-rich RNA in neurons and glia in learning." *Naturwiss.*, 53 (1966) 64–70.

45. Hydén, H. and Lange, P. W. "Differences in the metabolism of oligodendroglia and nerve cells in the vestibular area," in *Fourth international neurochemical symposium.* New York: Pergamon, 1960, pp. 190–99.

46. Hydén, H., and Lange, P. W. "Rhythmic enzyme changes in neurons and glia during sleep." *Science*, 149 (1965) 654–56.

47. Hydén, H., and Lange, P. W. "Rhythmic enzyme changes in neurons and glia during sleep and wakefulness," in Akert, K., Bally, C., and Schade, J. P. (eds.), *Progress in brain research*, Vol. 18. Amsterdam: Elsevier, 1965, pp. 92–95.

48. Hydén, H., and Lange, P. W. "The steady state and endogenous respiration in neuron and glia." *Acta. Physiol. scand.*, 64 (1964) 6–14.

49. Hydén, H., and Larsson, S. "A new scanning micro-analyser for data collection and evaluation from x-ray microradiograms," in *Proceedings of the second international symposium on x-ray microscopy and x-ray microanalysis.* Amsterdam: Elsevier, 1960, pp. 51–55.

50. Hydén, H., and Larsson, S. "The application of a scanning and computing cell analyser to neurocytological problems." *J. Neurochem.*, 1 (1956) 134–44.

51. Hydén, H., and McEwen, B. S. "A glial protein specific for the nervous system." *Proc. Nat. Acad. Sci.*, 55 (1966) 354–58.

52. Hydén, H., and Pigon, A. "A cytophysiological study of the functional relationship between oligodendroglial cells and nerve cells of Deiters' nucleus." *J. Neurochem.*, 6 (1960) 57–72.

53. Jacob, M., Judes, D., Michaelidis, P., Stevenin, J., and Mandel, P. *Int. Neurochem. Conf. Publ. Abstr.*, (1965) 52.

54. Jacob, M., Stevenin, J., Jund, R., Judes, C., and Mandel, P. "Rapidly labelled RNA in brain." *J. Neurochem.*, 13 (1966) 619–28.

55. Jacobson, A., Fried, C., and Horowitz, S. "Planarians and memory. I. Transfer of learning by injection of RNA." *Nature*, 209 (1966) 599–601.

56. Jarlstedt, J. "Functional localization in the cerebellar cortex studied by quantitative determinations of Purkinje cell RNA. I. RNA changes in rat cerebellar Purkinje cells after proprio- and exteroceptive and vestibular stimulation." *Acta. Physiol. Scand.*, 67 (1966) 243.

57. Katchalsky, A., and Oplatka, A. "Hysteresis and macromolecular memory." *Neurosci. Res. Progr. Bull.*, 3 (1965) 15–93.

58. Kierkegaard, S. A. *Philosophical fragments.* Princeton: Princeton Univ. Press, 1963.

59. Koenig, E., and Brattgard, S.-O. "A quantitative micro-method for determination of specific radioactivities of H^3-purines and H^3-pyrimidines." *Analyt. Biochem.*, 6 (1963) 424–34.

60. Konorski, J. "Mechanisms of learning." *Symp. Soc. exp. Biol.*, 4 (1950) 409–31.

61. Kuhn, T. S. *The structure of scientific revolutions*, Chicago: Univ. of Chicago Press, 1962.

62. Lajtha, A., and Toth, J. "Instability of cerebral proteins." *Biochem. biophys. res. comm.*, 23 (1966) 294–98.

63. Littau, V. C., Allfrey, V. G., Frenster, J. H., and Mirsky, A. E. "Active and inactive regions of nuclear chromatin as revealed by electron microscope autoradiography." *Proc. Nat. Acad. Sci.*, 52 (1964) 93–100.

64. Locke, J. *Essay concerning the understanding, knowledge, opinion and assent* (B. Rand, ed.). Cambridge: Harvard Univ. Press, 1931.

65. Luco, J. V., and Aranda, L. C. "An electrical correlate to the process of learning. Experiments in *Blatta orientalis*." *Nature*, 201 (1964) 1330–31.

66. Luttges, M., Johnson, R., Buck, C., Holland, J., and McGaugh, J. "An examination of transfer of learning by nucleic acid." *Science*, 151 (1966) 834–36.

67. Mahler, H. R., Moore, W. J., and Thompson, R. J. "Isolation and characterization of RNA from cerebral cortex of rat." *J. biol. chem.*, 241 (1966) 1283–89.

68. McCarthy, B. J., and Holland, J. J. "Denatured DNA as a direct template for *in vitro* protein synthesis." *Proc. Nat. Acad. Sci.*, 54 (1965) 880–86.

69. McConnell, J. V. "Memory transfer through cannibalism in planarians." *J. Neuropsychiat.*, 3, Suppl. 1 (1962) 42–48.

70. McEwen, B. S., and Hydén, H. "A study of specific brain proteins on the semimicro scale." *J. Neurochem.*, 13 (1966) 823–33.

71. Miani, N., Di Girolamo, A., and Di Girolamo, M. "Sedimentation characteristics of axonal RNA in rabbit." *J. Neurochem*, 13 (1966) 755–59.

72. Moore, B. W., and McGregor, D. "Chromatographic and electrophoretic fractionation of soluble proteins of brain and liver." *J. biol. Chem.*, 240 (1965) 1647–53.

73. Naora, H., and Kodaira, K. "Stimulation of amino acid incorporation *in vitro* by DNA: Different effects of aminoglycoside antibiotics in calf-thymus nuclear and bacterial ribosome systems." *Biochim. biophys. acta.*, 123 (1966) 425–27.

74. Oja, S. S. "Postnatal changes in the concentration of nucleic acids, nucleotides and amino acids in the rat brain." *Ann. Acad. Sci. Fenn.*, 125 (1966) 1–69.

75. Peterson, G. M., and Devine, J. V. "Transfers in handedness in the rat resulting from small cortical lesions after limited forced practice." *J. comp. physiol. Psychol.*, 56 (1963) 752–56.

76. Pevzner, L. Z. "Topochemical aspects of nucleic acid and protein metabolism within the neuron-neuroglia unit of the superior cervical ganglion." *J. Neurochem.*, 12 (1965) 993–1002.

77. Plato. *Meno* (R. S. Bluck, ed.). London: Cambridge Univ. Press, 1961.
78. Polanyi, M., in von Hayek, F. A. (ed.), *Proceedings of the analogy symposium*, Bellaggio, 1966. In press.
79. Ringborg, U. "Composition and content of RNA in neurons of rat hippocampus at different ages." *Brain Res.,* 2 (1966) 296–98.
80. Schadé, J. P., and Pascoe, E. G. "Maturational changes in cerebral cortex. III. Effects of methionine sulfoximine on some electrical parameters and dendritic organisation of cortical neurons," in Himwich, W. A., and Himwich, H. E. (eds.), *Progress in brain research,* Vol. 9. Amsterdam: Elsevier, 1964, pp. 132–54.
81. Shashoua, V. "RNA metabolism in goldfish brain during learning," *Mol. Neurobiol. Bull.,* 1 (1968) 8.
82. Tata, J. "Hormones and the synthesis and utilization of RNA," in Davidson, J. N., and Cohn, W. E. (eds.), *Progress in nucleic acid research and molecular biology,* Vol. 5. New York: Academic Press, 1966, pp. 191–251.
83. Ungar, G., and Oceguera-Navarro, C. "Transfer of habituation by material extracted from brain." *Nature,* 207 (1965) 301–02.
84. Von Hahn, H. P. "Distribution of DNA and RNA in the brain during the life span of the albino rat." *Gerontologia,* 12 (1966) 18–29.
85. Wang, T. Y. "Effect of DNA and histone on the nuclear ribosomal incorporation system." *Nature,* 212 (1966) 928–30.
86. Yamagami, S., Kawakita, Y., and Naka, S. "Some physical, chemical and biochemical properties of ribosomal RNA from guinea pig brain cortex." *J. Neurochem.,* 12 (1965) 607–12.

Consciousness, Memory,
and Man's Conditioned Reflexes

by Wilder Penfield

When I was invited to contribute an essay to the others that now make up this book, I was already at work on a chapter for *Modern Perspectives in World Psychiatry,* edited by John G. Howells. The editor had proposed the title "The Neurophysiological Basis of Thought" and had asked for "a personal assessment and one that is practical rather than academic." The Dean of the Harvard Graduate School of Education, in his invitation, was even more challenging. "Draw from physiological facts," he wrote, "some meaning that will serve the purposes of wisdom." To be specific, he suggested a discussion of memory and language.

In the end, this essay inevitably repeats briefly much that appears in *Perspectives.* The assessment I have now made is academic, rather than practical, and I have elaborated the argument in regard to consciousness, memory, and man's conditioned reflexes.

My approach to the concept of the stream of consciousness is intended, in part, as a tribute to Harvard's great psychologist, William James (8). I wish he could have joined us during the Burton Lecture. What a discussion would then have followed! (I am told that he intended to return to this world, if he could manage it.) There are exciting additions and modifications that could now have been proposed to him.

I have been gradually restudying the material that has to do with the brain's recording of the stream of consciousness. It was summarized in the Lister Oration at the Royal College of Surgeons, and the detailed case reports were added in *Brain* in 1963 (22). The same material was then reconsidered from different points of view in 1966 and 1967 (17, 6).

One cannot discuss memory, to say nothing of language, in any meaningful way without a very considerable preamble. Memory, for example, is not a simple recording; one is able to remember by drawing upon many different mechanisms of the brain, some of which we activate consciously, while others are activated for us subconsciously.

In this present writing, it is my desire to consider most especially the stream of consciousness beginning, as in the fourth section, with the relation of mind to the conditioned brain-mechanisms. But it is difficult to carry all readers along unless my own experience in this area of human neurophysiology is recapitulated. That is done in the first three sections. Thus I am free, in the two final sections, to consider mind and consciousness. I shall attempt, with far too little description of the work of others, to set down in personal perspective an outline of localization of function in the brain of man. I shall show which of the localized mechanisms is most intimately related to different aspects of speech, perception, motor skills, conscious control of attention, and thought itself. If I suggest certain hypotheses of interaction and integration, it should be remembered that hypotheses are no more than structural scaffoldings on which to work and build. We must use them for what they are. Without them, construction cannot begin.

Anatomical Preamble

The human brain and the spinal cord, which together constitute the central nervous system, can, of course, be looked upon as a functional unit (Figure 1). But they can also be studied as a collection of functional units coordinated and integrated by a remarkable system of electrical interconnections.

Among the cranial nerves, five provide man with special senses. They have specialized receptor nerve endings in the nose and mouth, eye, and also in the cochlea and labyrinth of the inner ear. Thus, in addition to somatic sensation that comes to him directly from the body as a whole, man is able to smell and taste, see, and hear and balance.

There are many units of automatic action. (1) Inborn reflex mechanisms are located in the brain stem and spinal cord. These are normally the same for all humans and many of the other mammals. (2) There are also acquired mechanisms, created by the process of conditioning in the cerebral cortex. These provide the automatic machinery that responds to direction by the ever-changing neuronal action, which is the counterpart of thought and awareness. Neuronal

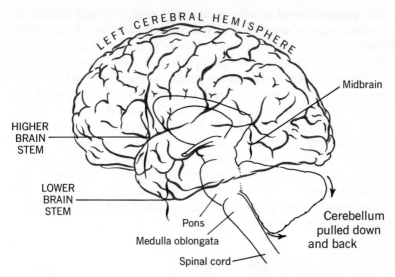

FIGURE 1 Left cerebral hemisphere of man. The darkly shaded brain stem and cerebellum and the spinal cord are shown as they would appear if the hemispheres were removed. The "higher brain stem" may be understood to include diencephalon, mesencephalon (midbrain), and probably the upper portion of metencephalon (pons). The thalamus on each side and the ventrally placed hypothalamus are included in the diencephalon. (SOURCE: W. Penfield and L. Roberts, *Speech and Brain-Mechanisms.* Princeton: Princeton Univ. Press, 1959, p. 15.)

action may be automatic or conscious; it is based on effective electrical activity in neurons and on conduction along their connections in a meaningful or purposeful pattern. Purpose, in this sense, may or may not be automatic.

A great deal of motor activity is involuntary and dependent on inborn reflex mechanisms in the higher brain stem, lower brain stem and spinal cord (Figure 1). Temperature control is managed by neuron circuits that include small centers of grey matter in the diencephalon (upper portion of higher brain stem). The same is true of sleep, as pointed out by Hess. We must conclude that there are within the diencephalon, in the grey matter covering the third ventricle, centers that control blood pressure, heart rate, vascular dilatation, sweating, salivation, lacrimation, pilomotor reactions, shivering, hiccoughing, and yawning (11). These are all motor activities dependent on specific reflexes and never activated, as far as my experience goes, by electrical stimulations of the cerebral cortex of patients during operations under local anaesthesia.

Consciousness, Memory, and Man's Conditioned Reflexes   **131**

The gastrointestinal system, on the other hand, is clearly influenced by certain areas of cerebral cortex in man. Penfield and Faulk (19) showed that the cortex covering the insula (Island of Reil) in man is related to sensation and movement in this tract from mouth to rectum.

In the spinal cord, reflex action produces inhibitions and contraction of muscle. It maintains muscle tone and produces reciprocal innervation of agonist and antagonist muscle. Spinal reflexes are, in general, local or segmental. Above the spinal cord, at the level of the lower brain stem, some of the reflex action begins to exert an influence over the musculature of the whole body. Thus, reflex mechanisms in the midbrain wield a powerful control over the posture and the coordinated movement of the whole body. They produce the muscle tone of standing and the walking rhythms and also the maintenance of positions adopted.

SENSORY AND MOTOR APPARATUS

The upper end of the brain stem presents two enlargements of gray matter, the right and the left thalamus. The cerebral hemispheres on each side are the outward projections of the thalamic nuclei. This is suggested by Figure 2.

It has often been assumed, because the cerebral cortex is a recent development, from a philogenetic point of view (and because, in man, it is comparatively such a vast ganglionic blanket), that the cortex is responsible for man's intellectual supremacy. This is no doubt true. But it has also been assumed that the cerebral cortex is the end station of the sensory afferents and the origin of the voluntary motor efferents, which is not true. The truth is that there are, in the cortex, separable sensory and motor areas, which serve as way stations to and from the higher brain stem. These are much the same for man and for other mammals.

The ganglionic target of the various afferent sensory tracts is in the thalamic nuclei. Auditory, visual, and discriminatory-somatic sensation make an essential detour from thalamus out to cortex and back to the end-target in the higher brain stem, instead of stopping there on first arrival. The currents of pain sensation, however, do not make a cortical detour. Head and Holmes (4) showed that the thalamus alone has to do, also, with the "physiological processes that underlie the crude aspects of sensations of contact, heat and cold." Thus the eventual rendezvous for all forms of sensory information brought to consciousness is in the higher brain stem.

If the brain and spinal cord are compared to a railway system, the

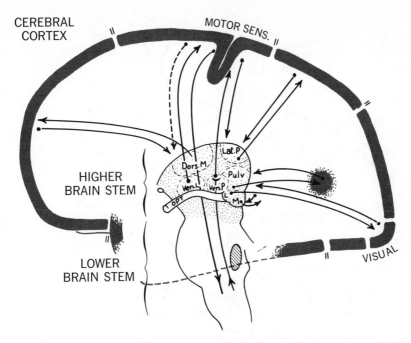

FIGURE 2 Diagrammatic scheme of left cerebral cortex, illustrating its direct connections with the underlying thalamic nuclei. The afferent somatic input is shown coming up through the spinal cord and lower brain stem. Passing through an interruption in the thalamus, it goes on to the sensory convolution of the cortex and back to the thalamus. The efferent voluntary output is shown coming through the thalamus to motor convolution and on out in the cortico-spinal tract to the muscles. (SOURCE: W. Penfield and H. Jasper, *Epilepsy and the Functional Anatomy of the Human Brain.* Boston: Little, Brown, 1954, p. 474.)

final "arrival platform" in "central station" is subcortical. The sensory detours to areas on the cortex are no more than way stations. Incoming traffic stops there but passes on into the subcortical arrival platform. The motor departure platform is likewise subcortical. The motor area in the cortex serves as a way station for outward-bound traffic. Much of the evidence that leads one to think in terms of the foregoing communication parable is to be found in the neurosurgeon's experience wtih the human cerebral cortex. The space limitation of this chapter, however, forbids description of the evidence (13, 15, 16, 21, 23).

The locations of the sensory areas in the human cortex are outlined in Figure 3, as worked out by cortical stimulation during operations under local anaesthesia and by planned excisions of cortex in

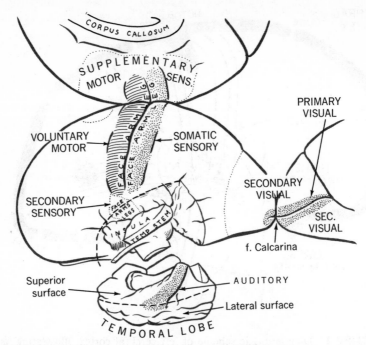

FIGURE 3 Primary sensory and motor areas of the human cortex (sensory are dotted and motor lined) with some secondary and supplementary areas in the cortex of the lateral surface of the left hemisphere. Localizations are derived from stimulation evidence during operation on conscious patients. Parts of the mesial surfaces are shown above and on the right. The temporal lobe has been cut and turned down to expose its superior surface (which is ordinarily hidden in the fissure of Sylvius) and the primary auditory area on the transverse gyrus of Heschl. No secondary auditory-sensory area is figured, since our stimulation evidence does not distinguish it from the adjacent interpretive cortex shown in Figure 9. (SOURCE: W. Penfield and L. Roberts, *Speech and Brain-Mechanisms.* Princeton: Princeton Univ. Press, 1959, p. 32.)

the treatment of focal epilepsy. It can be stated with certainty that unilateral removal of the cerebral cortex adjacent to and surrounding the precentral motor gyrus does not interfere with the ability of an individual to carry out delicate, normally directed voluntary movements in the contralateral limbs. It does, however, remove all transcortical connections to that gyrus.

It is necessary, therefore, to conclude that the outgoing efferent stream of electrical potentials, which controls voluntary movement,

Wilder Penfield

originates not in the cortex but in a more central area of the higher brain stem. One is forced to assume further that, in this same central area (diencephalon and perhaps mesencephalon), the integration that is prerequisite to planned movement takes place. This means that a patterned stream of nerve impulses passes out to the motor cortex area (of both hemispheres), as suggested by the broken lines in Figure 4.

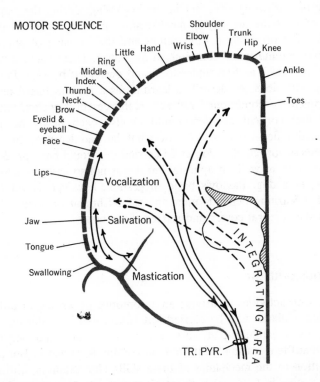

FIGURE 4 Voluntary motor system. A diagrammatic cross-section through the right hemisphere along the plane of the precentral gyrus is viewed from in front. The pathway of control of consciously directed movement is suggested as originating somewhere in the grey matter of the higher brain stem. The patterned message passes outward, as shown by the broken lines, to the motor transmitting strip of the precentral gyrus. From there, after elaboration, it continues down the cortico-spinal tract, as shown by the unbroken lines, toward the muscles. (SOURCE: W. Penfield and H. Jasper, *Epilepsy and the Functional Anatomy of the Human Brain.* Boston: Little, Brown, 1954, p. 60.)

It is clear that skills of hand and foot and mouth and vocalization are made possible by acquired mechanisms established in the primary (and probably also secondary and supplementary motor) somatic areas of the cerebral cortex.

When well learned, man's skills may be carried out while he is thinking of something else. But in the beginning, during the acquisition of each of the underlying mechanisms, he must focus his attention upon the proposition—the action and the focusing of attention are always voluntary and conscious at the outset. These become "conditioned reflexes," as first understood and described by Ivan Pavlov. Working with dogs, he described learning as a process based on the establishment of conditioned reflexes in the cerebral cortex, and he showed that cortical excision would abolish each newly acquired conditioned reflex—the animal lost what he had learned. In man, such heedless cortical excision as he carried out would have produced hand paralysis, as well, or aphasia, but it was not so with the paw, or the bark, of a dog. Pavlov's basic suggestion, however, is valid for man—that learning depends upon the establishment of acquired reflexes in the cerebral cortex and related thalamus.

CONSCIOUS GUIDANCE

In time, such activities as driving an automobile or writing or talking or playing a piano may be carried out subconsciously. Starting and stopping the mechanism, at least, is a conscious act, and one may assume that there is usually intermittent conscious guidance. But paying attention to the mechanics of these skills (for example, hitting a golf ball) may, in time, seem to interfere with the expertness of performance.

In this semi-independent activity, I surmise that no part of the cortex is ever acting quite alone without some control through back-and-forth connections from and to the higher brain stem. We may assume also, as will be pointed out, that conscious direction is never possible without neuronal action in some portion of the diencephalon.

As is suggested in Figures 2 and 4, the important nerve fibers that carry impulses to the cortex and those that return to the medulla and spinal cord are close to each other and run, for some distance, in parallel lines, although in opposite directions. Thus, ordinary pathological lesions interrupt both limbs of the motor efferent stream, which explains why the stream of impulses responsible for planned bodily action was so long considered to originate in the cortex.

Any pathological or surgical interference with a sensory or motor area of cerebral cortex interferes with its use, but the individual is still conscious and may well use other areas of cortex to carry out a selected plan. If the right hand is paralyzed or the right field of vision is blind, due to cortical injury, he "makes do" with the left hand or turns his eyes to expose more of the other side of the retina and so makes use of the normal field of vision remaining to him.

Indeed, any area of cerebral cortex can be destroyed or removed without loss of consciousness, but, when the higher brain stem is rendered inactive, there follows immediate unconsciousness. Neuronal action in this central area may be arrested by injury or tumor, by the discharge of an epileptic seizure, by the local loss of circulation during fainting, or by the more normal physiological alteration that comes with sleep.

CORTICAL EXCISION

Experimental physiologists have made most important contributions to knowledge of the functional anatomy of motor and sensory mechanisms in the animal brain. They have studied the integration of the inborn reflexes and the formation of conditioned reflexes. But there is a whole field of brain problems, which relate to the mind, that can be studied only when man himself is the subject.

Planned excision of cortical convolutions is a method of treating focal epilepsy that may, by chance, fulfill all the requirements of a scientific experiment. It is possible to remove convolutions from the brain, leaving the underlying white matter intact and without producing abnormality of circulation in the remaining convolutions. Thus, in selected patients, whose epilepsy is due to localized epileptogenic abnormality of the cortex, it is possible to remove the cause.

Cure by such a method must, of course, be balanced against loss of function of the excised convolutions, if they are still functional. In any case, the surgeon does well to make a preliminary survey of the cortex before removal, mapping out the function of the convolutions with the help of a stimulating electrode. He may also map out the extent of epileptogenic abnormality by means of direct electro-corticography. He must, of course, protect the patient from pain by local anaesthesia, and from anxiety by carrying on a calm running conversation with him. Surgery, in any case, should be reserved for selected cases. If a patient can lead a useful, happy life with the help of conservative medication and care, he should not be considered a candidate for craniotomy; but when medical therapy fails, and if there is evidence of a cortical focus, the chance of a cure by neurosurgery is good.

ELECTRICAL STIMULATION

The neurosurgeon can use electrical stimulation to reproduce any fit that ordinarily begins in an abnormal epileptogenic area of the cerebral cortex. (The patient will often say, "That is the way they begin.") But, if the surgeon is careful to use a mild stimulus, no after-discharge occurs, and no fit follows. The surgeon can also use an electrode to map out the normally responsive functional areas, thus increasing the accuracy and the safety of proposed surgical excision of the epileptogenic areas of cortex. The patient, who is inevitably well aware of the need for accuracy, can talk with him and guide his hand.

In a small book called *The Excitable Cortex in Conscious Man* (15), I undertook to study the significance and the interpretation of cortical stimulations. Some areas of cerebral cortex respond in a positive manner to electrical stimulation; others do not.

While the electrode is applied to an area of cortex, the patient cannot use the functional mechanism of which the area forms a part. While the electrode is producing, for example, flashing lights in one visual field by application to the contralateral occipital cortex, the patient is also blind to lighted objects in the field. While the electrode is causing movement of the right thumb, the patient has lost all control over it. When the electrode is applied to the speech cortex, there is no positive response; the patient is aware of nothing new. But, when he tries to speak, or read, or write, he finds himself aphasic.

In regard to the positive response, my final conclusion was this: "The principal cortical areas of the human brain that yield positive responses to gentle electrical stimulation may be placed in three groups: sensory, motor, and interpretive. The positive effects of stimulation seem to be due to dromic cortico-fugal conduction to distant but functionally connected nerve-cell groups."

"Dromic conduction" means passage of impulses from a nerve cell along its axon, as in normal neuronal activity, to some other cell or cells that may be at a distance. Neuronal action, then, is caused at the next ganglionic station. Conduction to it, in that case, is not by diffuse escape of current; it is axonal and, in a sense, physiological. Thus, stimulation of a sensory area of cortex activates, by its normal linkage, certain ganglion cells in the thalamo-diencephalic target, which was discussed above. Stimulation of the motor cortex activates, by efferent conduction, motor nuclei in the lower brain stem or the spinal cord.

Interpreting the results of electrical stimulation of the cortical speech areas calls for further consideration. The surprisingly different result of stimulating the homologous area of the cortex in the non-dominant hemsiphere also needs explanation. The structure of nerve cells and nerve-fiber tracts was, presumably, identical at birth on the two sides. But, after the child has learned to speak and to interpret the meaning of his environment, the functioning connections of the adult are obviously quite different on the two sides.

If the electrode has any effect (discoverable by surgeon or patient) when applied to the speech area, the result is interference aphasia. If it has any effect when applied to the other side, the result is a positive response—either a sudden interpretation of present experience or an equally sudden rerun of a strip of conscious experience from the past.

These are facts, not theories. One conclusion is clear: the initially uncommitted cortex of the temporal regions is programmed by the child during early years of life—programmed for speech, or for perception, but not for both. The functioning connections, which are established while the child is learning to speak and to perceive, are quite different. One must assume that, during the process of learning, the passage of electrical potentials (nerve impulses) along one of many possible collateral branches of a neuron, and through the junction of that branch with another cell, facilitates that pathway. In time, the facilitation becomes absolute, and the linkage of the cell is fixed.

Such are some of the data that have come to light through electrical stimulation of the cortex of the conscious patient. With the new evidence comes the new opportunity, indeed the responsibility, of considering what new light the facts may shed on the nature of thought and consciousness.

Speech

It was man's capacity to learn and to develop acquired skills that singled him out from other mammals during the later stages of mammalian evolution. We do not know when, in evolutionary time, he developed dominance for hand movements, but it was more than three and a half millennia ago. Russell Brain called attention to the fact that in the year 1406 B.C. there were in the Army of the Children of Benjamin, according to the biblical record, 700 chosen left-handed men who "could sling stones at an hair breadth, and not miss." At least 8.7 percent of the army were left-handers. Obviously, at that time, the great majority were right-handed. Man probably developed hand dominance as early as the appearance of organized language, but this is pure surmise.

BRAIN DOMINANCE

Dominance in favor of one extremity is characteristic of man. There is also a far more important cerebral dominance—that for speech. In the great majority of human beings, the left hemisphere is dominant for both hand and speech, but this is not invariable. When I refer to the dominant hemisphere, I shall mean the one in which the speech mechanism is located. Throughout the discussion of speech, I shall draw heavily on the work of others and on our own studies in Montreal, recorded and documented in previous writings (24).

Without quoting statistics, we can say that right-handers almost invariably are found to have the speech mechanism in the left hemisphere. Left-handers have speech sometimes in the right hemisphere, sometimes in the left. When there is injury to the cortical motor area of the right hand at birth, or during early childhood, hand dominance appears on the other side. Speech dominance does not shift with hand dominance unless there is also injury to the major speech area in the cortex or damage to the underlying nucleus in the thalamus.

APHASIA

If a child has already learned to speak, destruction of the speech mechanism in the left hemisphere produces complete aphasia. At the end of about a year of silence, the child begins to speak again, and he or she may learn to speak perfectly. The speech mechanism will then be found, newly established, in the other hemisphere. If brain injury occurs after the age of ten or twelve, however, such a complete transference does not take place. The adult who has become aphasic after a severe brain injury or hemorrhage involving the major speech area may improve, but he is no longer able to make a complete recovery. He cannot, it seems, set up a completely new mechanism for language in the other hemisphere.

There are probably two reasons for this: First, the young child has an amazing capacity for acquiring the basic units of the mother tongue (and other secondary languages at the same age, if he is allowed to hear them). He listens and imitates and, in so doing, establishes the *neuronal set,* the brain-patterning, of a language. From six years onward, he can add to his vocabulary with ease in any language that has already been set, but, from this time onward, he loses progressively the ready facility of establishing the basic brain pattern of a new language.

The second, obvious explanation of why a new speech mechanism cannot be set up on the nondominant side of the brain after the age of twelve is that the area has by then been appropriated for interpretation of another sort, perception. It has been given a nonverbal neuronal set. Before discussing the acquisition of nonverbal concepts and perception, however, I shall make a short detour to point out some self-evident conclusions about second-language learning.

SECOND-LANGUAGE LEARNING (AN ASIDE TO EDUCATORS)

The growing brain has in it a biological clock of learning aptitude. A mechanical computer can be programmed for new tasks, as I understand it, any time, but the brain must be conditioned for language according to the timetable of childhood. Given the opportunity, a child programs his own speech computer at the start, then adds vocabulary later.

This throws some light on the facility for language learning possessed by an individual who hears a second (and perhaps a third) language before, say, the age of six. He establishes a *set* for each language (in the dominant hemisphere) and develops a remarkable subconscious *switch* technique that turns on one language at a time. In later years, he can add at will to his vocabulary in any of the languages for which the set has been established, doing it easily and without an awkward accent.

The *set of a language* is established by the facilitation of nerve-impulse passage. It includes sound, inflection, and articulation. An infant listens to the mother tongue, which we may call Language A, for months before uttering the first word. He continues, of course, to modify his pronunciation progressively. When a new language (B) is presented to a young child, it does not fit the "set" established for A. The child begins at once, then, to elaborate a new set-mechanism. When he does start to speak in Language B, he does so as he did in A. The two sets do not fit, and so he switches back and forth repeatedly. Both sets are localized in the speech area of the dominant hemisphere. When Language C is heard, it fits neither, and the child waits. But soon he has a third set and begins to add vocabulary and facility of pronunciation in the third.

Switch Mechanism.   The man who was bilingual early in life seems to have less difficulty, later in life, in learning Languages C, D, and E than does the unilingual adult. The unilingual adult, when he begins a new language, does not switch it off but begins to translate through Language A. He seems to use A's brain set instead of waiting and imitating. Therefore, he speaks the new language with an easily recognizable accent. The accent of the Frenchman or Norwegian who learned English late in life is predictable and recognizable.

On the contrary, the individual who was early bilingual switches off the A set when he hears B spoken and thus approaches it directly, ready to imitate accurately as soon as he has heard new words for a little while.

When a bilingual adult approaches a completely new language, he can still approach it somewhat more directly than the unilingual adult, possibly because he has become so skilled in the switch-off mechanism. It is a conditioned reflex that is triggered normally by various learned signals. The switch-on mechanism is similarly conditioned, even by hearing a single word. Thus the switching-off and the switching-on are carried out as though the brain were a television set and the languages were to be reached on different channels.

THE BLANK SLATE

It was pointed out above that the second reason injury in adult life does not cause the speech circuits to shift to the other side is that the nondominant cerebral cortex has not been left idle during childhood. On the contrary, it gradually takes on a *set* of its own. It is programmed to serve the function of perception (nonverbal interpretation of present experience).

All learning is to be explained by the basic physiological fact that the movement of a train of nerve impulses down a path, through nerve-cell synapses and along nerve branches, facilitates the use of that pathway for subsequent passages. This facilitation effect is transient, as was pointed out by Sherrington, in the sensory and motor transmitting systems. In the cortical circuits responsible for conditioned reflexes, the facilitating effect easily becomes permanent. Thus, motor skills, speech mechanisms, and perception mechanisms are easily acquired and preserved through life.

The uncommitted cortex is peculiar, also, in that it adopts a *func-*

tional set in the early years of childhood. It may be for the interpretation and memory of speech, or it may be for memory of nonverbal concepts and the interpretation of nonverbal experience.

Much of the infant's temporal cortex may thus be compared to a clean slate. It will be utilized and written upon as the child grows older and *pays attention* to language and to experience. Speech and perception depend upon acquired ideational mechanisms established by the child in this great zone of cortex. The mechanisms come to serve the adult as an aid to interpretation—interpretation of speech posteriorly on the dominant side (speech cortex), interpretation of experience in the light of the individual's past in the other portions of both sides (interpretive cortex).

Consider the posterior temporal area of the cerebral cortex on the right (nondominant) side of any adult. This would have been used for speech if that function were not being established on the left: removal of this area on the right, if carried out in adult life, produces no interference with speech. It does, however, produce a loss of awareness of body scheme and of spatial relationships (Figure 5).

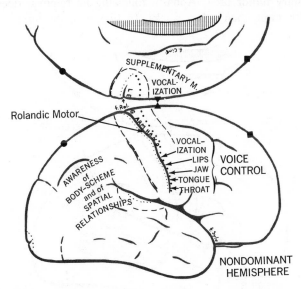

FIGURE 5 Nondominant hemisphere. The voice control is the same as on the dominant side. Its removal on either side produces no more than motor difficulty of enunciation. Removal of cortex about the posterior end of the fissure of Sylvius, if complete, produces loss of perception of spatial relationships. (SOURCE: H. Hécaen, W. Penfield, C. Bertrand, and R. Malmo, "Syndrome of Apractognosia due to Lesions of Minor Cerebral Hemisphere," *Archs. neurol. Psychiat.*, 75 [1956] 400.)

Consciousness, Memory, and Man's Conditioned Reflexes   **143**

This functional deficit has been described by many clinicians and summarized by Critchley. Riddoch (also Brain) referred to it as visual disorientation, Hécaen (5) as *troubles visuo-constructifs,* or apractognosia. Patients who have lost this area of the nondominant cortex in adult life are unable to interpret visuo-sensory information, unable to orient themselves in space.

CORTICAL SPEECH AREAS

Figure 6 presents the dominant hemisphere. The area, which was used on the other side to orient an individual in space, is here devoted to the ideational transactions of language. It is the major speech area originally described by Wernicke (28). The anterior speech cortex, as discovered by Broca (3), must be considered a secondary area. Aphasia follows its removal, but it clears up (after months or years, even in the adult) provided the major posterior area of Wernicke is intact. The third speech center, which we may call supplementary or superior, is still more dispensable (24). It is located in the general supplementary motor area. Aphasia following its removal does not continue for more than a few weeks. In Figure 6, the limits of the

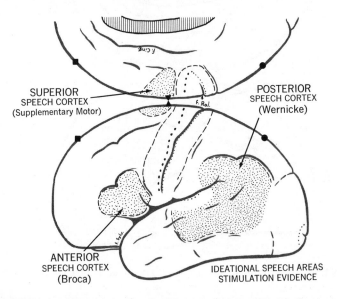

FIGURE 6 Speech areas of dominant hemisphere. This map is derived from a complete summary of the use of electrical interference to localize speech. (SOURCE: W. Penfield and L. Roberts, *Speech and Brain-Mechanisms.* Princeton: Princeton Univ. Press, 1959, p. 201.)

speech areas were established by summarizing the evidence derived from a long series of cases in which speech was mapped out by means of electrical interference.

Application of the electrode to a speech area produces no positive phenomena. It does produce aphasia, which the patient discovers only when called upon to speak or to read. The type and degree of speech interference is much the same regardless of which of the three areas is subjected to an interfering current, and it is equally irresistible. This suggests that the anterior and superior areas have effective axonal entrance into the thalamic nucleus, which has its direct connection with the major speech cortex. It suggests, too, that it is axonal conduction (not spread of current) from cortex to thalamus that produces the temporary interference.

Figure 7 shows, by broken lines, the connection of the posterior cortical speech area of the left hemisphere with the underlying thalamus (pulvinar). A destructive lesion there produces aphasia. (But if a lesion is placed more centrally, the syndrome of aphasia never appears. Instead, all awareness vanishes, and the patient is unconscious.) Something analagous occurs as the result of a lesion in the

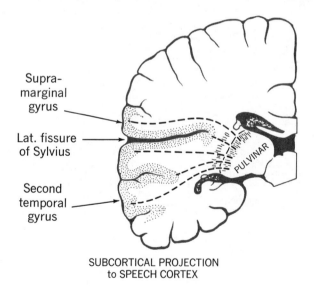

SUBCORTICAL PROJECTION
to SPEECH CORTEX

FIGURE 7 Cortico-thalamic connections for the posterior cortical area of the speech mechanism in the dominant hemisphere. Similar connections serve (presumably) the spatial perception mechanism in the nondominant hemisphere. (SOURCE: W. Penfield and L. Roberts, *Speech and Brain-Mechanisms.* Princeton: Princeton Univ. Press, 1959, p. 213.)

Consciousness, Memory, and Man's Conditioned Reflexes   **145**

homologous zone of thalamus in the nondominant hemisphere. There is loss of perception of space relationships. This, too, can be produced only in the cortex or in the thalamus, not more centrally. There is, we must conclude, a to and fro circuit.

The conclusion is obvious that these two cortico-thalamic mechanisms (speech and space orientation) can be activated normally—that is to say, used by an individual—as the result of neuronal action in the diencephalon. This action corresponds to conscious thinking and we may say the neuronal action accompanies thought. Here, then, are some of the neurophysiological mechanisms that form the *physical basis of thought.*

Compare Figure 8 now with Figure 5. The motor control of the throat, tongue, jaw, lips, and vocalization has a cortical area on each side. Removal of this sensori-motor area for voice control on the right produces no more than anarthria, to the extent of thickness of speech, which tends to clear up in time. We have also carried out (although rarely) excision of the same area on the left side, in order to remove an epileptogenic focus. This was done first with some misgiving, since it was sure also to interrupt whatever direct transcortical connection there

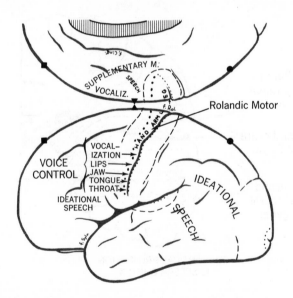

FIGURE 8 Dominant hemisphere of the human adult. Compare with Figure 5. There are no indispensable transcortical connections between the cortical speech areas and the motor areas for vocalization and verbal articulation. (SOURCE: W. Penfield and L. Roberts, *Speech and Brain-Mechanisms.* Princeton: Princeton Univ. Press, 1959, p. 213.)

might be between the anterior and posterior ideational speech areas. The result was temporary postoperative aphasia, but that cleared up, leaving only anarthria such as would have appeared following removal on the other side.

We have never removed any of the major speech cortex because of the fact that speech is never to be forfeited even in exchange for freedom from fits. But we have removed blocks of epileptogenic cortex in various positions all around the major speech area in the dominant hemisphere. None of these excisions produced an enduring aphasia. By summarizing them all, a map of the three cortical speech areas was produced. It corresponded closely with the map (shown in Figure 6) prepared by the method of electrical interference.

It must be clear, therefore, that the anterior and the superior areas of speech cortex play some sort of secondary role, analogous perhaps to the secondary visual cortex and the second somatic sensory cortex and the supplementary motor cortex. Wernicke's (posterior) area, which could be called "major," or perhaps "primary," is bounded by the visual cortex behind and in front by the audio-sensory and voice-control areas. Nevertheless, it is clear that transcortical intercommunication (however useful it may be) is not essential for speaking, writing, or understanding speech.

THE PATTERNING OF POTENTIALS*

Suppose one listens to the word "apple" spoken by a companion. The sound waves activate those nerve cells in the cochlea of the inner ear that correspond with each vibration frequency that has impinged upon the ear drum. The electrical potentials thus evoked make up an afferent auditory stream, a specific message pattern, which is flashed to the thalamic nuclei and on out to the audio-sensory cortex on both sides, then back into the circuits of central integration. From there the sound pattern is sent out again to the ideational speech mechanism in the cortex. A transaction that we may call "translation" must then take place in the speech mechanism. The message, now altered in its potential pattern, echoes back into appropriate circuits of the

---

* A word of explanation is called for here. Potential pattern refers to the arrangement of nerve impulses that are made to travel from certain nerve cells over nerve fibers to other nerve cells in sequence. The pattern must vary according to which nerve cells are activated and, no doubt, to the intensity of activation. *Afferent* flow of impulses means flow toward the central nervous system and into the zone of central integration; *efferent* flow is in the opposite direction.

central integrating system and evokes, in the mind, the idea of a familiar, rounded, colored, eatable fruit.

If the individual then chooses to repeat the word "apple," as a young child is apt to do, a stream of patterned potentials (nerve impulses) must pass out from the central integrating complex to the voice-control portion of the motor cortex on both sides and so on down to the appropriate motor nuclei in the pons and medulla oblongata, causing the word "apple" to be spoken.

For reading, a similar succession must be hypothecated: sight of the word "apple" written on a page sets off a corresponding afferent message and translation sequence, beginning this time in the visual system. The light waves activate nerve cells in the retina in a pattern that corresponds to the written word. The message pattern of potentials flash from the retina through the thalamus to the visual cortex, half the image on one and half on the other. Then they return through thalamic nuclei to the central integrating system, where the two patterned halves are combined. From there the message of patterned potentials goes out to the speech mechanism. Here it is translated and flashed back into appropriate central integrating circuits. Again, the idea of an apple is evoked.

What I have referred to as an "auditory message pattern" and a visual "message of pattern potentials," D. H. Hubel described more aptly, no doubt, as a coded arrangement of nerve impulses. Russell Brain referred cautiously to "schemata" in the realm of speech and of recognition of nerve impulse.

The child in the learning stage is conscious of the sound of the spoken word and the shape of the written word and is excited by the first evocation of the idea. Later, however, by the time the relationship is learned, a conditioned reflex has been set up, and the whole process by which an adult derives ideas becomes a subconscious one. When an adult listens to words, he comes in time to ignore all of the process described above and is aware only of the succession of ideas evoked.

When the process described above is reversed, the apple itself is presented, and the child sees it, speaks the word, learns to write it, quite conscious of each sound and shape. The adult, however, speaks the word on seeing the object, or writes it, oblivious to the intervening mechanism. Thus he is able to focus his attention on meanings or ideas. The important point is that the learner can only acquire a conditioned reflex in the full light of conscious attention.

Wilder Penfield

A child learns when he is paying attention—and only then. If he is keenly interested at the moment in something else, such as in an idea of his own, a desire of his own, or the appearance of an approaching dog, he will not hear the word "apple" or see the word, even if he seems to look at the page on which it is written. He may not even see the object if it is placed before him. Active inhibition of incoming streams of information is obviously a part of the neuronal mechanism of the focusing of attention. Inhibition (or blockage of messages) seems to be exerted at some point quite early in the input sequence, a fact that need not be discussed here.

Language learning may be looked upon as the process of setting up conditioned reflexes in certain parts of the uncommitted cortex of the dominant hemisphere. Thus a speech mechanism is created. But another brain mechanism must be created, for nonverbal perception and for concept recognition.

Perception and the Interpretive Cortex

Words are symbols. Before a child can speak and know what he is saying, he must have a concept of what, for example, an apple is. A parrot uses words, but doubtless without understanding and without connecting words to corresponding concepts—translation fails. Animals in general interpret meanings in the world about them. A puppy, for example, learns faster than a baby in the early months of life. But when the baby speaks, the dog is left behind.

Capacity for perception and speech are normally acquired at the same stage in the child's life, step by step. During the process, the initially uncommitted cortex is conditioned by the child and his teacher. Thus, an area on one side, the *speech cortex,* is conditioned for speech. The remainder of the initially uncommitted cortex (which we have called *interpretive cortex*) is programmed to serve the purposes of perception.

Two brain mechanisms are thus being established. A stimulating electrode, applied to the speech cortex of the adult, produces only interference-aphasia, without loss of nonverbal perception. From the interpretive cortex, electrical stimulation may produce positive psychical phenomena, a vastly different process, although the cerebral cortex on one side was the exact counterpart of the other at the outset.

PSYCHICAL RESPONSE

The word "psychical," as used here, was borrowed from Hughlings Jackson (7), who recognized that fits, derived from discharges in either temporal region, might have an "intellectual aura."* He referred to such fits as "dreamy states"; we may call them psychical seizures. They are of two kinds: one is an illusion during which there is a sudden change in the patient's interpretation of present experience. He calls the environment "familiar" or "strange" or "frightening," etc. Objects may seem to come near or to recede. In the second form, the patient has a hallucination, which comes to him like a dream. In it, some previous period of time is reexperienced.

The positive responses that we have produced by stimulation at various points in the interpretive cortex are like these "dreamy state" fits. We see now that the hallucinations are, in reality, experiential flashbacks from the past, while the illusions are sudden interpretive conclusions about the present. See Table 1.

TABLE 1 Psychical responses to electrical stimulation of interpretive areas of cortex.

Experiential flashback:	Random reenactment of a conscious sequence from the patient's past
Interpretive signaling:	Production of sudden interpretations of the present experience, such as *familiar, strange, fearful, coming nearer, going away*

INTERPRETIVE SIGNALS

Take as an example of interpretive signaling (10) the following: the patient (on the operating table under local anaesthesia) remarks suddenly, when the electrode is applied to an anterior point on the nondominant temporal lobe, "This all seems familiar, as though it happened before, and I even know what is coming next." Under normal circumstances, such a judgment of familiarity often proves to be true. To make that possible, it must follow that there is a mechanism in the brain that enables the individual to make an instantaneous, subconscious review of similar experiences in his past.

* We now realize that during such fits there is local electrical discharge. It can produce the same activation or interference as that which would be produced in the cortex if an electrode were applied to it.

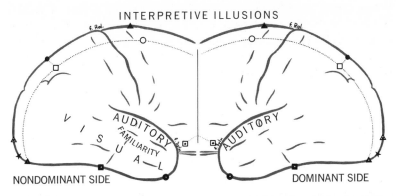

FIGURE 9 Summarizing map areas from which electrical stimulation produced illusions of interpretation. Changed interpretation of things heard (auditory) was produced by stimulation of the first temporal convolution on either side. A change in interpretation of things seen (visual) was produced in the nondominant side only (dominant being the side on which speech was localized). The feeling that this had all happened before (*déjà vu*, familiarity) was also produced in the nondominant side. (SOURCE: S. Mullan and W. Penfield, "Illusions of Comparative Interpretation and Emotion," *Archs. neurol. Psychiat.*, 81 [1959] 269.)

In another example: "People seem to be getting smaller . . . you both look more distant." In another case, stimulation caused the patient to say that he had a sudden feeling that objects seen were coming closer and that things heard were growing louder. These are common judgments of things that approach or go away.

Illusions that were strictly visual, as well as interpretations of space, were produced when the nondominant temporal cortex was being stimulated (Figure 9), and rarely, if ever, from the other side. This may well bear some relationship to the fact that disorientation in space is produced by posterior temporal excisions on that side.

In one patient, this area on the nondominant side was removed completely (zone in Figure 5 bearing the words "awareness of body scheme and spatial relationships"). In the years that followed the operation, the patient's epileptic attacks stopped. He was able to earn his living, but he had a penalty to pay. With his eyes closed, he had no conception of his position in space. On leaving his house in the village where he lived, he seemed to be well oriented until he turned a street corner. After that he was lost. To get back home, it was necessary for him to ask the direction from a passerby.

This man had no functional defect except that he had lost the capacity to construct in his mind a concept of spatial relationships.

Consciousness, Memory, and Man's Conditioned Reflexes   **151**

When called upon to make a drawing, he showed a loss of understanding of the relationships of external objects to each other as well as to himself. The loss was as absolute and as discrete as the aphasia would have been if the homologous area of cortex (Figure 8) had been excised on the dominant side.

EXPERIENTIAL RESPONSE OR FLASHBACK

The flashback responses to electrical stimulation are altogether different. They bear no relation to present experience in the operating room. Consciousness for the moment is doubled, and the patient can discuss the phenomenon. If he is hearing music, he can hum in time to it. The astonishing aspect of the phenomenon is that suddenly he is aware of all that was in his mind during an earlier strip of time. It is the stream of a former consciousness flowing again. If music is heard, it may be orchestra or voice or piano. Sometimes he is aware of all he was seeing at the moment; sometimes he is aware only of the music. It stops when the electrode is lifted. It may be repeated (even many times) if the electrode is replaced without too long a delay. This electrical recall is completely at random. Most often, the event was neither significant nor important. The details of all examples of experiential response are included in our final summary of them (22).

When all the points from which experiential responses were produced were summarized on a brain map, Figure 10 resulted. The general distribution is the same as that from which interpretive illusions were elicited. This we have called the "interpretive cortex." It avoids the speech area and skirts the visuo-sensory and audio-sensory areas. When the purely visual and purely auditory experiential responses were summarized, the diagram shown in Figure 11 was produced. The additional experiences that were both auditory and visual were elicited from points on the first temporal convolution of both sides.

These are facts collected from carefully preserved records of craniotomies under local anaesthesia. They have been critically studied and presented on these maps by my associates (Sean Mullan, interpretive illusions, and Phanor Perot, experiential responses). These operations, as I have said, were not planned experiments. But chance did fulfill, from time to time, all the conditions of controlled experimentation. These are not epileptic phenomena. Ordinarily when the current was switched off during deep stimulation, or the electrode was removed following superficial stimulation, the psychical response stopped instantly. If not, this response was given no localizing value since a

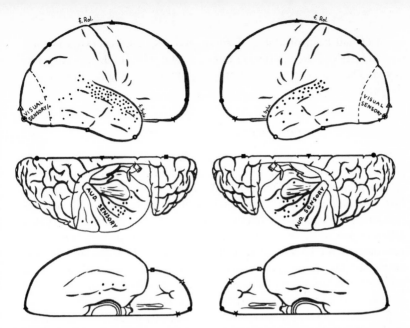

FIGURE 10 Flashbacks. Points of stimulation that produced experiential responses. Hemisphere partly excised to show superior surface of temporal lobe. (SOURCE: W. Penfield and P. Perot, "The Brain's Record of Auditory and Visual Experience. A Final Summary and Discussion." *Brain*, 86 [1963] 595.)

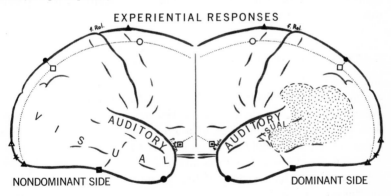

FIGURE 11 Experiential responses to stimulation shown for the lateral surfaces of both hemispheres. The temporal speech area (compare with Figure 6) is stippled. The number of experiential responses that are visual in character is much greater on the nondominant side and nearer the occipital cortex. No positive experiential responses followed stimulation of the speech area. (SOURCE: W. Penfield, "Speech, Perception and the Uncommitted Cortex," in J. C. Eccles [ed.], *Brain and Conscious Experience*. New York: Springer-Verlag, 1966, pp. 217–37.)

Consciousness, Memory, and Man's Conditioned Reflexes **153**

small fit had been produced. Experiential responses occurred in forty cases (forty different patients) out of a total series of 1,132 cases surveyed. There was no such response to stimulation in any other area of the brain.

THE UNCOMMITTED CORTEX

Consider for a moment the two homologous areas of originally uncommitted cortex—ideational speech (Figure 8) and awareness of spatial relationships (Figure 5). We may assume that at the time of birth the anatomical detail was identical, right and left, and the connections of cortex to thalamus were similar. Yet the child makes a different use of the two sides. It has already been pointed out that if you destroy the ideational speech area on the left at the age, for example, of five years, previously learned speech goes with it. But it returns to normal after a year or more of aphasia, and the major speech area is then (in our experience) established on the right.

Speech is apparently served best by a strictly unilateral mechanism. If there is destruction of the original speech cortex after the age of ten or twelve, we must assume that the slate that was once blank on the nondominant side is so no longer. After the age of ten or twelve, the writing on it can no longer be erased. Thus, with the posterior temporal region destroyed on the dominant side, restoration of speech will be no more than partial.

INTERPRETIVE CORTEX

Let me recapitulate the evidence from stimulation of the speech cortex and the interpretive cortex. We have had almost no cases of cortical stimulation before the age of ten. But it is apparent that after that time the neuronal paths open to a stimulating electrode in the two areas are quite distinctly different. On the speech side, a gentle current sends axonal impulses from any one of the three cortical speech areas to the pulvinar nucleus of the thalamus and blocks the speech mechanism effectively.

On the other (nondominant) side, a similar current applied similarly to the temporal cortex, if it has any effect, produces a positive phenomenon. Whether it brings an interpretation of the present or a recall of the past, the surgeon's electrode has evidently activated a small part of an automatic mechanism. The mechanism is involved in nonverbal perception. In the right posterior temporal region, it deals particularly with pure visual experiences from the past and with present spatial relationships. On the other hand, the cortex of the first temporal convolution on both sides deals with pure auditory experience and with combined auditory and visual experience.

How does this interpretive mechanism work? What are its parts? One can only give partial answers, of course. It is clear that there is a neuronal record of the stream of consciousness. It seems to be complete and detailed during conscious life from childhood onward. It is located, not in the temporal cortex, but at a distance from the cortex.* Conscious effort gives any individual only limited access to this record. With rare exceptions, it fades progressively beyond voluntary recall and may be replaced by memory's generalizations, to be discussed below.

What we have termed the interpretive cortex is apparently used in the subconscious mechanism that summons previous experience for comparison with present experience. The mechanism is constantly employed in scanning the past for similar or related experience. The strips of the stream of previous consciousness that we have been able to summon electrically are largely concerned with visual and auditory phenomena, together with the previously attendant emotions and reactions. (Whether there is a mechanism for recall of other phenomena in life's experience that are predominantly nonauditory and nonvisual is not clear.)

PERCEPTION

Perception, for the normal adult, may be defined as interpretation of present experience in the light of past experience. For example, when someone on the street is recognized as a man, that is the beginning of perception; a general concept has been summoned. When the man speaks, perhaps the sound is familiar. Then the subconscious mechanism signals something like "heard before." If that voice had been heard before with fear, the observer would probably feel the fear now. Then comes a more specific recognition. The man is suddenly remembered, and details of that man come to mind and with such clarity that one realizes exactly what changes have occurred—a different bearing perhaps, a moustache, signs of advancing age. A past record has been summoned subconsciously. The particular concept of that man, having come clear, is presented now to the speech mecha-

* One may hazard a guess that the record itself is closely related to the hippocampus of both sides together with their connecting central circuits. It may be that the hippocampus, with its strange structure, plays a role in *recall* rather than *storage* of the record. I shall discuss this, with other aspects of memory, presently.

nism, where the idea is translated automatically into the name. Both man and name are remembered, and they emerge again in consciousness.

Relation of Mind to Brain-Mechanism

The programming or conditioning of the uncommitted cortex that goes on in childhood produces two automatic brain-mechanisms that are separable functionally. Their interaction and their relationship to the neuronal action that accompanies conscious thought must now be faced.

A PATIENT'S INTROSPECTION

The case of C. H., which I am about to discuss, has been reported fully elsewhere. But it brings us directly to the problem of the relation of mind to brain. Under local anaesthesia, a large part of the left hemisphere of this patient had been exposed. As a guide to cortical excision, I undertook to outline clearly the limits of the major speech area in the temporal region. To that end, one of my associates began showing him a series of pictures. C. H. named each picture accurately. While this was going on (and without the patient's knowledge), I applied an interfering current by means of an electrode placed on the speech area. When the next picture was shown to him, he remained silent. But he snapped his fingers as though in exasperation. Presently, I withdrew the electrode.

"Now I can talk," he said. "Butterfly. I couldn't get that word 'butterfly,' so I tried to get the word 'moth.' "

It is clear that while the speech mechanism was temporarily blocked, he could still perceive the meaning of the picture of a butterfly. He made a conscious effort to "get" the corresponding word. Then, not understanding why he could not do so, he summoned another concept which he considered the closest thing to butterfly. He presented that to the speech mechanism and drew another blank.

When trying to understand the interdependence of brain and mind, I have often recalled this quiet moment in the operating room. The patient's simple statement startled me. He was calling on two automatic brain-mechanisms alternately and at will. I had it in my power to inactivate one mechanism, that of speech, without altering his ability to use other mechanisms of the brain and certainly without making it difficult for him to think. I could do this at will. *Conscious thought* and *brain action* seemed suddenly within reach of one's understanding.

This patient, wanting to help the surgeon, had turned his complete attention to the task, ignoring all else even in this strange operating-room environment. We may assume that he was inhibiting all the unrelated streams of sensory information that might otherwise have reached the place from which he was *sending* the patterned potentials that carried the idea of a butterfly to the speech mechanisms. Now that one had some idea of where the acquired cortico-thalamic mechanisms were, it was necessary to ask where the messages were coming from and where the pattern had been put together. The question may be asked another way: where did the nerve impulses come from that activated the nerve cells that would carry the concept "butterfly" (the pattern also that would mean "moth") when it reached the speech mechanism?

Somehow the patient had held the line of communication open. He waited. When no answer came, he turned to the nonverbal perception mechanism again, seeking the nearest substitute for butterfly. The concept of moth was forthcoming and he compared it "in his mind's eye" with the concept of butterfly. Then he sent off a different message, so patterned that it should mean "moth" to the speech mechanism. When again there was no automatic response, he made a movement of exasperation with his hand.

Now, while C. H. was making this effort to direct the action of his brain, his stream of consciousness was certainly being recorded. It is more accurate to say that the neuronal action that accompanied and made possible the stream of consciousness was recorded so that it might be reproduced when summoned later, consciously or unconsciously. Meanwhile, all the other contemporary neuronal activity came and went without leaving a record, like a million moving lights that twinkle for a moment on as many circuits and go out.

DUALITY OF APPROACH

Before going on to a discussion of memory, attention, and the stream of consciousness from the physiological point of view, I propose to make a short philosophical detour. In the foregoing discussion I have said *he* wanted to help, *he* turned his attention, *he* summoned another concept, *he* chose, *he* presented, *he* was exasperated—as though he and his mind were one, while the brain was something else, a machine to be used. I have said *I* was startled, *I* could activate his speech mechanism, *I* could do this at will. In all of this, I was clearly thinking of the persons, him and me, as distinguished from brain and brain-mechanisms. There is no other language a scientist can use.

Science has not explained the mind, the person, or the personality. A neurophysiologist can study the central nervous system with its in-born reflexes, its lines of communication, and its acquired brain-mechanisms. He can point out the parallelism between the electrical activity in neurons and the changing content of the mind. But he cannot study the mind directly. There is no method.

A biographer may describe the changing behavior of a man all through his life. His objective is to picture what he considers to be a changing personality, and he assumes that the person who is the subject of his book is something more than a collection of reflexes. Someone looks out of the eyes of his subject, listens through the subject's ears, makes decisions, laughs, and weeps. Like the scientist, a biographer must use the language of duality. There is no other way. There is no other way for a man to describe himself or to work out his own belief about his Creator.

ANOTHER SCHOOL

The revelations of biological evolution and the history of the planets serve the purposes of science. But there is another school and a far more ancient scholarship, which have to do with social evolution and the history of moral and religious thinking. Wise men, parents, poets, prophets, priests, philosophers, and common men have glimpsed spiritual and moral truths that are no less important to man than the discoveries of science. There is a vast accumulation of knowledge in this school that has to do with the nature of man. There are depths of good and bad in human nature. Man is teachable, loyal to ideals and traditions, and yet capable of critical and creative thinking.

To say that such characteristics are hidden in a man's genes, chromosomes, and nucleoprotein molecules explains nothing. It points merely to one of the approaches science may well make to the problem. When Pavlov's early work was reported, it was said (although not by him) that conditioned reflexes could explain the mind and disprove the existence of a spirit of man or God. But the saying was wrong—Pavlov's work threw light on the cerebral mechanisms, not on the nature of the mind. Physicians must make a double approach to the problem of man, for there is no thoroughfare of cause and effect between the brain and the mind of man, and there will be none until a new bridge is built. It is our present task to lay a solid footing for a bridge from both sides. But all the while we must bear in mind "the possibility," to use the words of Sir Henry Dale, "that man's mind may never be able to achieve for itself an understanding of its own relation to the function of the brain."

The Integrative Action of the Nervous System, by Charles Sherrington, was reprinted by the Physiological Society in 1947, 41 years after its original publication—"to be read by all students of physiology and to be reread by their teachers." Sir Charles contributed a foreword to that reprinting in which he considered this problem that I have skirted, the problem of the mind and the brain. "Each waking day," he remarked, "is a stage dominated for good or ill, in comedy, farce or tragedy, by a *dramatis persona,* the 'self.' And so it will be until the curtain drops." In the end, after seventeen pages of discussion, he came to no final pronouncement. He was far too honest for that—too honest as a philosopher and too knowledgeable as a physiologist. The final paragraph of his foreword was this: "That our being should consist of *two* fundamental elements offers I suppose no greater inherent improbability than that it should rest on one only."

Conscious Man

Physicians are called upon to care for the unconscious as well as the conscious. In cases of coma not due to toxic agents or drugs, the doctor's problem is to discover where the interference with brain function may be located, as well as what it is. To that end, he turns his attention at once to the diencephalon, since hemispheral lesions do not produce coma.

Neuronal action may be described as the passage of nerve impulses (electrical potentials) in meaningful patterns over appropriately selected lines of communication within the brain. Since, in some cases, neuronal action clearly accompanies the corresponding sequence of thoughts and awareness that flow through the mind of a conscious man, the scientific hypothesis is this: all mental phenomena are associated with corresponding neuronal action. On that assumption, then, what has been called "the stream of consciousness" must be accompanied by a corresponding stream of neuronal action.

Charles Sherrington, when addressing a lay audience, gave us a fanciful and often-quoted description of the brain of a man as he wakes from sleep. He said:

> Picture to yourself a scheme of lines and nodal points gathered at one end into a great ravelled knot, and brain. . . . Imagine activity

in this shown by little points of light. . . . Should we continue to watch . . . the great top-most sheet of the mass, where hardly a light had twinkled or moved, becomes now a sparkling field of rhythmic flashing light points with trains of travelling sparks hurrying hither and thither. . . . Swiftly the head mass becomes an enchanted loom where millions of flashing shuttles weave a dissolving pattern, always a meaningful pattern though never an abiding one. The brain is waking and with it the mind is returning.

When the mind returns after sleep or after coma, a man is conscious. Consciousness returns. One might object that neither mind nor consciousness can return, since no one can say where they are at any time. But consciousness does return when normal movement returns in certain nervous pathways of the brain. While there is light, the stream of light waves that impinge upon the human retina must be forever renewed. There is no light without vibratory movement, and there is no evidence of consciousness without neuronal action.

The content of a man's consciousness is never twice the same. It resembles a melody, which must advance to be a melody. In the waking state, the shuttles of the brain weave "a meaningful pattern though never an abiding one." The changing content of man's thinking corresponds with continuing neuronal action in meaningful patterns in the higher brain stem and the cerebral hemispheres. The action is never an abiding one, and yet that action is recorded with great fidelity and can be used and recalled in various ways. Consciousness is awareness. The individual is not aware of all that is going on in the brain. He is aware only of what lies within the focus of his attention, and here is the heart of the matter.

SENSORY INPUT

The sensory in-flow is remarkably varied. The succession of nerve impulses that makes up the afferent stream of electrical potentials brings into the thalamus, from the special sense organs, the sights and the sounds, the written and the spoken words, and all the meanings of social life. Together with the afferent impulses from the body, it makes available a very great amount of information of the environment. But only a small portion of the available information is selected and admitted to consciousness at any one time. By turning or directing his attention, each individual selects for himself, and that selecting is an act that may be considered voluntary.

Wilder Penfield

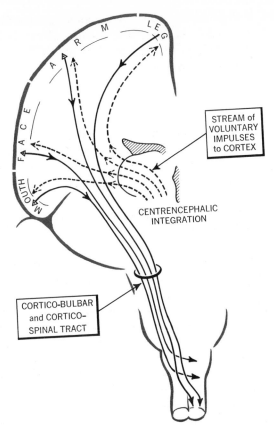

FIGURE 12 The motor path of nerve impulses that produce voluntary movement. The broken lines show the course of the hypothetical stream of patterned potentials from diencephalon to motor cortex. The unbroken lines show the stream from the cortex onward. (SOURCE: W. Penfield, *The Excitable Cortex in Conscious Man.* Liverpool: Liverpool Univ. Press, 1958, p. 17.)

ORIGIN OF MOTOR OUTPUT

The supposition is inescapable that the efferent stream of impulses, which produces the purposeful use of the motor system, arises within the higher brain stem (Figure 12). This directing current passes out to motor cortex and, from there, doubles back and goes on down through medulla or spinal cord to the muscles. Within the diencephalon and the reverberating circuits that link it to the cerebral cortex, the decisive neuronal action takes place. This action must precede the sending out of impulses in a meaningful motor pattern. The neuronal action that precedes the pattern formation selects data from sensory input and formulates the pattern. This action is an accompaniment of consciousness and thought.

MOTOR SKILLS

As already pointed out, man's motor skills are acquired in the full light of consciousness. But they quite rapidly become semiautomatic and even "subconscious." In spite of that, they may still be started and modified and stopped consciously. Although one may say, as Pavlov did, that conditioned reflexes are established in the cerebral cortex, it must always be remembered that these reflex circuits are cortico-thalamic and that they depend upon subcortical connections for initiation and modification. Thus, the circuit of a learned skill, when it is operating subconsciously, is still not cut off from subcortical interplay. But it is, for the time being, not receiving conscious directives.

It is clear then that Figure 12 is vastly oversimplified. The broken lines, for example, refer to the course of messages that formulate voluntary muscular action at certain times. At other times, they initiate, modify, or arrest semiautomatic mechanisms. The experiment described below is one example in which what may be called voluntary changes in electrical potentials were recorded.

Certainly man is the subject best suited for the study of such questions, and experimentation in the case of man is sometimes justifiable when it does no harm. The following experiment (from Jasper and Penfield, 9) was reported only in the Jubilee Volume dedicated to a German scientist, Hans Berger, and has been ignored as far as I am aware. (It was Berger's exemplary human experiments that proved the importance of the initially derided "Berger Rhythm" and established electroencephalography as a scientific discipline.)

Here is the experiment: in the case of a conscious patient whose cerebral cortex was exposed, for a therapeutic purpose, under local anaesthesia, a line of recording electrodes was placed along the precentral gyrus. The patient was then asked to squeeze with the opposite hand. The so-called resting beta rhythm of neuronal activity, which was being recorded all along the convolution, was disturbed only in the hand area. The disturbance disappeared after he had clenched his fist. It reappeared when he was asked to stop clenching. He was then asked to get ready to clench at the word "now," but not to clench. When the surgeon said "now," the same disturbance of rhythm occurred at the electrode placed on the hand area (and only there), but no hand movement resulted.

Such an observation does not prove anything. It is entirely consistent, however, with the hypothesis of electrical potential messages moving out to selected points in the cortex as indicated in Figure 12. And one must accept the conclusion that conscious thought in the mind of that patient preceded the dispatch of nerve impulses, along a selected path in the brain, to that part of the motor gyrus capable of controlling the hand in the way the patient had in mind.

The message, thus carried by a change of electrical potential, came from a subcortical source. It may be said that the message was an "action potential," but after the second command, the message seemed to carry to the hand area both an action potential and a countermanding inhibitory potential. Controlling messages, then, do come to the voluntary motor system from the diencephalon. They *cannot* conceivably come from anywhere else.

STREAM OF CONSCIOUSNESS

The psychologist William James (8) said of consciousness that "it flows." "A 'river,' " he added, "or a 'stream' are the metaphors by which it is most naturally described . . . the stream of thought, of consciousness, or of subjective life." But James's description may well be misleading. There is an inevitability about the content of a river that does not characterize consciousness. An observer cannot influence the river as he stands on the bank; he *can* control the stream of conscious experience. It comes to him out of the future; it passes and moves on into the past. The movement is inexorable, but each person modifies the content to some extent. Each man selects for himself, paying attention to a small portion of the sensory input, admitting that portion to the stream of his awareness. The rest vanishes without effect. It "dries like rain drops off the stones," leaving no neuronal record. Of course, there are things no man can exclude from notice. An explosion near at hand cannot be denied. It enters consciousness. But even then the man, though frightened, makes his own addition to consciousness. He considers instantly what it means to him, looks about, and discovers how best to escape.

The movement of the stream of awareness continues through each man's waking day until drowsiness intervenes and sleep closes the gate. The gate does not always close completely. There are leaks, especially at the beginning and end of sleep. Awareness seems to trickle in, and dreams come. The material of those dreams, the background or the ~tage setting, if you like, is drawn from the brain's record of the stream of consciousness during some period in the past. It may be distant or near at hand, like the flashbacks evoked by the surgeon's electrode. What happens in the foreground of the dream-land stage is a subject that would carry us far beyond the problem of attention and memory. When a man awakes from sleep, the gate of awareness opens wide. He begins to select again, at least in part, the stuff that is to be woven into consciousness.

ATTENTION

When one seems to have little purpose, his attention ranges. Discomfort, curiosity, interest, desire, purpose, all influence his decision, but the focusing of attention is always to some extent a voluntary act. There must be, accompanying it, a corresponding neuronal action with nerve impulses passing over appropriate paths. The focusing of attention signifies activation of certain brain-mechanisms and inhibition or blockade of many others. The patterns of activation and blockade in the brain of an individual differ widely when he writes a letter, listens to a lecture, watches television, or plays a sonata. Blockade and arrest permit neuronal traffic in the area selected for attention.

What, one may ask, is the anatomy of attention? The physiological anatomy, I suppose, is, in the end, the same whether the pattern of the attention is initially established as an involuntary or a voluntary act. In either case, it has a specific pattern. The pattern may be maintained for long periods until, perhaps under the influence of fatigue, it melts away. It may, of course, be modified or replaced by other patterns at any time.

One may ask: Is the pattern of neuronal action formed within the diencephalon at the time of initiation, and do messages emerge to the cerebral cortex like those that serve to direct voluntary motor activity? No firm answers can be given to these questions. But the assumption must be made that initiation of the pattern of attention has a corresponding neuronal action somewhere. Where else can it be but in the diencephalon?

Attention has been compared to the beam of a searchlight moving about in the dark. It may focus on the world without or on inner thoughts and fancies. But the act of paying attention is much more than the focusing of a searchlight. It selects and draws into the foreground, while initiating neuronal action on the stage of consciousness. Other action may go on off stage. Off-stage action is not arrested, but

Wilder Penfield

it is ignored—*only what happens on stage is recorded and remembered.*

MEMORY

I have pointed out that the focusing of attention is prerequisite to the establishment of conditioned reflexes, whether these are in the cortical mechanism of motor skills or in the peculiar mechanisms of speech or of perception. Attention then determines what skills a learner is to remember, also what words and what nonverbal concepts are to be stored away in his memory.

There is another kind of memory aside from these conditioned reflexes, which is related to the sequential record of the stream of consciousness. We have already described it in this paper and pointed out that a stimulating electrode, applied to the surface of the interpretive cortex of a conscious man, sometimes selects a moment in past time and causes the stream of consciousness to flow again. This record apparently includes all that the individual was aware of at the time, things seen and heard in normal detail, things felt and believed. The flashback strips of experience, which have been summoned thus from the past, include, as far as one may judge, all of the individual's awareness and nothing of what he ignored.

It is clear that the neuronal action that accompanies each succeeding state of consciousness leaves its permanent imprint on the brain. The imprint, or record, is a trail of facilitation of neuronal connections that can be followed again by an electric current many years later with no loss of detail, as though a tape recorder had been receiving it all.

Consider now what happens in normal life. For a short time, a man can recall all the detail of his previous awareness. In minutes, some of it has faded beyond the reach of his command. In weeks, all of it seems to have disappeared, as far as voluntary recall is concerned, except what seemed to him important or wakened in him emotion. But the detail is not really lost. During the subconscious interpretation of later contemporary experience, that detail is still available. This is a part of what we may call perception.

But man's memory has a still broader meaning beyond his skills, his words, his general concepts, his interpretations, and his recall of hour-to-hour events. Most of what he calls to mind voluntarily is made up of generalizations. He recalls a song but does not remember, perhaps, any of the times he heard it or sang it. He may recall a person. But the person has become a generalization, for he may be able to recall few if any periods of time shared with that person. Thus we have come back to the process of establishing concepts. A man can summon a generalization of a butterfly or a moth and the word symbol for each. The concept is established in the perception mechanism. The word is remembered, thanks to the speech mechanism. He uses these mechanisms at will, and what emerges in consciousness he calls a memory.

Generalizations, then, may be called concepts. They are built up gradually. The child sees a succession of butterflies, and thus the concept is progressively elaborated. The same is true of words. The meaning of a word, its pronunciation, and even its spelling change through the years. The same is true of motor skills. The skills of a golfer are added to, or altered, as time passes. They depend upon cortico-thalamic reflexes, conditioned reflexes.

A man can start and stop and modify these neuronal mechanisms. He can think of other things while using, for example, the concept mechanism and the speech mechanism, as the patient C. H. did in the operating room. He can employ one of a hundred skills, from writing to the execution of a concerto, while turning his mind to something else. What he turns his mind to will be preserved in the brain's sequential record. The concomitant doings, which were subconscious, are not recorded, at least not in the same way.

All the things that a man can call to mind, and all the skills a man can use, were established with materials that once formed a part of his awareness, that appeared in the stream of his consciousness. There is no evidence, as far as I am aware, that any of the things he ignored are stored away—at least not in any available form—in the central nervous system. Thus, a man, in selecting what he will attend to, selects what is to be preserved not only in the sequential record of experience but in the numerous mechanisms of the brain.

CONCLUDING REMARKS

I have looked at the human brain and the mind of man from my own perspective of experience after an interval of years. I have talked of consciousness and of the many aspects of memory and the many different mechanisms of the brain. I see now that they have a common basis of automatic availability. I have talked of attention. If I had another life to devote to human neurophysiology, I would like to devote it to the neuronal mechanism that makes possible the focusing of attention.

The unclassified cortex of the anterior frontal lobes of man has for function the planning of initiative, and this, I suppose, will someday be seen in its relation to the voluntary uses of attention.

The temporal cortex, so much of which is devoted to speech or to perception, makes it possible for man to speak and understand, using automatic mechanisms that are cortico-thalamic. Similarly, the vastly enlarged human motor cortex for hand and for vocal articulation provide him with a place in which motor skills can have their semiautomatic establishment. All of these mechanisms can be developed only in the focused light of conscious attention.

Finally, to put the matter simply, I think of the mind, or the spirit, as acting with some degree of independence. One assumes, in ordinary talk, that the mind and the individual are one and the same thing. I conclude this must be the truth. By selecting what he will attend to, the child conditions his own cortex. Thus, as the years pass, the child, with the help of parents and teachers, may be said to create his own brain-mechanisms. The man continues the process.

Until the day (if that day ever comes) we understand the nature of the mind, we can say only that each man uses his mind to condition and to program his brain. The spirit, then, is really father to the brain. And our thoughts, we may be sure, will go on breeding other thoughts, through the brains of other men.

REFERENCES

1. Adrian, E. D. "Consciousness," in Eccles, J. C. (ed.), *Brain and conscious experience*. New York: Springer-Verlag, 1966.
2. Bazett, C., and Penfield, W. "A study of the Sherrington decerebrate animal in the chronic as well as the acute condition." *Brain,* 45 (1922) 185.
3. Broca, P. "Sur la siège de la faculté du langage articulé." *Bull. Soc. anat.,* 2nd Series, 6 (1861) 355.
4. Head, H., and Holmes, G. "Sensory disturbances from cerebral lesions." *Brain,* 34 (1911) 102.
5. Hécaen, H., Penfield, W., Bertrand, C., and Malmo, R. "Syndrome of apractognosia due to lesions of minor cerebral hemisphere." *Archs. neurol. Psychiat.,* 75 (1956) 400.
6. Howells, J. G. (ed.). *Perspectives in psychiatry.* Edinburgh: Oliver and Boyd, 1967.
7. Jackson, J. H. "On the anatomical, physiological and pathological investigation of the epilepsies." *West Riding Lunatic Asylum Medical Reports* 3 (1873) 315.
8. James, W. *The principles of psychology.* New York: Holt, Rinehart and Winston, 1910.
9. Jasper, H., and Penfield, W. "Electrocorticograms in man: effect of

voluntary movement upon the electrical activity of the precentral gyrus." *Psychiat. Nervkrankh.*, 183 (1949) 163.

10. Mullan, S., and Penfield, W. "Illusions of comparative interpretation and emotion." *Archs. neurol. Psychiat.*, 81 (1959) 269.

11. Penfield, W. "Diencephalic autonomic epilepsy." *Archs. neurol. Psychiat.*, 22 (1929) 358.

12. Penfield, W. "Bilateral frontal gyrectomy and post-operative intelligence." *Proc. Ass. Res. Nerv. Ment. Dis.*, 27 (1947) 519.

13. Penfield, W. "The supplementary motor area in the cerebral cortex of man." (Published as part of the 75th and 80th birthday volume for Oskar and Cécile Vogt.) *Arch. psychiat. Nervkrankh*, 185 (1950) 670.

14. Penfield, W. "Epileptic automatism and the centrencephalic integrating system." *Proc. Ass. Res. Nerv. Ment. Dis.*, 30 (1952) 513.

15. Penfield, W. *The excitable cortex in conscious man.* Liverpool: Liverpool Univ. Press, 1958. Also, Springfield, Ill.: Thomas, 1958.

16. Penfield, W. "A surgeon's chance encounters with mechanisms related to consciousness." *J. R. Coll. Surg. Edinb.*, 5 (1960) 173.

17. Penfield, W. "Speech, perception and the uncommitted cortex," in Eccles, J. C. (ed.), *Brain and conscious experience.* New York: Springer-Verlag, 1966.

18. Penfield, W., and Evans, J. "The frontal lobe in man: a clinical study of maximum removals." *Brain*, 58 (1935) 115.

19. Penfield, W., and Faulk, M. E., Jr. "The insula: further observations on its function." *Brain*, 78 (1955) 445.

20. Penfield, W., and Jasper, H. "Highest level seizures." *Proc. Ass. Res. Nerv. Ment. Dis.*, 26 (1947) 252.

21. Penfield, W., and Jasper, H. *Epilepsy and the functional anatomy of the human brain.* Boston: Little, Brown, 1954.

22. Penfield, W., and Perot, P. "The brain's record of auditory and visual experience. A final summary and discussion." *Brain*, 86 (1963) 595.

23. Penfield, W., and Rasmussen, T. *The cerebral cortex of man.* New York: Macmillan, 1950.

24. Penfield, W., and Roberts, L. *Speech and Brain-Mechanisms.* Princeton: Princeton Univ. Press, 1959. Also New York: Atheneum, 1966.

25. Sherrington, C. S. *The integrative action of the nervous system.* London: Cambridge Univ. Press, 1947.

26. Sherrington, C. S. *Man on his nature.* New York: Macmillan, 1941. Also, London: Cambridge Univ. Press, 1941.

27. Walker, A. E. *The primate thalamus.* Chicago: Univ. of Chicago Press, 1938.

28. Wernicke, C. *Der aphasische Symptomencomplex.* Breslau: Max Cohn and Weigert, 1874.

Advances in Brain Research with Implications for Learning

by H. W. Magoun

In Amsterdam, on the last day of the year 1686, the English scholar-physician John Locke completed the fourth and concluding book of his *Essay Concerning Human Understanding* and, with it, opened contemporary approaches to study of the learning process. He had been occupied with this work for two years in Holland, having in 1684 been expelled from Oxford by the English king, who was "given to understand that Mr. Locke had upon several occasions behaved himself very fractiously and undutifully to the government" (13). Locke had left England shortly before "this harsh command" and, though rumor implicated a Dutch mistress, had chosen Holland because the climate suited his health and because, as he pointed out, "there was but little beer in France."

In the section of his *Essay* "Of Ideas," Locke drew attention to the essential role that input from the senses plays in learning when he wrote:

> Let us then suppose the mind to be, as we say, white paper, void of all characters, without any ideas; how comes it to be furnished? Whence comes it by that vast store, which the busy and boundless fancy of man has painted on it with an almost endless variety? To this I answer, in one word, from experience. In that, all our knowledge is founded! . . . I think it will be granted easily that if a child were kept in a place where he never saw any other but black and white till he were a man, he would have no more ideas of scarlet or green than he, that, from his childhood, never tasted an oyster or a pineapple, has of those particular relishes.

A variety of contemporary studies have begun to move a short way through the great door opened by Locke's *Essay,* to explore the manner by which brief recurring signals, generated by environmental changes at peripheral organs of sense, influence the subsequent per-

171

formance of the brain and so contribute to psychobiological development. A number of areas of recent study have relevance for this question.

A long-term study of differences in the brains of rats reared in enriched or restricted environments, and thus subjected to high or low experiential influences, has been undertaken by Bennett, Diamond, Krech, and Rosenzweig (7). On sacrificing the animals at maturity, they found the major changes in the cerebral cortex. Though the number of neurons remained the same in the two groups, the enriched rats displayed an increased cortical acetylcholinesterase activity, as well as a greater weight and thickness of the cortex, attributed both to an augmented growth of neuronal dendritic processes and to an increase in the number of glial cells. The cortical responses to environmental enrichment identified in these studies—the multiplication of dendritic, synapse-bearing branches of cortical neurons and the increment in transmitter biochemistry serving their functions—are thus reciprocal and obviously advantageous for expediting learning.

Moving from the rat to man, the report of the late President Kennedy's Panel on Mental Retardation (32) pointed out that in only a quarter of the large number of mentally retarded in this country is the condition attributable to so-called organic disturbance of the brain. The remainder show no evidence of biologic dysfunction detectable by present methods of medical diagnosis. The prevalence of these functionally retarded in disadvantaged population groups suggests that lack of environmental enrichment and limited intellectual stimulation and challenge had contributed significantly to the etiology of their condition.

Remarkable remedial advances are being made in such disadvantaged groups by providing the missing "experience," to which Locke made reference, in the education of children of Middle Eastern immigrants to Israel and comparable children in the Soviet Union. Such activities are now being extended in this country, where the initial efforts of Kirk, Martin Deutsch, and others have blossomed into Head Start and other early school-enrichment programs designed to restore the high-calorie experiential diets needed for optimal psychobiological development in early childhood.

Next, with respect to actual alimentary diets, a number of studies of protein-calorie malnutrition, both in Asia and Latin America, have identified mental retardation as a conspicuous feature of such malnourished children; and, again, subsequent provision of the missing input, in the form of protein-rich food products, goes a long way toward ameliorating the retardation (14).

172

These studies identify two highly important factors in mental development—first a rich diet of experiential and cognitive stimulation and, second, a viable protein metabolism, presumably of the brain. They even suggest that modification of cerebral protein metabolism may constitute the mechanism by which environmental and ideational stimulation promotes psychobiological development, for this work has been undertaken against the background of current advances in molecular and cellular biology that are identifying the biochemical mechanisms of genetic encoding and readout.

> Geneticists far and wide have come to accept the dogma of the Holy Trinity—DNA, RNA and protein—according to which, in all organisms, the ultimate store of genetic information lies in the DNA contained within the nucleus of each cell. Its message is conveyed to the RNA of the cytoplasm and there presides over the synthesis of proteins and enzymes. (20)

There are a number of contemporary neuroscientists who propose that nature has not been profligate enough to have evolved more than a single mechanism for information coding in biology. They postulate a comparable role of nucleic acid and protein in encoding and readout in the nervous system. Learning and memory, in their view, depend upon the specification of brain RNA and/or protein, as a consequence of bombardment by afferent signals from the external world—the more varied, intense, and frequent the bombardment, the more rapid and pronounced the specification. Such specified and replicated RNA or protein is proposed, in turn, to provide the template for elaboration of enzyme-like neuronal transmitter substances, responsible for consequent patterns of neuronal firing, serving behavior.

> The environment normally does not alter the DNA molecule except for rare and random genetic mutations. Rather, it selects one or another group of these molecules in terms of the relative degree of their adaptation to the environment. This is Darwinian evolution—natural selection of certain molecules from an array of possible DNA molecules. But when a given DNA molecule starts to produce RNA and proteins and enzymes and, ultimately, behavior, some step or steps in this sequence seem to be under fairly direct control by the environment, but just where in the sequence it acts, we do not know. (18)

When the neuron is examined with the electron microscope, the ubiquitous Nissl substance of its cytoplasm is seen to consist of interlacing membranes, on the profiles of which is a rich profusion of myriads of RNA granules. This, together with recent biochemical studies, indicates that neurons are among the most active protein-synthesizing cells of the body. An increase of neural RNA can be induced by trans-synaptic bombardment of cortical pyramidal cells within the animal brain (35). Hydén (25, 26, 27) has been able to dissect individual nerve cells from the rabbit brain, most recently from the hippocampal cortex, and their microanalysis has revealed both a high resting level of neuronal RNA and its considerable increment following stimulation of the animal preceding sacrifice. During ordinary stimulation, the newly formed RNA is unchanged in composition; by contrast, during learning situations, the newly formed RNA differs biochemically from that previously encountered (see pp. 108–13, above).

Hydén has extended these findings to the formation of a hypothesis of learning and memory, whose successive stages propose: first, that neuronal RNA is specified as a consequence of afferent signals; second, that this altered or specified RNA provides a template for the subsequent production of proteins and transmitter substances; and, last, that these transmitter substances subsequently excite postsynaptic neurons in patterns like those that initially induced the change. From a statistical point of view, he points out, the molecules of the brain can be estimated to furnish the necessary permutation possibilities to store the learning and memory experience of a lifetime. In this regard, it may be significant, too, that the neuron is one of the few cells in the body that, once formed, never subdivides again throughout the life of the individual and so avoids a jumbling of the file of codes. Additionally, it has been proposed by Schmitt (41) that specified RNA provides a template for transformation of proteins at receptor sites beneath synaptic junctions and thus, by means like those of immunochemistry, induces a specification of the affected neuron in learning that enables it to respond to the initial pattern of input signals, whenever repeated, but not to other patterns of excitation.

Others are testing the role of RNA and protein metabolism in learning by injecting antibiotics or other antimetabolites known to interfere with such metabolism. The Flexners and Roberts (17) have abolished learning and memory in animals by intracerebral injections of puromycin. After bilateral injections into the temporal region, recent learning was lost; loss of longer-term memory required injections involving, in addition, most of the remainder of the cortex. Spread of the memory trace from the temporal region to wide areas of the cortex appeared to require 3 to 6 days. It was initially thought that puromycin destroyed memory permanently, perhaps as a consequence of combining with essential messenger RNA. From more recent study, it appears that puromycin may block the expression of memory without substantially altering the process that maintains the basic memory trace.

In this regard, Cohen, Barondes, and Ervin (11, 12) found that puromycin blocks normal electrical activity and may induce local seizures in the hippocampus, events that themselves are likely to interfere with memory. These investigators have been able, however, to inhibit cerebral protein metabolism without these effects by injection of cycloheximide and to abolish long-term memory. From study of the influence of both these agents and of actinomysin-D upon learning and memory in the goldfish, Agranoff (4) has concluded:

> Short-term memory is a palimpsest; if behavioral information is not fixed, it is lost. . . . From our present limited knowledge, it would seem that short-term or temporary memory involves electrical state, conformational changes in protein, or other readily reversible phenomena, while long-term or permanent memory formation requires metabolic changes of which protein synthesis is a part.

These findings suggest applied goals toward which research might profitably move. If the nucleic acid or protein metabolism of neurons can be changed by external stimulation, in a Lamarckian kind of fashion, and the alteration preserved so as to continue to influence performance on a long-term basis, it might be possible to transfer learning from one brain to another by chemical extraction. Additionally, it might be possible to expedite learning by pharmacological means and so accelerate the educational process. Following up the initial findings, which have been disputed, of McConnell with flatworms, Jacobson and others (6) have reported that injection of RNA from the brains of trained rats appears to advance learning in naive rats in the direction of the original training, though not in other directions; but a number of other investigators have been unable to confirm these findings. In more complex experiments, Albert (5) trained rats in which one hemisphere was transiently blocked by spreading depression. After a consolidation period of at least 8 hours, the medial cortex of the functional hemisphere, in which learning had occurred, was then removed and an extract of it injected intraperitoneally into the same animal. The rat was then retrained, with only the previously blocked hemisphere functional, and performed demonstrably better at its learning task than did controls without injection.

Some time ago Cameron and Solyom (10) observed an improvement in the impaired memory of elderly individuals upon feeding of yeast RNA. More recently, it has been reported (19) that magnesium pemoline has the capacity to stimulate the natural synthesis of RNA in the brain. Slow-learning rats, given magnesium pemoline, learned conditioned avoidance responses four or five times more rapidly than controls and retained this learning for considerably longer periods than did untreated ones (40). Again, a number of investigators have been unable to confirm these findings. In the meantime, however, Cameron has tested the memory-enhancing effects of magnesium pemoline in elderly patients and has reported significant improvements of memories for visual presentations and word-pairing, while others have found this substance ineffective in enhancing learning and memory in student-age subjects. My personal interest and concern lies, of course, with the presenile group, and as soon as more support for magnesium pemoline becomes available, I intend to try some of this medicine myself.

In another direction, it is Adey's view that the significant extracellular space, recently demonstrated around and between the neuronal and glial elements of the brain, is filled with a protein-rich glue, alterations in the macromolecules of which may modify the functional properties of the membranous surfaces of neurons to which they adhere. Adey (1, 2, 3) has been able to record marked shifts in impedance, attributable to such changes, from relevant cerebral sites during learning and the elicitation of learned behavior. The magnitude of these shifts increases at high levels of training, and the shifts disappear during extinction of the response. Moreover, their variance declines at high performance levels, increases temporarily upon cue reversal, and again declines progressively with retraining. The brain mucoids, particularly the glycoproteins and lipoproteins associated with neural membranes and synapses, have been proposed by Bogoch (8) as molecules especially qualified for coding experiential information in learning and memory.

In still another direction, John (28) has advanced a view of memory storage alternative to the connectionistic or deterministic concepts of most current theories. Starting with the premise that the rate of protein synthesis in the neuron can be regulated by the concentration of ionic substances, John postulates a model in which a set of cells involved in coherent activity for a time after an event undergo a common change in cellular chemistry. This proposed change involves no specific coding of molecular structure but, rather, establishes the possibility that the set will subsequently display coherent activity. The memory is stored as a probability of coherence.

John's current studies of the electrical activity of the brain during learning and performance

> reveal that extensive neural regions acquire an invariant component of response during conditioning. Similar wave-shapes are evoked in

many brain areas upon presentation of the conditioned stimulus. Errors in performance are accompanied by failure of certain regions to display this common pattern of activity. Such data suggest that a particular pattern of neural activity through time comes to be established in many brain regions during learning, and such patterns of activity are released when retrieval of information occurs.

If we agree, then, with Locke, that input from the senses provides the only route to learning, and look to modification of some aspect of neurochemistry as the ultimate substrate of its process, let us consider what insights can be applied to the practical aspects of expediting learning in everyday life. In efforts toward this goal, educational psychology earlier proposed a number of influential factors, which ultimately became memorialized in so-called Laws of Learning. It may be of interest to review briefly the background of their development and to begin again with Locke's *Essay*.

In his chapter "Of Retention," Locke wrote: "Attention and repetition help much in the fixing of any ideas in the memory. But those which naturally at first make the deepest and most lasting impression are accompanied with pleasure or pain." In a later edition, Locke added a chapter, "Of the Association of Ideas," that was exceedingly influential in stimulating the thinking of the eighteenth- and early nineteenth-century school of British Associationists, whose members one after another elaborated the factors promoting ideational association. The implications of their conclusions for learning and pedagogy continue to be as relevant today as at the time of their elaboration.

These conceptual developments were launched vibrating into motion by David Hartley in his *Observations on Man, His Frame, His Duty and His Expectations* (1749). Hartley wrote:

> It is easy to conceive that the medullary substance of the brain should be endowed with a proper subtle ultimate structure, for the purpose of retaining a state that is frequently impressed. One may guess also that it is better suited to this purpose during its growth than afterward. Each brain region may easily be conceived to lean sometimes to the vibrations from one object, sometimes to those from another, according to the strength, frequency and novelty of the impression. . . . When the pleasure or pain attending any sensations and ideas is great, all the associations will be cemented sooner and stronger than in common cases.

Later, Thomas Brown remarked in his *Lectures on the Philosophy of the Human Mind* (1822):

> When I reduce under a few heads those modifying circumstances which seem to me as laws on which associations depend, first is the length of time. . . . The longer we dwell on objects, the more fully

do we rely on our future resemblance of them. Second, the parts of a train are more closely and firmly associated, as the original feelings have been more lively. . . . That strong feeling of interest and curiosity, which we call attention, not only leads us to dwell longer on certain objects, but also gives more vivacity to them— and, in both these ways, tends to fix them more strongly in the mind. Third, the parts of any train are more readily suggested, in proportion as they have been more frequently renewed. Fourth, the feelings are connected more strongly in proportion as they are more recent.

Shortly thereafter, James Mill, the father of John Stuart Mill, commented in his *Analysis of the Phenomena of the Human Mind* (1829): "The causes of strength in association seem all to be resolvable into two; the vividness of the associated feelings and the frequency of their association." By vividness, Mill implied "pleasureable or painful sensations and their ideas, as compared with those which are not; and the case of the more recent, compared with the more remote." "Frequency or repetition," he added, "are, however, the most remarkable and important cause of the strength of our associations."

In the late nineteenth century, the Associationist movement passed imperceptibly into what today we call psychology and neurophysiology. Indeed, the Pavlovian paradigm of conditioned reflexes (37), actually called "associational reflexes" by his contemporary, Bechterew, may be considered a direct extension of Associationist principles. In a similar manner, one can trace earlier emphasis upon the importance of pleasure or pain in establishing association, through Thorndike's (46) studies of the Law of Effect, to type II, free, operant, or instrumental conditioning, in which Miller and Konorski (34) and Skinner (43) devoted appropriate emphasis to the role of reinforcement in promoting learning. It will be noted that a high degree of conceptual convergence marked the development of these principles by successive Associationists over more than a century. The more frequently emphasized factors were: repetition, that aspect of intensity related to attention and to pleasure and pain, and recency and contiguity as well.

It is appropriate now to discuss current advances in brain research that have identified central neural mechanisms and functions related to and serving these principles. In this connection, let us think of the brain as really being made up of several closely interrelated "brains." One is the classic brain we learned about in school, comprising the lateral surface of the cerebral cortex and the long ascending and descending pathways that course to and from it, up and down the neuraxis. This is sometimes called "Pavlov's brain" because it contains his "analyzers" (37). It is this brain that deals with the transmission and processing of specific information and with the analysis and differentiation of that information. A second brain, occasionally called "Magoun's brain," makes up the central core of the neuraxis, with rostral extensions into the medial and basal parts of the hemisphere outside of the areas of Pavlov's analyzers (31). Like its sometime namesake, this brain is highly nonspecific and seems to deal largely with generalizations. Moreover, and here the analogy ends, it has a powerful ability to raise or lower the excitability of the rest of the central nervous system.

These two "brains" are intimately associated functionally in orientation and attention to novel afferent signals, in perception of these signals, and in habituation to their monotonous and stereotyped repetition. They serve these functions by providing dual routes over which inputs from the senses reach, and are able to influence, the activity of higher neural levels. The first of these routes comprises the specific afferent pathways to the receiving areas of the cortex. As signals ascend these collective paths, they contribute polysensory excitation to parallel ascending nonspecific connections, distributed through the central core of the brain. The functions served by these specific and nonspecific cortical input channels are supplementary. The specific one conveys the informational content of the afferent message, for its signals are both modality- and locality-related. The core system, lacking these features, provides instead for behavioral and EEG arousal underlying an orientation and attention to the message.

In addition, excitation of this nonspecific system has been found to exert a powerful facilitating influence upon specific afferent signals reaching the cortex over the classical sensory paths. Sensory cortical responses double or triple in amplitude during the concomitant stimulation of the nonspecific core system of the brain (9, 16). This pronounced, but short-lived, facilitation of input signals appears identical with that which occurs naturally whenever novel afferent stimuli provoke the orienting reflex. These information-promoting aspects of the orienting reflex are obviously of capital importance for the expedition of learning, but, in one important respect, such orientation is in conflict with the law of repetition.

Unlike signal transmission in specific afferent paths, that in the nonspecific system, leading to the orienting reflex and facilitation of cortical input, attenuates rapidly and disappears upon stereotyped repetition of the evocative stimulus (42, 23, 24). With recurring presentation of the same signals, which initially provoked orientation, arousal and related changes become progressively reduced in intensity and duration, until they fail to occur at all and a stage called habituation ensues. This is not attributable to fatigue or other generalized impairment of the nonspecific system, for, during habituation, whenever signals regain a novelty, by some change in their parameters, full-blown orientation is again evoked. These findings indicate that the nonspecific system, which magnifies input signals and provokes orientation and attention to them, is built to respond only to novel signals. They imply, further, that the brain contains a converse mechanism that responds to the stereotyped repetition of stimuli by actively blocking their transmission to the nonspecific system and so preventing orientation and attention to them.

The prepotent role of novelty in evoking the orienting reflex suggests that this response is initiated not directly by a stimulus, in the customary sense of the term, but rather by a change in its intensity, pattern, or other parameters. A comparison of present with previous stimulation seems of prime significance, with an orienting reflex being evoked by each point of disagreement. The concept of a cortical neuronal model has been proposed by Sokolov (44) to account for this induction of the orienting reflex by stimuli whose characteristic feature is their novelty. This model preserves information about earlier stimuli, with which aspects of novel stimulation may be compared. The orienting reflex is evoked whenever the parameters of the novel stimulus do not coincide with those of the model. This discordance, it is suggested, generates cortical discharge to the nonspecific core brain, triggering the orienting reflex. In contrasting situations, when recurring stimuli are accordant with the established cortical model, feedback inhibition from the cortex blocks afferent input to the core system and promotes habituation.

These concepts suggest a major conflict between a primary law of learning and the way the brain actually works. They plainly imply that repetition is the first law, not of learning, but of habituation, whose influence upon learning is a negative rather than a positive one. Obviously, the promotion of novelty rather than of repetition should become a primary law of learning. Whenever afferent signals are repeatedly presented in a learning situation, each should be made adequately distinctive, in some respect, from that preceding it so as to avoid habituation and, by provoking a recurring series of orienting reflexes, utilize their powerful amplification of cortical input signals as a resource for achieving learning. Should this prove impossible, recourse may be had, next, to a second law of learning—reinforcement—which has a built-in mechanism for preventing habituation.

Recent research has disclosed a third brain, different from the two just considered but closely interrelated with them. This third, or limbic, component may appropriately be called "Olds' brain," for his major contributions to our knowledge of its function. Olds and others (36, 15) have identified reciprocal regions in the cephalic brain stem and the bordering area of its attachment to the hemisphere, the direct experimental stimulation of which reproduces all the features of primary reward or punishment. When electrodes are placed in the positively reinforcing part of this limbic "brain" and the animal is trained to press a lever to stimulate the site of implantation, it repeatedly excites its own central nervous system, to the exclusion of all other activities, for long periods of time. Once an animal has stimulated the aversive part of this region, however, it will never do so again. Moreover, it will repeatedly press a lever to avoid recurring stimulation, by the experimenter, of this negatively reinforcing mechanism.

These limbic regions for positive and negative reinforcement are closely associated functionally with adjacent neural mechanisms serving the life- and race-preserving goals of innate behavior, whose impelling nature is probably to be accounted for by the powerful degree to which the consummation of such behavior is reinforced. To whatever degree these reinforcement systems can be involved in a learning situation, their intrinsic potency and related immunity to habituation can provide a powerful resource in the acquisition and maintenance of learned behavior.

For a half-century before the physiological basis of reinforcement was understood, it had been utilized effectively in the studies of conditional learning by Pavlov (37), in avoidance conditioning by Bechterew, and in the subsequent elaboration of operant conditioning by Konorski (34) and Skinner (43). The feature essential for the initiation and acquisition of these types of learned behavior was reinforcement: the positive reinforcement of a food reward in the case of approach learning, or the negative reinforcement of a noxious shock to the foot in the case of avoidance learning. Moreover, such reinforcement proved essential for the maintenance of learning, once acquired. When learned behavior had been established, subsequent withdrawal of reinforcement led to a kind of negative learning—or learning not to respond—called extinction, which tended to pass into the relaxation, drowsiness, and sleep of Pavlovian internal inhibition.

The powerful expedition of learning, either by positive or negative reinforcement, may depend in considerable part upon the marked facilitation and generalization of afferent signals, which such reward or punishment promotes. John and Killam (29) have demonstrated a pronounced increase in the amplitude of afferent signals, and a generalization of their distribution in the brain, when either positive or negative reinforcement is introduced into a learning situation. In this respect, reinforcement resembles the orienting reflex, but the facilitation of input by reinforcement is far more persistent and, unlike that of the orienting reflex, does not attenuate or habituate upon repetition, short of that leading to consummation and ensuing satiety.

Indeed, when an afferent signal, initially facilitated by the orienting reflex, is repeated monotonously until habituation occurs, the introduction of reinforcement immediately overcomes habituation and augments the signal far beyond its original amplitude and central distribution. These striking capabilities for the amplification and generalization of afferent signals within the brain, resisting and overcoming habituation, are testimony to the great influence reinforcement can exert in the promotion of learning. Ideally, learning should be initiated by orientation and then followed up to criterion and maintained by reinforcement, in the application of the renovated laws proposed.

In functional terms, then, the lateral sensory-motor cortex making up "Pavlov's brain" supplies information about the external world. Arousal, orientation, and attention to these incoming signals are served by the nonspecific core "brain." Motivational and reinforcement factors are referable to activity in the limbic "brain" of Olds.

Another major field of current study is exploration of the genesis of learning. The classical efforts of Pavlov to determine the mechanism of learning were limited by the technical developments of his time. His concepts of the central neural events involved had necessarily to be derived largely from observations of behavioral performance. By contrast, contemporary technical advances provide means of investigating the learning process more directly by recording changes in electrical activity within regions of the brain where the events are actually proceeding. In much the same way that isotope-tagged chemicals are now introduced into and traced through metabolic processes in biochemical research, recent studies of learning have employed repetitive flashes of light as tracer stimuli and monitored sequential changes in frequency-tagged responses during avoidance learning or conditioning to a paired tone (47, 29). In these studies, the first photically labeled responses to be elicited by the tone alone—that is, the first associated or "learned" responses—were recorded from the nonspecific core of the brain stem. Only later did tagged responses appear in the cortex, initially with a widespread distribution that gradually became restricted to the projection area of the uncondi-tioned signal.

Contrary to Pavlov's view that the cerebral cortex is the site of formation of novel temporary connections during learning, these find-ings imply that the nonspecific or polysensory nature of the subcorti-cal brain serves in establishing the first transmodal links underlying stimulus equivalence, which secondarily become transferred to the cortex. Once the cortex is involved, however, the initially widespread and subsequently focal distribution of tagged responses confirm the succession of initial generalization and later differentiation identified by Pavlov in the establishment of all conditioned reflexes. Considered broadly, the sequence of events suggests a subcortical focus of and role in the initiation of conditioned learning, as well as in its succeed-ing generalized transference to the cortex. The cortex is doubtless in-volved preeminently, however, in subsequent differentiation, probably by a gradual extinction, in the pattern of Sokolov's model of feedback inhibition (44), of all nonreinforced components. Ultimately, labeled responses persist only in the cortical projection area of the uncondi-tioned signal—i.e., in the analyzer with which reinforcement, immune to habituation, has become associated (29).

Once learning has been acquired, it is stored in and can be re-trieved, as we say, from "memory." The processing of information into storage and its subsequent readout implicate a number of parts of the brain, but the temporal lobe of the cerebral hemisphere is espe-cially involved. For his many contributions to its functions (38, 39), this region can be designated "Penfield's brain."

It has long been known that temporal-lobe seizures in man are associated with auras of familiarity or recollection, while during the seizure the processing of experience into memory is blocked, with subsequent retrograde amnesia or loss of recall. In neurosurgical studies, Penfield has found it possible, by direct stimulation of the exposed temporal lobe at operation, to induce the experience of ac-tual earlier events that are reported by the patient as vividly as though they were happening again. With deeper stimulation, typical temporal-lobe seizures were provoked, with the conspicuous disturbances of memory just described.

In other patients, with bilateral injury to or surgical ablation of the temporal lobes, there is a paradoxically severe impairment of recent memory, along with preservation of that for earlier periods. Although "Penfield's brain" must serve importantly in the processing of current information into storage, as well as in initial consolidation and recall of this information, it obviously cannot provide the storehouse for all memories once induced. As mentioned earlier, the storage and retrieval of such long-term memories doubtless involve widespread participation of the higher levels of the brain.

In electrophysiological studies, Adey (1, 2, 3) has found that all categories of novel experiential input induce a characteristic wavelike theta rhythm in the temporal region, generated and best recorded from a deep-lying component called the hippocampus. With routine stimulation, the amplitude and frequency of this rhythm is irregular, and its distribution is widespread. During learning, when discriminative performance has been acquired, the rhythm becomes conspicuously regular and more focal. This theta rhythm can be proposed to serve the role of a phase comparator or carrier wave, which, in combination with specific input signals, leads to the involvement of additional regions of the cerebral hemisphere. Whenever the affected neuronal populations of these more disseminated regions are subsequently reexcited, they are proposed to discharge in a manner like that induced by the original experience and by so doing subserve subjective recall.

The significant interval of time required for the consolidation of this "memory trace" is supportive of its biochemical nature, as are also the changes of impedence in the hippocampus that Adey has recorded during learning. The process appears to be a migratory one, involving first the temporal cortex adjacent to the hippocampus and later more distant parts. During the initial stages of this fixation period, measurable in minutes, alterations that are ongoing are exceedingly susceptible to interference with neuronal metabolism, and the process, once initiated, can be blocked by antibiotics, anesthesia, or electroshock (33).

In addition, at this stage consolidation can be effectively blocked physiologically by intervening orientation to distracting stimuli. During the orienting reflex, the focus of attention is promoted both by the amplification of signals at its center and, additionally, by contrast-enhancement through feedback inhibition of all competing central neural activity related to inputs from the periphery (23). This latter was called "external inhibition" by Pavlov, who identified its blocking effect upon the retrieval of recently learned behavior. The block appears to work against the fixation of novel input as well.

This and other data suggest a potentially inhibitory relationship between the nonspecific core system, serving orientation and attention to signals so long as they are novel, and the temporal lobe system, which continues to process these signals into storage long after they

H. W. Magoun

have ended and which serves also in their subsequent recall. In programming a learning situation, consideration should be given to this potentially antagonistic relation between Magoun's and Penfield's "brains" by avoiding the possibility of orientation to irrelevant and distracting stimuli during consolidation, as well as by providing adequate time for the fixation of each successive stage of learning before directing orientation to the next.

Further, and in the same direction, excessively vigilant attention may impede the free-flowing retrieval of previously stored material leading to innovative associations (21). The most significantly productive of creative ideas, relating disparate information and providing a new insight or synthesis, have often been reported to be generated, not in the intensity of strained, focused concentration upon the subject or problem, but rather during a contrasting state of mind, as when performing a stereotyped activity, or gazing hypnotically into a glowing fireplace, or even during sleep itself, in dreams. A large number of such ideational conjunctions have occurred in what is called a preconscious state, differing from an unconscious one in being potentially available to consciousness and communication. Such testimony suggests that the creative process can often be advanced by the unfocusing of orientation and attention, permitting the welling-up and coalescence into new configurations of readouts from the multiple data-storage systems of the brain. Such relaxation of vigilant attention and its lateral inhibition is seldom cultivated in pedagogical situations, but it appears to be of great importance for the stage of synthesis and creative ideation in learning.

The types of experimental learning discussed above have been arranged by Hernàndez-Péon (22) in a hierarchy of neurophysiological complexity, in which habituation is the simplest, classical conditioning is next, and instrumental conditioning is the most complex of the basic learning paradigms. In keeping with this view, Thompson (45) has independently identified these same learning paradigms as representative of three successive stages of increasing capability for learning during individual maturation.

Thompson points out that age, by itself, is an empty variable in maturation and, alternatively, constructs a model around the differentiation of input and output systems. He proposes three axioms: (1) differentiation increases with age; (2) it increases both on the input and on the output sides, these being operationally separable; and (3) it increases at a faster rate on the input than on the output side. "Given distinctive rates of increment on input and output sides," he states, "it is immediately obvious that three qualitatively different age-zones may be defined: (1) lack of differentiation both on input and output sides; (2) differentiation on the input side and lack of it on the output side; and (3) differentiation on both input and output sides."

The advances in brain research discussed above may be related to these stages of behavioral differentiation during development, as follows: At stage one, the differentiation both of stimulus and of response is exceedingly limited. All stimuli are relatively nonspecific, with their only variable that of intensity. Responsiveness is comparably generalized, and the chief capability for learned modification of behavior is along the spectrum between habituation, on the one hand, and affective arousal, on the other, as the stimulus intensity is low or high. At this stage, only Magoun's and Olds' "brains" are available to the individual, both on the input and the output sides of the central nervous system.

At stage two, there is afferent, but no motor, differentiation. The individual has become able to distinguish cues, but responsiveness continues to remain generalized. Classical conditioning is possible, enabling orientation and affective responsiveness to become attached to conditioned, as well as to unconditioned, signals. At this stage, Pavlov's and Penfield's "brains" have been added to the central nervous system of stage one, but only on the input side.

At stage three, motor, as well as afferent, differentiation has been acquired. The individual is able to distinguish between responses as well as stimuli; he can do the appropriate thing in response to a particular signal and relate appropriate behavior to particular cues. Feedback from differentiated responses can now guide future behavior, and present performance can be related effectively to past experience. In the human species, coping behavior and cognitive learning become possible. At this stage, Pavlov's and Penfield's "brains" have been added to the central nervous system of stage one on the output, as well as on the input, side.

"Let us then suppose," again with Locke, "the mind to be, as we say, white paper, void of all characters, without any ideas, how comes it to be furnished? When comes it by that vast store, which the busy and boundless fancy of man has painted on it with an almost endless variety?" The efforts of many investigators have provided some insight into these routes to and processes of the mind, which Locke was seeking. Starting with the organs of sense, coded information about the environment is carried into the central nervous system, where the fate and impact of its message involves a number of component "brains."

First are the specific sensori-motor areas of the lateral cerebral cortex, concerned with analysis and differentiation of incoming messages, together with the initiation of specific responses to them.

Second are the nonspecific systems in the core of the brain, serving orientation and attention to incoming messages, as well as promoting their amplification and dissemination so long as they are novel, and contributing to turning them down or off if they are not.

Third are the limbic systems for positive and negative reinforcement, which also amplify and generalize incoming messages, whether or not they are novel, for limbic involvement can prevent or overcome habituation to monotonously repeated messages.

Fourth are temporal-lobe systems, which promote transmission of incoming messages into storage and are involved, as well, in their subsequent recall and, therefore, in their association with other earlier messages.

These findings push open Locke's door, at least a little way. They suggest that benefits from manipulation of a number of brain mechanisms and processes that have now been identified can provide significant ways of promoting learning and advancing educational goals —whether in or out of school.

REFERENCES

1. Adey, W. R. "Brain mechanisms and the learning process." *Fed. Proc.,* 20 (1961) 617–27.
2. Adey, W. R. "Hippocampal mechanisms in processes of memory: thoughts on a model of cerebral organization in learning," in Brazier, M. A. B. (ed.), *Brain function.* Vol. II, *RNA and brain function: Memory and learning.* Berkeley, Calif.: Univ. of California Press, 1964, pp. 233–76.
3. Adey, W. R. "Intrinsic organization of cerebral tissue in alerting, orienting, and discriminative responses," in Quarton, G. C., Melnechuk, T., and Schmitt, F. O. (eds.) *The neurosciences.* New York: Rockefeller Univ. Press, 1967, pp. 615–33.
4. Agranoff, B. W. "Agents that block memory," in Quarton, G. C., Melnechuk, T., and Schmitt, F. O. (eds.), *The neurosciences.* New York: Rockefeller Univ. Press, 1967, pp. 756–64.
5. Albert, D. J. "Memory in mammals: evidence for a system involving nuclear RNA." *Neuropsychologia,* 4 (1966) 79–92.
6. Babich, F. R., Jacobson, A. L., Bubash, S., and Jacobson, A. "Transfer of a response to naive rats by injection of ribonucleic acid extracted from trained rats." *Science,* 149 (1965) 656–57.
7. Bennett, E. L., Diamond, M. C., Krech, D., and Rosenzweig, M. R. "Chemical and anatomical plasticity of the brain." *Science,* 146 (1964) 610–19.

8. Bogoch, S. *The biochemistry of memory.* New York: Oxford Univ. Press, 1968.

9. Bremer, F., and Stoupel, N. "Facilitation et inhibition des potentials évoqués corticaux dans l'éveil cérébral." *Arch. internat. Physiol.,* 67 (1959) 240–75.

10. Cameron, D. E., and Solyom, L. "Effects of ribonucleic acid on memory." *Geriatrics,* 16 (1961) 74–81.

11. Cohen, H. D., and Barondes, S. H. "Puromycin effect on memory may be due to occult seizures." *Science,* 157 (1967) 333–34.

12. Cohen, H. D., Ervin, F. and Barondes, S. H. "Puromycin and cycloheximide: different effects on hippocampal electrical activity." *Science,* 154 (1966) 1557–58.

13. Cranston, M. *John Locke, a biography.* London: Longmans, Green, 1957.

14. Cravioto, J. *Nutrition deprivation and psychobiological development in children* (Res. 4/8). Washington, D.C.: Pan American Health Organization, 1965.

15. Delgado, J. M. R., Roberts, W. W., and Miller, N. E. "Learning motivated by electrical stimulation of the brain." *Am. J. Physiol.,* 179 (1954) 587–93.

16. Dumont, S., and Dell, P. "Facilitation réticulaire des méchanismes visuels corticaux." *EEG clin. Neurophysiol.,* 12 (1960) 769–96.

17. Flexner, L. B., Flexner, J. B., and Roberts, R. B. "Memory in mice analyzed with antibiotics." *Science,* 155 (1967) 1377–83.

18. Gerard, R. W. "Summary and general discussion," in Fields, W. S., and Abbott, W. (eds.), *Information storage and neural control.* Springfield, Ill.: Thomas, 1963, pp. 353–76.

19. Glasky, A. J., and Simon, L. N. "Magnesium pemoline: enhancement of brain RNA polymerases." *Science,* 151 (1966) 702–03.

20. Glass, B. "The establishment of modern genetical theory as an example of the interaction of different models, techniques and inferences," in Crombie, A. C. (ed.), *Scientific changes.* London: Heinemann, 1963, pp. 521–41.

21. Graubard, S. R. (ed.). "Creativity and learning." *Daedalus,* 94, (1965).

22. Hernàndez-Péon, R. *Current concepts of the neurophysiology of learning* (Res. 4/8). Washington, D.C.: Pan American Health Organization, 1965.

23. Hernàndez-Péon, R. "Reticular mechanisms of sensory control," in Rosenblith, W. (ed.), *Sensory communication.* New York: Wiley, 1961, pp. 497–520.

24. Hernàndez-Péon, R., and Brust-Carmona, H. "Functional role of subcortical structures in habituation and conditioning," in Delafresnaye, J. F. (ed.), *Brain mechanisms and learning.* Oxford: Blackwell, 1961.

25. Hydén, H. "Biochemical changes accompanying learning," in Quarton, G. C., Melnechuk, T., and Schmitt, F. O. (eds.), *The neurosciences.* New York: Rockefeller Univ. Press, 1967, pp. 765–71.

26. Hydén, H. "Biochemical changes in glial and nerve cells at varying activity," in Brucke, F. (ed.), *Biochemistry of the central nervous*

system. *Proceedings of the 4th internat. meeting biochem.* New York: Pergamon, 1959.

27. Hydén, H. "RNA—a functional characteristic of the neuron and its glia," in Brazier, M. A. B. (ed.), *Brain function.* Vol. II, *RNA and brain function: Memory and learning.* Berkeley, Calif.: Univ. of California Press, 1964, pp. 29–68.

28. John, E. R. *Mechanisms of memory.* New York: Academic Press, 1967.

29. John, E. R., and Killam, K. F. "Electrophysiological correlates of avoidance conditioning in the cat." *J. pharm. exper. Therap.,* 125 (1959) 252–74.

30. Locke, J. *An essay concerning human understanding.* Cleveland: Meridian, 1964.

31. Magoun, H. W. *The waking brain,* 2nd ed. Springfield, Ill.: Thomas, 1964.

32. Mayo, L. W. (chm.). *A proposed program for national action to combat mental retardation.* Washington, D.C.: U.S. Government Printing Office, 1962.

33. McGaugh, J. L. "Time-dependent processes in memory storage." *Science,* 153 (1966) 1351–58.

34. Miller, S., and Konorski, J. "Sur une forme particuliere des réflexes conditionnels." *Compt. Rend. Soc. Biol.,* 99 (1938) 1155–57.

35. Morrell, F. "Lasting changes in synaptic organization produced by continuous neuronal bombardment," in Delafresnaye, J. F. (ed.), *Brain mechanisms and learning.* Oxford: Blackwell, 1961, pp. 375–92.

36. Olds, J., and Milner, P. "Positive reinforcement produced by electrical stimulation of septal area and other regions of rat brain." *J. comp. physiol. Psychol.,* 47 (1954) 419–27.

37. Pavlov, I. P. *Conditioned reflexes. An investigation of the physiological activity of the cerebral cortex* (1927), Anrep, G. V. (trans. and ed.). New York: Dover, 1960.

38. Penfield, W. "The role of the temporal cortex in recall of past experience and interpretation of the present," in Wolstenholme, G. E. W., and O'Connor, C. M. (eds.), *Neurological basis of behavior.* London: Churchill, 1958, pp. 149–74.

39. Penfield, W., and Jasper, H. H. *Epilepsy and the functional anatomy of the human brain.* Boston: Little, Brown, 1954.

40. Plotnikoff, N. "Magnesium pemoline: enhancement of learning and memory of a conditioned avoidance response." *Science,* 151 (1966) 703–04.

41. Schmitt, F. O. "Molecular neurobiology in the context of the neurosciences," in Quarton, G. C., Melnechuk, T., and Schmitt, F. O., (eds.), *The neurosciences.* New York: Rockefeller Univ. Press, 1967, pp. 209–19.

42. Sharpless, S., and Jasper, H. "Habituation of the arousal reaction." *Brain,* 79 (1956) 655–80.

43. Skinner, B. F. *The behavior of organisms.* New York: Appleton-Century-Crofts, 1938.

44. Sokolov, E. N. "Neuronal models and the orienting reflex," in Brazier,

Advances in Brain Research with Implications for Learning   **189**

M. A. B. (ed.), *The central nervous system and behavior*. New York: Josiah Macy, Jr. Foundation, 1960, pp. 187–239.

45. Thompson, W. R. *Development and the genetic expressivity of behavior*. Presented at the New England Psychological Conference, 1964.

46. Thorndike, E. L. "Animal intelligence. An experimental study of the associative process in animals." *Psychol. Monogr.* 2 (1898) 1–109.

47. Yoshii, N., Pruvot, P., and Gastaut, H. "Electroencephalographic activity of the mesencephalic reticular formation during conditioning in the cat." *EEG clin. Neurophysiol.,* 9 (1957) 595–608.

H. W. Magoun

The Four R's of Remembering

by Karl H. Pribram

Introduction

The four R's of remembering, which I want to discuss, are representation, reconstruction, registration, and rearrangement. All of these, as well as "remembering" itself, begin with "re-"—a prefix that denotes repetition. To say that the educational process involves repetition may seem self-evident, but a fresh look at the variety of forms that repetition can take is in order. In fact, the study of the structure of repetition reveals an unsuspected richness and importance that has, for the most part, been ignored in scientific investigations.

The technical term for repetition is "redundancy." The concept is derived from information-measurement theory, which for the past two decades has contributed many of the major advances in thinking about problems in the behavioral sciences. Most of these have come from the precision given the term "information" by communications engineers and their ability to construct computers—devices that process information. "Information" conceived in this fashion is akin to what in ordinary language we mean by "novelty"—with the provision that novelty almost always refers to something new about something familiar (as expressed, for example, by the fact that the words "invent" and "inventory" stem from the same root). The recent concern in the behavioral sciences has been with information measurement, information processing, and even information storage. And so, in teaching and learning, the emphasis has been on ways of imparting the novel, the facts, the latest facts, to our students. Because the computer can handle masses of such facts, the major question persistently posed of educators in this post-Sputnik space age has been: how can we make our students into better "computers"—i.e., better information-processing organisms?

This approach has, to my mind, missed half the problem. Wolfgang Köhler once wrote a book entitled *The Place of Value in a World of Fact* (27). In this spirit, perhaps I should have entitled this paper "Redundancy in a World of Information" or, better yet, "Memory in a World of News." The point is that values, redundancy, memory— the enduring aspects of the world we live in—have been given short shrift of late in our scientific thinking. Every psychologist who has explored the problem has found that the context, the set of events in which information occurs, is as important a determinant of the outcome of his experiment as the information-carrying signal itself. And yet it is usually this context that remains unspecified, unstudied, and often hopelessly shrugged off as being impossible to study.

Why? Most likely because the enduring is so often carried in the organizational system of an order higher than the one the scientist is studying. Culture is enduring—culture carries values and is endowed with memory. Behavioral scientists of the hard-headed variety rarely want to take such a large system into account, for this would only point up the limitations of their data. Organisms also endure and so bring values and memories to each situation, whether it be a classroom or a conditioning experiment. The behavioral scientist already has enough to think about—this complex biological organism is altogether too much. Yet, as so clearly sensed by those who have invited us here, how can we be successful educators when we know not the capacities of those whom we are trying to lead, or, for that matter, out of where we are leading them?

The work of my laboratories has, over the past two decades, been devoted to unraveling some of the mysterious organizations educators try to educate. These studies of brain and behavior indicate that there are at least two major classes or modes of organization into which repetitiously experienced events are coded. Each of these encoding processes appears to be intricately interwoven with another that decodes and makes usable the memory mechanism involved. I will adduce some of the evidence for the existence of each of these four processes (representation, reconstruction, registration, rearrangement) and suggest a model for each of the two memory mechanisms (spatial and temporal) by way of analogy with an operational physical artifact whose characteristics have been independently studied.

Representation: A Spatial Encoding Process*

Let me begin by detailing an apparent paradox concerning habit and habituation. If we are repeatedly in the same situation, in a relatively invariant environment, two things happen. One is that if we have consistently to perform a similar task in that environment, the task becomes fairly automatic—i.e., we become more efficient. We say the organism (in this case, ourself) has learned to perform the task; he has formed *habits* regarding it. But at the same time the subject habituates, by which we mean that he no longer produces an orienting reaction; he no longer notices the events that endure, are constant, in his environment. His verbal reports of introspection, his failure to move his head and eyes in the direction of the stimulus—electrophysiological measures such as galvanic skin response, plethysmography, and EEG—all attest to the disappearance of orienting with repetition of unvarying input in an unvarying situation.

Habituation, however, is *not* an indication of some loss of sensitivity on the part of the nervous system. Sokolov (56), for example, has demonstrated that if he decreases the intensity of a tone that has been given repeatedly to a subject, orienting or alerting will recur. Further, if he again habituates the subject and then shortens the duration of the tone, orienting again will take place, but this time to the unexpected silence. These findings led Sokolov to propose that a neural model of the environment is produced in the nervous system. This model then constitutes an expectancy, a type of memory mechanism against which inputs are constantly matched. The nervous system is thus continually tuned *by* inputs to process further inputs.

It is hardly necessary to state that the habitual performance of the organism is also due to neural activity. The point to be kept in mind is this: in the case of expectancy, there is a diminution of neural activity with repetition, while in the case of performance, enhancement seems to occur. So the question becomes: what is the difference between these two kinds of neural activity that appear at first sight to be

---

* The biological coding process is, of course, a two-way street, and what one chooses to call encoding or decoding is largely arbitrary and depends on where one enters the process. This is especially the case in the recognition mechanism. I have here chosen to call "encoding" the process that *distributes* information in the brain and to call "decoding" the process that allows *use* to be made by the organism of the information so distributed. I could as easily have chosen the more common view that encoding involves storage and decoding the readout from storage. In that case the observations reported would be arranged somewhat differently but the resulting "image" would, of course, be essentially the same.

inversely related to each other? Neurophysiology provides us with some sound clues.

Graded potential changes at synapto-dendritic junctions in nerve tissue, on the one hand, and nerve impulses, on the other, are available as two kinds of processes that could function reciprocally. The channeling of nerve impulses obviously is related to performance. Junctional neural events are therefore left as candidates to account for the orienting reaction of the organism and its habituation.

A synapse does not work by itself. Nerve impulses arrive at many synapto-dendritic junctions simultaneously. In essence, such arrivals occur in patterns that generate stationary wavefronts (5), which, once established, can interact and produce patterns similar to moiré (41) or interference effects. These effects act as immediate analogue cross-correlation devices to produce new figures from which departure patterns of nerve impulses can be initiated. The orienting reaction could well be a function of such interference effects.

Subjectively, the orienting reaction is correlated with awareness, habituation with unawareness. What evidence do we have to suggest that the graded electrical activities of the central nervous system are involved in awareness? Kamiya (24) at the University of California Medical School in San Francisco has shown, using instrumental-conditioning techniques, that people can be aware of whether their brains are producing alpha rhythms or not. Specifically, the hypothesis reads that we are indeed able subjectively to tell one pattern of junctional potential changes from another. My suggestion is, therefore, an old-fashioned one: that we experience some of the events going on in the brain, but not others. The point is an important one; if accepted, it carries with it a corollary—viz., that nerve impulse activity and thus behavior (including verbal behavior) per se are not directly and immediately available to awareness. More experiments of the kind Kamiya has performed are urgently needed.

But in order for recognition to be effected, some more permanent alteration of substrate must act to influence the configuration of arrival patterns. If one looks at EEG records coming from an EEG machine for a number of hours during the day, and then goes home to sleep, what happens? The day's records go by in review; but note—they go by *in reverse!* This is known as the "waterfall effect."

Obviously, some neural change has taken place to allow the record to be re-viewed, but also obvious is the fact that the re-viewing takes place from a vantage point different from that of the original viewing. The record must therefore have "stereo"-like properties that provide parallax and allow it to be examined now from this, now from that, standpoint. This re-viewing from various vantage points must not lose its identity relative to the entire record: a familiar face gains, rather than loses, its familiarity and recognizable identity by being viewed from different angles.

Recently, important new advances have been made in the study of interference effects. Moiré patterns, as mentioned above, have been explored, and unexpected varieties of figures have been produced by the interaction of relatively simple grids. Even more startling in their similarity to perceptual processes are the results of a new photographic process, which produces images by way of a record called a hologram. The hologram does not visually resemble the original object—rather, it is an encoded record of the wave patterns emitted by or reflected from an object.

This process is radically different from conventional photography that records only the intensity of the image focused on the photographic plate and records detail that produces equal intensity at the film plane as equal shades of gray. Hologram photography was first used by professor Denis Gabor of Imperial College, London, in 1948, to record and then reproduce the actual wavefronts of light that issue from an illuminated object.

Professor Gabor studied the propagation of light from the viewpoint of information theory, deducing from Huygen's wave theory of light that all the information in an image must exist in every plane between the object and the photographic plate. Thus, he reasoned that it might be possible to extract the information at any arbitrary plane and then recreate an image without the necessiy of using a lens.

The wave nature of light had been demonstrated more than a century earlier by Thomas Young, who showed that light waves have amplitude and phase characteristics, and that this description obeys simple laws of superposition that can be used to describe the propagation of light mathematically. From this early work, Gabor knew that both the amplitude and phase of light must be recorded. Light amplitude is only measured indirectly by the eye, film, or photodector, the energy sensitive devices that record the square of the amplitude of the incident light. Phase information is not recorded in conventional photography.

Gabor's brilliant invention was to superimpose on the arbitrary recording plane a reference beam of light derived from the same source so the phases of light would reveal themselves by changes in intensity. The interference pattern produced by the light scattered by the object and the reference wave serves to store both the amplitude and the phase of the scattered light. In this way, Gabor produced on film a record of information in an arbitrary plane; such a record he called a hologram because it contained the "whole" information. Furthermore, when the hologram was reilluminated by the same or a similar reference beam, the light emerging from the hologram emulsion formed an image of the object. Gabor realized that in this process, the wavefronts of light at original exposure time were being reconstructed.

A quasi-monochromatic light source that can be used for supplying the object illumination and coherent reference beam is required for recording and reconstructing holograms. The development of the laser in 1960 provided a convenient source of the high-energy light required and hence added an enormous stimulus to holographic research. Thus today, research in holography is being carried out by more than 100 laboratories. This research has provided a wide variety of basic techniques useful for making records with extremely high information content. (62)

These records can be thought of as a "freezing" of the information contained in the amplitude and phase relationships of wave patterns; the patterns remain frozen until such time as one chooses to reactivate the process, whereupon the waves are "read out" of the recording medium. As noted above, holograms are produced by virtue of interference effects obtained by splitting a beam of coherent light, using the major portion as a reference beam and allowing the minor portion to be reflected from the object to be photographed. A photographic recording of these effects will yield a gating-like, gridlike structure

> that can be regarded as a two-dimensional analogue of the sinusoidal wave produced by an electric oscillator. The important point of this analogy is that just as an electric wave can be modulated to serve as a carrier of information . . . so can the inferometrically produced wave pattern be modulated to serve as a carrier of information about the light waves that produced it. (30)

There are many startling attributes of holograms. Among these, the following are of greatest interest to us in our search for the mechanism by which experience can be experienced.

First, the image seen by looking through the hologram is complete, three-dimensional.

> As the observer changes his viewing position the perspective of the picture changes, just as if the observer were viewing the original scene. Parallax effects are evident between near and far objects in the scene: if an object in the foreground lies in front of something else, the observer can move his head and look around the obstructing object, thereby seeing the previously hidden object. . . . In short, the reconstruction has all the visual properties of the original scene and we know of no visual test one can make to distinguish the two. (30)

Second, holograms have the property that

> several images can be superimposed on a single plate on successive exposures, and each image can be recovered without being affected

by other images. This is done by using a different spatial-frequency carrier for each picture. . . . The gating carriers can be of different frequencies . . . and there is still another degree of freedom, that of angle. (30)

Third, today holograms can be constructed and reconstructed (10) without the use of lasers. Further, when two or more objects are present in making the hologram, any one of them can serve as a source to reconstruct the others, which appear as "ghosts"—a simple mechanism for producing associative memory.

Finally,

each part of the hologram, no matter how small, can reproduce the entire image, thus the hologram can be broken into small fragments each of which can be used to construct a complete image. As the pieces become smaller, resolution is lost. (30)

However, as successively larger parts of the hologram are used for reconstruction, the depth of field of image decreases, i.e., focus becomes narrowed, so that an optimum size for a particular use can be ascertained. These curious properties derive from the fact that

each point on the hologram receives light from all parts of the subject and therefore contains, in an encoded form, the entire image. (30)

These properties of the hologram are just those demanded by the facts of brain physiology as they pertain to perception. One of the most puzzling experimental findings, one that led Lashley initially to propose a neurological-interference theory, is that removal of as much as 80 percent of the sensory input mechanism fails to impair pattern perception (29). This is especially odd since the anatomical arrangement within these systems is such that a topological point-to-point correspondence exists between peripheral sensory receptors and the cortex. On the basis of the evidence of relatively intact perception in the face of removal of as much as 80 to 90 percent of their volume (38), these anatomical connections cannot conceivably be assumed in the intact individual to produce ordinary isomorphic or ikonic images. On the other hand, if these essentially parallel receptor-cortical connections are conceived as constituting a neural reference beam for the construction of a holographic representation, the dilemma is resolved. For holograms have the most unusual property, as already noted, that any small part can be used for reconstruction of the entire image. Any part of the hologram contains all the information necessary to reconstruct the whole.

I have already made the suggestion that arrival patterns in the brain constitute wavefronts that, by virtue of interference effects, can serve as instantaneous analogue cross-correlators to produce a variety of moiré-type figures. Now, by means of some recording process, a temporary storage mechanism derived from such arrival patterns and interference effects must be envisioned. Could the conformation of protein and even longer range anisotropic orderings of protein structure be altered in one direction during exposure and then later reversed, such that, as it were, "the tape plays backward"? And would this "drift" in protein memory produce a reverse drift in the synaptically produced patterns?

What is the relevance to education of a spatially encoded neural representation? Could it be that the academic community has centered too much on the teaching of skills and habits to the neglect of image? Is there something to be gained from the techniques developed by Madison Avenue? If indeed image formation is an important form of memory mechanism, should we not listen to these experts, the image makers?

Two processes dear to image makers are identification and imitation. In our recent endeavors to program learning, are we not neglecting these powerful processes for the purpose of educating? Learning through reinforcement is an important mode, and I will discuss it shortly; but learning through image-making is equally potent. A simple experiment performed in my laboratory by Dr. Patrick Bateson (4) illustrates this point. Bateson trained monkeys to discriminate between two letters of the alphabet by the usual reinforcement techniques. He then placed a third letter so as to be always in view in the home cage of the monkeys. After some months of such exposure and with the appropriate control procedures, the "home-exposed" letter and one of the previously "reinforced" letters were each paired with a new one in a standard discrimination. To our surprise, the "home-exposed" letter proved to be discriminated more rapidly. Perhaps we should not have been so surprised—my four-year-old daughter can point to and "read" the names of cereals, soaps, and other goods displayed in the supermarket. When asked how, she replies, "I learned it at home—on television." My plea is, therefore, that we not lose sight of the picturesque, for the brain is built to work with pictures.

In summary, I suggest that the perceptual mechanism is constituted in such a way that neural holograms are produced and that images can be reconstructed from the interactions of the holographic patterns. Let me now turn to this reconstruction process.

Karl H. Pribram

Reconstruction

The hologram is an excellent method for encoding neural events initiated by input or as the representation of patterns of neural interaction to be read out. But as a mechanism for permanent storage, the hologram accomplishes too much too soon—a plethora of memories would plague our every moment were there not some more parsimonious way to store and identify those events useful to the organism. A mechanism must exist that can extract, from the "holographic" representation, information relevant to the continuing needs and interests of the organism. This information must be stored in such a way that when subsequent input is appropriate an image can be reconstructed from the permanent remnant. How is this accomplished?

I have so far omitted from discussion the formation of a screen onto and through which inputs are projected to produce an image. The necessity for invoking such a "screen" concept comes from many sources—the simplest observation is the fact that intrinsic movement of the eyes results in a stable perception, while extrinsic movement, as by digital pressure on the eyeballs, produces a moving perception. Only by moving the screen to keep up with the projected input can the perception become stable.

To indicate some of the complexity of makeup of this screen, let me present a summary of the results of an experiment recently accomplished in my laboratory (52). Monkeys were trained to pull a lever by which a display of one of two patterns (circle, vertical stripes) was initiated. The display lasted for one millisecond and was centered on a translucent panel split down the middle. The monkeys could press either the right or the left half of the panel to close a microswitch that would initiate the delivery of a banana pellet if the correct panel had been pressed. The panel on the right was correct when the circle had been displayed; the one on the left was correct when the vertical stripes appeared.

Records were made of the electrical activity occurring in the monkey's brain (see Figure 1) while he was solving this problem. From the wave form of these records we could distinguish whether the monkey saw the circle or the vertical stripes; whether he made the correct response or an error; and whether he intended to press the right or the left half of the panel once he knew the problem. All of these differential electrical responses occurred in the visual cortex

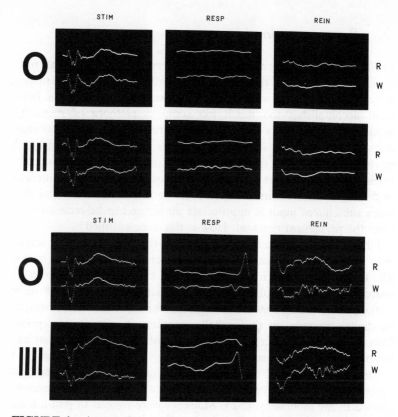

FIGURE 1 Averaged recordings of electrical activity obtained from the occipital cortex of monkeys performing a differential discrimination: circle as opposed to vertical stripes. A standard 500 msec of activity is represented in each trace; the amplitude represented is variable, however, and depends on how many more signals were obtained when the monkey made a correct response than when he made an error during criterion performance. The records under STIM are the waveforms evoked by a display lasting 1 msec; the records under RESP were generated just prior to the response; the records under REIN were generated after the response and during the period when reinforcing events occurred. The upper six panels were made from records obtained while the monkey was performing at chance; the lower six panels were made from records obtained after the monkey attained an 85 percent criterion (200 consecutive trials). The records in line with R were made when the monkey performed correctly; those in line with W were made when the monkey was wrong. The waves generated just prior to response (the intention waves) are similar whenever the monkey is about to press the right half of the panel, regardless of whether this is for the circle or vertical stripes, and regardless of whether this response proves to be correct or wrong.

Karl H. Pribram

(that part of the brain which also receives the visual input), though different electrodes recorded different events. Apparently, experience and current input converge in the input system.

This experiment suggests that some form of recoding takes place within the input system, making possible a longer-term storage of experience. A clue as to the nature of this recoding process comes from the theoretical analysis of Beurle (5), who has demonstrated that waveforms of the sort that constitute the neural hologram (plane waves) tend to "focus" whenever they occur in an absorptive medium (e.g., brain). The waveform is thus capable of exciting a highly localized aggregate of neurons—or even a single unit. This amounts to extracting a single dimension, a single "sinusoidal" wave and the particular information carried on it, from the multidimensional hologram. Thus the impulse configuration, the firing characteristics of a specific constellation of neurons, can be influenced by and can in turn influence the interference patterns that constitute the hologram. Unit recordings, as by Jung and his group (23), Mountcastle (35), Maturana (33), Lettvin (31), and, of course, Hubel and Wiesel (21), have amply demonstrated this specificity. From these studies it appears likely that each of the columns of cells constituting the cerebral cortex is, either innately or by experience (through the operation of the hologram), tuned to one or another specific function. Subsequent to tuning, each such column would tend to resonate—i.e., produce an identifiable output whenever the same or a similar input pattern occurred.

In my laboratory, Dr. Spinelli (57) has developed the details of a model of a memory mechanism based on these assumptions. Spinelli approaches the problems posed by the neurological evidence by focusing on the need for (1) a distribution of information in memory and (2) a simple device to decode and store the complexities of the input. Distribution of information is the major accomplishment of the neural hologram, which can realistically be derived from the operation of a Fourier transform on nerve impulses performed at synaptic junctions. Decoding is accomplished by reversing this procedure: neural units are assumed to be sensitive to two characteristics of the wave pattern, its amplitude and its phase angle. In the Spinelli model these two characteristics determine the size of the receptive field and some simple property of its configuration.

Pattern recognition has been accomplished by computer in just this fashion. By programming a device that codes amplitude and phase angle, the basic similarities of sets of complex patterns can be identified, leaving flexible a considerable range of leeway in minor

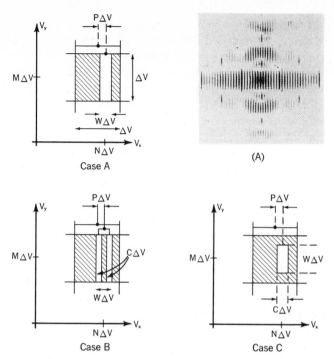

FIGURE 2 Three ways of constructing a cell from which a hologram can be reconstructed and an example of a Fraunhofer hologram that corresponds to Case A. Slit width and height, as well as the cell size, are the adjustable parameters.

differences between configurations (7). The manner of coding used in this device is shown in Figure 2 and displays remarkable similarity to the visual receptive fields of neurons in the visual system.

Long-term storage of amplitude and phase information is conceived by Spinelli to occur by timing an ensemble of units to respond more readily to those characteristics by which they have been most frequently excited. The tuning is conceived to take place by means of the mechanism of self-inhibition within the ensemble of lateral inhibition between ensembles. A diagram of the Spinelli unit is shown in Figure 3.

The characteristic essential to both the hologram and the Spinelli unit is that access to the memory mechanism is gained through a host of channels, nerve pathways, working simultaneously and in parallel. This is not to deny the importance of hierarchical organizations within the nervous system (e.g., see next section) or even within the input channels. But the fact remains, as was pointed out in the last section,

Karl H. Pribram

that the anatomy and function of the input systems to the brain are to a large extent organized in parallel. In this respect they differ from the commonly used serial processing computers available today.

This contrast with hardware computers provides another attribute of biological memory. Today's computers are structurally addressed —i.e., the "address" of an item is coded in terms of its location in memory. Through the hologram, information becomes distributed, and the evidence upon which the Spinelli unit is based shows that storage remains distributed. Since the hologram and its anatomical substrate provide simultaneous parallel access to all parts of the system, location of items becomes irrelevant. The chances are, therefore, that biological memory is content addressed; i.e., as already indicated, inputs with a particular characteristic will call forth (through resonance) outputs from neuronal aggregates that are tuned to the same or similar characteristics. We have all shared the common experience that a few bars or phrases of a song or a poem will start the reconstructive mechanism going and the whole will come pouring out. It may well be that Professor Penfield is providing just the right waveforms to his patients' temporal lobes to initiate such a process.

Decoding the neural holographic representation, the reconstruction of an image, is in this fashion conceived to be similar in many respects to the formation of "ghost images" in ordinary holography: the input configuration contains at least a part of the total information to be used in reconstruction.

But there is more to the reconstructive process than this. Man is not completely at the mercy of the input patterns that surround him. He can focus on this or that aspect, change what he chooses to attend to and to identify. For this operation also, a neural mechanism must exist—and indeed there is a good deal of evidence as to what it might be like.

There exist, in the primate brain, regions of cortex that, although associated with each of the input systems, operate more or less independently of the input. A good deal of my own research efforts over the past twenty years has been devoted to deciphering the functions of these associated regions. The detailed results of this research are reviewed elsewhere (42, 43), but the essential findings can be summarized as follows: contrary to popular opinion, these regions do not appear to serve as intersensory association mechanisms. Rather, there is one such area associated with each of the major sensory modes. How each area serves its sensory-specific functions remains a puzzle, but my neurobehavioral and neurophysiological results suggest that the associated areas exert their influence, via corticofugal fibers,

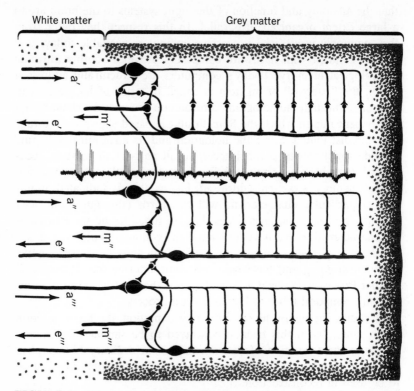

White matter   Grey matter

FIGURE 3 Diagram of the Spinelli unit, which operates much as does a Computer for Average Transients (C.A.T.). Thus, just as the C.A.T., it stores only the incoming activity that synchronously repeats itself. Maximum output will therefore be produced by neuron e′ only when the incoming activity matches exactly the stored pattern. Neuron m′ is essentially a comparator; it receives the input activity from neuron a′ through an inhibitory interneuron and the activity from neuron e′ through an excitatory connection. Because the assumption is that there will be an output from e′ only when there is a match, an incoming signal will go through totally, in parts, or not at all, with the result that neuron m′ will be disinhibited, partially inhibited, or strongly inhibited. Neuron m′ will signal a match or a partial match independently from the strength of the signals; its action is essentially that of a differential amplifier or of a comparator with an integrative action over a time span of unspecified duration. In addition, the ensemble is connected by inhibitory neurons that function much as does lateral inhibition in the retina. Assuming the memory to be initially blank, this feature prevents all memory neurons from storing the same items. The amount of reduplication in the storage of one item is, therefore, inversely related to the amount of lateral inhibition. There is an added twist to the lateral inhibition: if there is an output from the middle neuron, for example, the lateral inhibition impinging on its neighbors is enhanced. The effect of this is

on the neural activities occurring within the relevant input systems. In the visual system (51, 52), for instance, the electrical activity of single neurons in the optic nerve, lateral geniculate nucleus, and cortex is altered by electrical stimulation of the visually associated area (Figure 4). In the auditory system, the corticofugal pathways involved in influencing electrical activity in the auditory system have been traced as far peripherally as the cochlear nucleus (12, 13, 37).

What is accomplished by these corticofugal fibers? Removal of the cortex of their origin impairs choice among alternatives (8, 47, 60). This impairment is due to a restriction in the sample size out of which choices are made—a restriction in the organism's field of attention. The neurophysiological explanation of this alteration of attention rests on our experiments as noted above. Specifically, stimulations and removals of the corticofugal fibers from the associated cortex were interpreted to show that redundancy could be changed by altering the number of nerve pathways used at any moment by any particular input (58, 59). Thus the *rate* of input processing can be regulated by the associated cortex.

Adjustment of the rate of information processing is thus one of the functions of the neural "screen." The inhibitory mechanisms of the Spinelli unit allow just such control to be exercised on it at the cortical level, and a somewhat similar neuronal configuration could be involved at subcortical stations (15, 48). In these locations, the screen acts more as a filter or lens than as projection surface. To return to the hologram analogy, the extent of the neural hologram at any moment is determined by these corticofugal influences. As in the

---

(again assuming memory to be initially blank) that when an item is presented to the whole memory, only a selected few memory neurons will become active, and each one will be surrounded by an area of inhibition. The spatial arrangement of the excited neurons and of surrounding inhibited areas is determined only by chance. Upon repeated excitation, some memory neurons will begin to output, thus enhancing the surround inhibition with the result that from then on these neurons will have a higher probability of being the foci of excitation (being "open" to that item) and of preventing memory neurons all around them from learning that item any further. From a behavioral standpoint, a learning curve should have at least two components; the first one around chance levels would be correlated with the building up of memory cells in which the activity produced by the learning situation emerges more and more from "noise"; the second, starting from above chance, should be much steeper and would be the expression of the fact that the activity produced in the memory neurons is well above "noise" and can, therefore, attract further activity of that kind to the *same* memory neurons.

The Four R's of Remembering   **207**

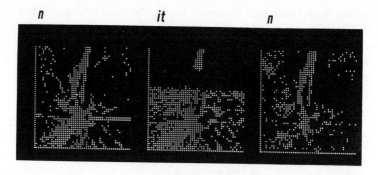

FIGURE 4 Effects of stimulation of the posterior "association" cortex of a cat on a visual receptive field recorded from a neural unit in the optic tract. These records are made by moving a spot with an *X-Y* plotter controlled by a small general-purpose computer (PDP-8), which also records the number of impulses emitted by the unit at every location of the spot. The record shown is a section parallel to the 2 S.D. above the background firing level of the unit. Note the dramatic change in the configuration of the receptive field, especially after stimulation of the posterior "association" cortex (IT, inferotemporal).

photographic hologram, the larger the extent, the shallower the depth of field and the greater the resolution of the parts of the image in focus (30). In other words, increasing the number of nerve pathways occupied by input at any moment increases the extent of the representative process and thus the focus of any particular aspect of the image, much as does the use of a telephoto lens. Conversely, decreasing the extent of the representative process brings into simultaneous focus a larger field (a greater number of items), much as does the use of a wide-angle lens in an ordinary camera.

The mechanism for changing the focus of attention by regulating the redundancy of the input channels was discovered by us in monkeys. However, the process appears to be a ubiquitous, primitive neurophysiological mechanism. An entirely independent series of studies on crayfish (64) has led to the demonstration in this invertebrate of a mechanism remarkably similar to the one outlined here for the primate, which attests to its biological importance.

So much for the experimental evidence obtained in the laboratory. These experiments leave unanswered the question of whether the rate of input processing is qualitatively as well as quantitatively alterable by the operation of the "associated" cortex mechanism. Here, the experiments detailed by Professor Penfield for this audience provide a partial answer. Electrical excitation of the associated cortex in man

Karl H. Pribram

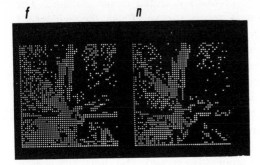

_f_   _n_

gives rise, in the scarred brain, to sequentially ordered remembrances. This observation has been taken further in a study by Mahl (32), where implanted electrodes were used so that the stimulations could be carried out repeatedly over the course of weeks. Mahl found that the events remembered varied according to the set and setting produced by the experimenters prior to and during the electrical stimulation. An hour's conversation about childhood experiences would result in stimulation memories dating to childhood; a discussion of current marital problems would result in stimulation memories associated with the marriage. Thus, the same electrode placement and stimulus parameters could give rise to different sets of memories. The conclusion to be reached from these observations is this: the re-membering process, in this case initiated by the electrical stimulation, must operate by assembling from their distributed locations the variety of fragments dis-membered during storage (much as a sequence-control program does for a computer). Apparently, the qualitative differences are determined by the set and setting of the moment and its immediate antecedent, not by the reconstructive process per se.

We have all made this observation. Events dimly remembered become vivid when we return to the scene of the experience. Meeting old friends, hearing familiar music, rereading in a long-neglected topic, all call forth reconstructive powers thought long since gone. We are little aware of the amount of our memory that is carried "out there"—not in our brains but in our homes, jobs, and libraries. Given these highly structured inputs, the machinery of our brains can restructure—reconstruct—a remembrance from the bits and dabs actually stored in the head. The process is somewhat similar to that familiar to us in a desk calculator—or, less familiarly, a computer. Given the appropriate input, these machines can perform herculean feats of memory: they will, for instance, repeatedly compute correctly the product of 3767 × 1564 and for that matter _any_ combination of four numbers. Yet none of these products is stored in the machine! The operation of multiplication is reconstructive. From the evidence I have reviewed here, it appears likely that a great deal of what we call remembering is in like manner reconstructive.

For education, the moral is clear. Instruction (shared discovery of structure) should supplement teaching (showing). The tools for structuring and restructuring must be developed by the pupil; the machinery of reconstruction must be put together. The techniques of analysis and of synthesis are to be empasized. The simple repetition of loosely connected facts ought to give way to the search for structure in the material to which the student is exposed. The short-answer test, which explores the number of items retained (ever so briefly and meaninglessly), ought to be recognized for what it is—a labor saving, featherbedding procedure to process the students through the school system with the least possible effort on anyone's part.

As an educational experience, term papers, take-home examinations, and group test efforts produce an infinitely greater impact. How many of you still have in your files somewhere that paper you wrote in high school of which you were so proud, and still are? How many of you have had the experience of reading of a recent statement by Toynbee, or the expression of some other famous person in the news media, and exclaiming: "Why, you know, I said something like that in a paper I wrote in that history course back in 19XX"? The writing of the paper was educational, and today's reconstructive experience is possible and meaningful only because the paper was accomplished. The likelihood is slight that any one of the 500,000 short-answer questions you have had to answer during your school life has had much effect other than the deleterious one of dulling interest.

In summary, the understanding achieved by research on brain function in my laboratory suggests that the present educational effort is deficient in the techniques of image making and in the lack of emphasis on the reconstructive aspects of remembering. The real possibility exists that these deficiencies account for the fact that so many gifted individuals' schooling becomes a dull routine to be escaped as rapidly as possible. But, before the full impact of this suggestion can be explored, I must detail some of what we know about the workings of the brain in the more standard learning situation—the mechanism by which events become registered in memory.

Karl H. Pribram

Registration: A Temporal Encoding Process

The holographic image is a spatial representation of experience in the nervous system. As such, it is momentary. Yet, as discussed in the section on reconstruction, aspects of this spatial representation become enduring. From these enduring fragments the image can be reconstructed whenever subsequent input is appropriate and sufficient to the task. The observation was also made that the reconstructive process was not just quantitative—that qualitative attributes have been identified. From this observation, it follows that there must be a brain process that functions to encode in a temporal mechanism the redundancies experienced. To begin the exploration of such a temporal encoding process, it is necessary to return to the studies on the habituation of the orienting reaction.

The work in my laboratory on this topic began (26) by repeating Sokolov's experiments and extending (3, 25) the findings to monkeys, on whom brain operations could readily be performed. These studies uncovered the unexpected finding that the orienting reaction is not all of a piece. Rather, the several measures of orienting—EEG, GSR, heart and respiratory rate, and orienting movements—were dissociated into two categories by the brain lesion (1). Further, the results of the experiments showed that the absence of one class of orienting responses was correlated with a deficiency in habituation and in classical conditioning (2). As shown in Figure 5, this deficiency is related to a failure to anticipate the consequences, the effects, of the event experienced. There appears to be a failure of normally recurring rehearsal of the conditioning events. We have therefore labeled this class of orienting responses indications of "registration." In the absence of "registration," the mapping, encoding, of experience into temporal dimension fails to occur.

The results of these experiments mirror an everyday experience shared by most of us. There are times during which we are preoccupied, when our spouses or friends rattle on, only to become aware at last that we are not attending to their words. Piqued, they exclaim: "You're not listening." We immediately try to reassure them by repeating to them the last phrase or sentence that they expressed. Our representation-reconstruction process has saved us for the moment. But, if asked some time later what the "conversation" was all about, we might well reply, "What conversation?"—with predictable results.

In man, a permanent memory defect of just the sort that is nor-

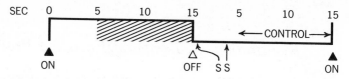

TRIALS	GRP	5–10 SEC ON	10–15 SEC ON	5–10 SEC OFF	10–15 SEC OFF
FIRST 40	NORM	3.7	7.0**	3.9	7.0
	AMX	3.2	3.3	3.9	6.3
SECOND 40	NORM	5.7**	8.8*	6.2	4.5
	AMX	2.7	4.8	3.5	4.3
ALL 80	NORM	9.3	14.5*	10.3	7.0
	AMX	5.8	8.2	7.3	6.3

*=p<.08
**=p<.05

MEAN NO. GSRS IN PERIODS PRECEDING SHOCK
(ANTICIPATORY RESPONSES)

FIGURE 5 The top of the figure shows a conditioning paradigm in which a light is turned on, then turned off after 15 sec. Following this by 3 sec is the onset of shock. The table shows the number of anticipatory responses made during the first and second forty trials, which show in the shaded area of the diagram above. Note that normal S's make more and more anticipatory responses and that these occur earlier and earlier. Note also that monkeys who have been amygdalectomized show no such anticipatory response.

mally shown during periods of preoccupation has been related to lesions of the same parts of the brain ablated in our monkey orienting-reaction experiments—the medial portions of the temporal lobes, which include the limbic structures amygdala and hippocampus. Such patients have been studied extensively (55, 61) with behavioral techniques, as have monkeys with similar lesions (11, 40). Detailed reviews of this work are available (14, 16), and this is not the occasion for analyzing the complexities of the results. This general statement may be made, however: all of these studies show that these parts of the brain become important in situations that demand of the organism an active organizing process entailing rehearsal and relation in some new fashion of his past experience to the current circumstance. The process can be conceived to encode and distribute redundancy in a temporal mechanism much as the neural hologram achieves the distribution of redundancy spatially. When this active organizing process is engaged, events are promptly registered in memory. Without the operation of this mechanism, items must be repetitiously presented to the organism before they become "memorized."

I have elsewhere (45) presented evidence for the suggestion that this organizing process is what takes place in behavioral experiments when an organism is reinforced. The involvement of these limbic temporal-lobe structures in reinforcement is well documented (39, 54). However, before proceeding further with the analysis of the temporal-lobe contribution to reinforcement, let me turn to the neuronal level for a suggestion as to the direction inquiry into the mechanism of this organizing process might take.

The suggestion is that the reinforcing process accomplishes in the nervous system what the mechanism of induction achieves in the embryo (17, 18). The superficial descriptive similarity between induction as studied in embryological tissue and reinforcement as studied in conditioning situations has been presented in another manuscript (46) and is reviewed briefly here:

> (a) Inductors evoke and organize the genetic potential of the organism. Reinforcers evoke and organize the behavioral capacities of organisms. (b) Inductors are relatively specific as to the character they evoke but are generally non-specific relative to individuals and tissues. Reinforcers are relatively specific in the behaviors they condition but are generally nonspecific relative to individuals and tasks. (c) Inductors determine the broad outlines of the induced character; details are specified by the action of the substrate. Reinforcers determine the solution of the problem set; details of the behavioral repertoire used to achieve the solution are idiosyncratic to the organism. (d) Inductors do not just trigger development; they are more than just evanescent stimuli. Reinforcers do not just trigger behavior; they are a special class of stimuli. (e) Inductors must be in contact with their substrate in order to be effective. Contiguity is a demonstrated requirement for reinforcement to take place. (f) Mere contact, though necessary, is insufficient to produce an inductive effect; the induced tissue must be ready, must be competent to react. Mere contiguity, though necessary, is insufficient to produce reinforcement; shaping, deprivation, readiness, context, expectation, attention, hypothesis—these are only some of the terms used to describe the factors which comprise the competence of the organism and without which reinforcement cannot become effective. (b) Induction usually proceeds by a two-way interaction—by way of a chemical conversation (6). Reinforcement is most effective in the operant situation where the consequences of the organism's own actions are utilized as the guides to its subsequent behavior.

A good deal of experimentation and speculation has been aimed at this problem. Much of it, unfortunately, has been concerned not with reinforcement but with inhibition. But this is not too different from the emphasis in experimental embryology, which has been almost totally concerned with the problem of segregation.

In short, embryogenesis is dependent not only on the inherited and inherent properties of the genetic constitution of the organism; rather, these properties are evoked and organized by the inductive capacity of the milieu in which the cells grow. The inductive capacity is itself specific, but in a somewhat different sense than is the genetic potential. The *genetic capability* is individual-, species- (and genus- and order-) specific. Hereditary factors prescribe commonalties with the past and future, while assuring variation within any single generation. *Inductors,* on the other hand, are nonspecific with respect to individuals, species, and so forth. They are relatively simple chemicals—RNA's— common to all living organisms (36). Inductors thus provide the existential commonalty that allows the possibility of modification of whole generations according to the exigencies of the time.

But when this much has been said, the question still remains: do these descriptive similarities point to homologous mechanisms? My hypothesis states that they do. What evidence is there in support? What neural processes become operative during learning?

The story of the experimental findings in the embryological field is paralleled by results in the field of learning experiments. You have been given an extensive review of this story by Professor Hydén. His view, based on the beautiful series of experiments accomplished in his laboratories, holds that RNA "induces" the derepression of genomes in central neural tissue just as RNA induces the formation of structures in embryonic tissue. The nature of the neural "structures" induced remains to be clarified; but I have elsewhere (49) suggested that, among other possibilities, actual neuronal growth may take place. This growth could readily be guided, in the central as it is in the peripheral nervous system, by surrounding glia. According to this hypothesis, secretion of RNA from a repetitively stimulated neuron induces surrounding glia to divide and open a pathway for the neuron's growth cone.

If we return now to the temporal-lobe mechanism, it is clear that any induction-like process needs time to take place. I have already noted that segregation is important to the occurrence of embryological induction. In the nervous system, inhibition has a somewhat similar function. It has been well established (19), both for the retina and for the cerebral cortex, that an externally derived excitation at any locus will produce inhibition in the surrounding tissue—i.e., the frequency of spontaneously occurring electrical discharges of the inhibited cells will diminish. This "surround" or "lateral" inhibition will tend to isolate the focus of excitation and enhance the contrast between stimulated and nonstimulated regions. Such isolation is necessary for differentiation to be accomplished neurally and behaviorally as well as embryologically. In addition to lateral inhibition, other inhibitory processes are known to occur (e.g., recurrent or Renshaw inhibition). These act as mechanisms of self-inhibition, "segregating" one neural occurrence from another in time, much as the lateral inhibition mechanism accomplishes spatial segregation. There is, in fact, good evidence that the limbic structures of the temporal lobe have a great deal of influence on these inhibitory mechanisms (9, 20, 48). Further, neurobehavioral studies, taken in conjunction with the physiological studies already presented, have made it likely that the orienting reaction is a function of lateral inhibition, while habituation is a function of the longer lasting self-inhibitory process (15). We have thus come full circle: the organizing process of registration, which we call reinforcement, is made possible by the "segregation" of neural events through the operation of the mechanisms of the orienting reaction and its habituation.

This is borne out in fact by studies, extensively reviewed by Magoun for this series, in which direct electrical intervention in the nervous system was shown capable of guiding and modulating behavior. Electrical stimulation with alternating or pulsed currents, or polarization with direct currents, speeds or slows learning according to the parameters of stimulation used. Especially effective guides to behavior are brain excitations that the organism itself can produce in the temporal lobe and related structures. Such self-stimulations are, if anything, more potent than extrinsic reinforcers.

In summary, registration is thought to involve two related processes. One is control over afferent neural inhibition (see Figure 6), in the form of an orienting reaction and its habituation, which allows the spatial and temporal segregation of an event. The other is a reinforcement mechanism, which guides the development of the neural structures that in turn program behavior. Orientation and habituation are believed to minimize interference among events, allowing time for a process similar to rehearsal of an experience to take place. As a result, an RNA-induced reinforcement mechanism could become operative to encode successive patterns of events in the brain, either as actual neuronal growth, or by some alteration in membrane properties, or both. Such a course of events is but one route, albeit a plausible one, by which experience can become registered and capable of subsequent influence on the psychological process. As data accumulate, other routes will undoubtedly be suggested.

The relevance of the registration mechanism to education may be discerned in the effect on learning of medial temporal-lobe lesions in

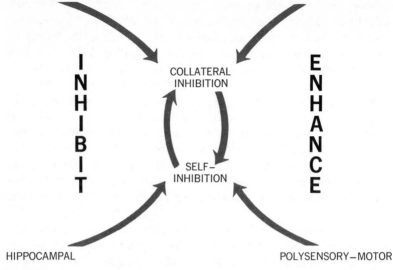

FRONTOTEMPORAL   SENSORY–SPECIFIC/INTRINSIC

I N H I B I T

COLLATERAL INHIBITION

SELF– INHIBITION

E N H A N C E

HIPPOCAMPAL   POLYSENSORY–MOTOR

FIGURE 6 A model of corticofugal control over input processing. Collateral inhibition is considered the basic process for the orienting reaction; self-inhibition is the basic process for habituation. Two corticofugal systems enhance and two inhibit this basic mechanism of afferent neural inhibition. For details see text and (15).

monkeys. These monkeys can still learn: provided the experimental conditions are repeated over and over, the task is mastered, and, once mastered, it is not forgotten. But the learning is slowed.

Similarly, we can drill our students to attain never-to-be-forgotten skills. My father quoted the first chapter of Caesar's *Gaul* to me in Latin without error decades after he had first memorized the words. He had been exposed to 14 grueling years of Latin. I decided after this episode that for me even 2 years was too much—and the academic community has since supported my decision. How much of what we now teach our youngsters looks to them as Latin did to me? How often do we ask of them that they learn by rote what they might better achieve by engaging their registration mechanism?

Only this morning I read a Berlitz advertisement in the newspaper. "Learn any language by total immersion in 10 *days*" the blurb proclaimed. I tend to believe in the efficacy of their method—the registration process is sure to be taxed by any such procedure. Perhaps the learning is incomplete, and perhaps it is not altogether permanent— but then how much do you remember of your 10 (or 100) *weeks* of high-school French?

216   *Karl H. Pribram*

I give these examples not to indicate that one or another method of instruction is better or worse than another. For some purposes memorization is ideal, as when an aspiring physician must quickly master drug dosages. Rather, my question is: "Can the material presented to our students be made relevant to their aspirations and values?" Once this is done, we can "immerse" them in the material and let them proceed in their own way and at their own speed. The advent of programmed instruction has given this approach new feasibilities where repetition and practice are necessary, as in the development of skills. However, even in the past, once engaged, the student found his way to those stacks of condensed programs—the libraries.

Thus, teachers will never be superfluous. Responsible and enthusiastic educators serve as models for identification and imitation as already noted. And instructors must help decode and recode the flux of material as it is registered, or else the registration process becomes quickly overburdened and grinds to a halt. It is to the teacher that the burden of relevancy falls.

Rearrangement

Decoding the temporal structure of redundancy poses as complex a problem as does the encoding of it. Take this essay for instance. It is made up of multiple rearrangements of almost infinite repetitions of only twenty-six characters, the alphabet. How do we proceed to decode this stream of symbols?

McCulloch has provided us with a clue in a by-now famous illustration of the problem. He presents the following puzzle for deciphering:

INMUDEELSARE
INCLAYNONEARE
INPINETARIS
INOAKNONEIS

How much time it takes to make sense of this conglomeration of letters. But how easy it becomes when written or spoken as:

IN MUD EELS ARE
IN CLAY NONE ARE
IN PINE TAR IS
IN OAK NONE IS

In a similar vein, Miller (34) has pointed out that what constitutes an item or event in a biological information-processing system varies according to how the information is "chunked."

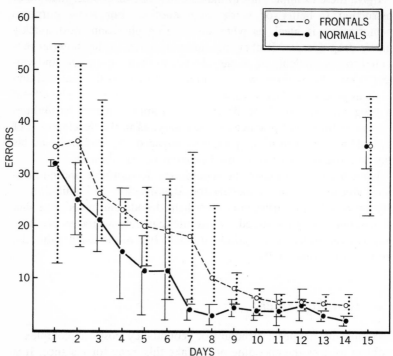

FIGURE 7 Graph of the average number of errors made by monkeys having ablations of the frontal cortex and by their controls. Bars indicate ranges of errors made. For day 15, records are shown of the number of errors made on return to the classical 5-sec alternation task.

As a first step therefore, it appears that decoding temporal structure involves a proper division, a partitioning—parsing—process. I put this idea to test in a simple experiment. In monkeys, a very specific difficulty in problem solving occurs after ablation of the anterior frontal cortex—an operation similar to the once popular lobotomy procedure performed as psychosurgery in man. This difficulty is manifest as an inability to perform a variety of sequential tasks, the simplest of which is a right-left alternation (22, 51). The precise nature of the difficulty has resisted clarification despite much effort (50). In view of the importance of parsing and chunking in decoding verbal material, I ventured to parse artificially the alternation task for frontally ablated monkeys by inserting a 15-second pause between each right-left couplet. Thus, the task that was right-left-right-left, etc., was parsed to read right-left, pause, right-left, pause, etc. As can be seen in Figure 7, the monkeys immediately began to solve the problem.

The conclusion to be reached from this experiment is that ordinarily the anterior frontal cortex supplies a mechanism that decodes the flow of events by inserting "pauses" at the appropriate time, thus providing a grammar, as it were, for the psychological process and behavior (53).

On the basis of the results of other neurobehavioral experiments, I ventured a few years ago to suggest that the anterior frontal cortex functions much as does a "flexible noticing order" in a computer program (50). In the computer, such a device acts as an executive, giving priority now to this, now to that, set of events being processed by the computer. Since the time this suggestion was made, computer science has progressed considerably. Executive routines based on "flexible noticing orders" have become important tools for allowing time sharing—i.e., the use of a single computer by a number of users. Time sharing is a decoding operation: items must be sorted and separated according to the user, despite the fact that both the input and the events in the computer become temporally intermixed.

We have met a similar problem in the discussion of reconstructive remembering. There the issue was to reassemble items distributed spatially in the nervous system; here the task is to arrange in some order items distributed temporally. As in the case of the reconstructive process, a great deal depends on the appropriate structure—or structuring—of the input. This is clearly indicated by the jumble resulting from unparsed verbal material even in us, who presumably possess creation's finest executive organ, the human frontal lobe.

What do we know about the neurophysiological operation of the temporal decoding mechanism? As already noted, electrophysiological experiments have shown that input processing can be slowed by electrical stimulation of the frontal cortex. This slowing results from an increase in effective redundancy within the input channel, which also has the effect of reducing interference among the events being processed. In this respect frontal-lobe function is similar to that of the medial temporal structures.

But, aside from these initial findings, practically nothing is yet known. There is some hope that new insights will come from the recently discovered Contingent Negative Variation, a slow potential change that originates somewhere in the front of the brain whenever the organism is preparing to respond (28, 63). This and our finding of a wave preceding meaningful response in the input systems (already noted) provide indicators of intentionality and so allow exploration of the mechanism of temporal decoding. After all, a great deal is already accomplished when we know where to look and have some tools with which to do the looking.

These experimental results suggest that a great part of the educational process, except for the acquisition of skills, lies in arranging and rearranging one's experiences. When I was in college, as today, there were individuals who "cribbed" during exams. One of the most effective methods was to condense the most important material onto small cards or even onto the inside of the shirt cuff. I was impressed and envious—identification and imitation quickly suggested itself. But as I began to work studiously through the course material in order to compress the relevant facts and ideas adequately, I found that I could go the "cribbers" one better. The arranging and rearranging of notes constituted a superb review. And the aim toward parsimony in expression left me with a few key cards, which could now easily be committed to memory, since a context had been provided by the review. With one stroke, rearrangement had given me superiority: not only did I remember the material for the examination; I gained knowledge of enduring value and didn't have to risk disruption of my social fabric or of my conscience.

According to this view, lecturers should present but few facts that are to be remembered, unless these are unobtainable elsewhere (in which case precise note-taking is to be encouraged or handouts given ahead of time). Rather, a lecturer should arrange and even rearrange material that the student can, with informed guidance, find for himself. Each set of lectures should provide a framework, a core idea on and around which the student can build for the remainder of his life. Further, the student must be prompted by his instructors to make his own rearrangements. He can do this in term papers and in research endeavors, and he will, of course, use his instructor's lectures as models. If these are sufficiently flexible in approach, the student's work will reflect this. These are some of the lessons to be learned from the study of how the brain functions in remembering, although they may seem fairly tame to those involved daily in the educational process.

I have had nothing to say (although some things are known—e.g., 44) about such important topics as transfer, which allows knowledge gained in one situation to be applied in another. Nor have I discussed (because there is as yet so little to discuss) symbol manipulation, a process basic to most human educational effort. And, when it comes to creativity and originality, the neuropsychologist today has nothing solid to offer. But I am far from discouraged by these deficiencies. Only a little over a decade ago Lashley had to admit that, according to the neurophysiological and neurobehavioral facts then available, learning and remembering were simply impossible. What a difference

Karl H. Pribram

today, when we can look at the details of the spatial and temporal coding mechanisms reviewed here, the possibility of analysis into encoding and decoding processes, the richness of data and of analogous and relevant hardware from which we can derive precise and testable hypotheses. No, I am encouraged that indeed we are finding man's brain to work as it must, to produce the behavior we encounter. We often observe that man's destiny is in the hands of its educational process. But the currency of education is based on brains. When we knew little of brain function except that it controlled the body's economy, we were apt to pit man's baser nature against his ennobling culture or play the reverse theme of the noble savage and degrading civilization. The scientific as well as the humanistic literature is full of unfounded allusion to the primitive, the older neurological processes that have become overlaid with the mechanisms that distinguish man from beast. There is, of course, some truth in these assertions. However, the mammalian visual apparatus is as hoary as is the apparatus that regulates hunger and sex, and the truth is that the neural formations and psychological processes that regulate appetite in man have developed easily as much as have his mechanisms of vision. There are no subhuman gourmets, nor have the beasts as yet produced a Marquis de Sade—they just don't have the brains.

The simple fact is that our view of the world depends in large part on our view of ourselves. And the organ crucially involved in viewing is, of course, the brain. Better we know it well, how it represents the world and reconstructs its images. Better also that we know well the tricks that can be played on us by our memories—how registration can occur and how it can fail. And we must come to know the limits of resolving power when our brains are faced with temporally organized codes.

These then are the frontiers of mind: developments in neurobehavioral science that permit man to evolve his understanding of man.

REFERENCES

1. Bagshaw, M. H., and Benzies, S. "Multiple measures of the orienting reaction to a simple non-reinforced stimulus after amygdalectomy in monkeys." *Exp. Neurol.,* 20 (1968) 175–87.
2. Bagshaw, M. H., and Coppock, H. W. "GSR conditioning deficit in amygdalectomized monkeys." *Exp. Neurol.,* 20 (1968) 188–96.
3. Bagshaw, M. H., Kimble, D. P., and Pribram, K. H. "The GSR of monkeys during orienting and habituation and after ablation of

the amygdala, hippocampus and inferotemporal cortex." *Neuropsychologia*, 3 (1965) 111–19.

4. Bateson, P. P. G. "Ear movements of normal and amygdalectomized rhesus monkeys." Submitted to *Nature*.

5. Beurle, R. L. "Properties of a mass of cells capable of regenerating pulses." *Philos. Trans. Royal Soc. London*, 240 (1956) 55–94.

6. Bonner, J. "Molecular biological approaches to the study of memory," in Gaito, J. (ed.), *Macromolecules and behavior*. New York: Appleton-Century-Crofts, 1966, pp. 158–64.

7. Brown, B. R., and Lohmann, A. W. "Complex spatial filtering with binary masks." *Applied Optics*, 5 (1966) 967–69.

8. Butter, C. M. "The effect of discrimination training on pattern equivalence in monkeys with inferotemporal and lateral striate lesions." *Neuropsychologia*, 6 (1968) 27–40.

9. Clemente, C. D., Green, J. D., and deGroot, J. "Studies on behavior following rhinencephalic lesions in adult cats." *Anat. Rec. Am. Ass. Anat.*, 127 (1957) 279.

10. Cochran, G. "New method of making Fresnel transforms with incoherent light." *J. Optical Soc. of America*, 56 (1966) 1513–17.

11. Correll, R. E., and Scoville, W. B. "Performance on delayed match following lesions of medial temporal lobe structures." *J. comp. physiol. Psychol.*, 60 (1965) 360–68.

12. Dewson, J. H., III. "Efferent cochlear bundle: some relationships to noise making and to stimulus attenuation." *J. Neurophysiol.*, 30 (1967) 817–32.

13. Dewson, J. H., III, Nobel, K. W., and Pribram, K. H. "Corticofugal influence at cochlear nucleus of the cat: some effects of ablation of insular-temporal cortex." *Brain Res.*, 2 (1966) 151–59.

14. Douglas, R. J. "The hippocampus and behavior." *Psychol. Bul.*, 67 (1967) 416–42.

15. Douglas, R. J., and Pribram, K. H. "Learning and limbic lesions." *Neuropsychologia*, 4 (1966) 107–220.

16. Gerbrandt, L. K. "Neural systems of response release and control." *Psychol. Bul.*, 64 (1965) 113–23.

17. Hamburger, V. "Experimental embryology." *Encyclopaedia Britannica*, Vol. 8 (1961), pp. 973–80.

18. Hamburger, V., and Levi-Montalcini, R. "Some aspects of neuroembryology," in Weiss, P. (ed.), *Genetic neurology: Problems of the development, growth, and regeneration of the nervous system and of its functions*. Chicago: Univ. of Chicago Press, 1950, pp. 128–60.

19. Hartline, H. K., Wagner, H. G., and Ratliff, F. "Inhibition in the eye of limulus." *J. gen. Physiol.*, 39 (1956) 651–73.

20. Haider, M., Spong, P., and Lindsley, D. B. "Attention, vigilance and cortical evoked potentials in humans." *Science*, 145 (1964) 180–82.

21. Hubel, D. H., and Wiesel, T. N. "Receptive fields, binocular interaction and functional architecture in the cat's visual cortex." *J. Physiol.*, 160 (1962) 106–54.

22. Jacobsen, C. F., and Nissen, H. W. "Studies of cerebral function in primates. IV. The effects of frontal lobe lesions on the delayed

alternation habit in monkeys." *J. comp. physiol. Psychol.*, 23 (1937) 101–12.

23. Jung, R. "Neuronal integration in the visual cortex and its significance for visual information," in Rosenblith, W. (ed.), *Sensory communication.* New York: Wiley, 1961, pp. 627–74.

24. Kamiya, J. "Conscious control of brain waves." *Psychology Today*, March 1968.

25. Kimble, D. P., Bagshaw, M. H., and Pribram, K. H. "The GSR of monkeys during orienting and habituation after selective partial ablations of the cingulate and frontal cortex." *Neuropsychologia*, 3 (1965) 121–28.

26. Koepke, J. E., and Pribram, K. H. "Habituation of the GSR as a function of stimulus duration and spontaneous activity." *J. comp. physiol. Psychol.*, 3 (1966) 442–48.

27. Köhler, W. *The place of value in a world of fact.* New York: Liveright, 1938.

28. Lacey, J., in Kimble, D. P. (ed.), *Readiness to remember.* Proceedings of the Third Conference on Learning, Remembering, and Forgetting. In press.

29. Lashley, K. S. "Functional interpretation of anatomic patterns." *Res. Publ. Assoc. Nerv. Ment. Dis.*, 30 (1952) 537–39.

30. Leith, E. N., and Upatnieks, J. "Photography by laser." *Scientific American*, 212 (1965) 24–35. Copyright © 1965 by Scientific American, Inc. All rights reserved.

31. Lettvin, J. Y., Maturana, H. R., Pitts, W. H., and McCulloch, W. S. "Two remarks on the visual system of the frog," in Rosenblith, W. A. (ed.), *Sensory communication.* New York: Wiley, 1961, pp. 757–76.

32. Mahl, G. F., Rothenberg, A., Delgado, J. M. R., and Hamlin, H. "Psychological responses in the human to intracerebral electrical stimulation." *Psychosom. Med.* 26 (1964) 337–68.

33. Maturana, H. R. "Efferent fibers in the optic nerve of the toad (*Bufo Bufo*)." *J. Anat.*, 92 (1958) 21–26.

34. Miller, G. A. "The magical number seven, plus or minus two, or, some limits on our capacity for processing information." *Psychol. Rev.*, 63 (1956) 81–97.

35. Montcastle, V. B. "Modality and topographic properties of single neurons of cat's somatic sensory cortex." *J. Neurophysiol.*, 20 (1957) 408–34.

36. Niu, M. C. "Current evidence concerning chemical inducers," in *Evolution of nervous control from primitive organisms to man.* Washington, D.C.: Pub. No. 52 American Association for the Advancement of Science, 1959, pp. 7–30.

37. Nobel, K. W., and Dewson, J. H., III. "A corticofugal projection from insular and temporal cortex to the homolateral inferior colliculus in cat." *J. aud. Research*, 6 (1966) 67–75.

38. Norton, T., Frommer, G., and Galambos, R. "Effects of partial lesions of optic tract on visual discriminations in cats." *Fed. Proc.*, 25 (1966) 2168.

39. Olds, J. "Physiological mechanisms of reward," in Jones, M. R. (ed.),

Nebraska symposium on motivation. Lincoln, Neb.: Univ. of Nebraska Press, 1955, pp. 73–138.

40. Orbach, J., Milner, B., and Rasmussen, T. "Learning and retention in monkeys after amygdala-hippocampus resection." *Arch. Neurol.,* 3 (1960) 230–51.

41. Oster, G., and Nishijima, Y. "Moiré patterns." *Scientific American,* 208 (1963) 54–63.

42. Pribram, K. H. "A neuropsychological analysis of cerebral function: an informal progress report of an experimental program." *Canadian Psychologist,* 7 (1966) 326–67.

43. Pribram, K. H. "Memory and the organization of attention and intention," in Hall, V. P. (ed.), *Brain function and learning.* Berkeley, Calif.: Univ. of California Press, 1967, pp. 79–121.

44. Pribram, K. H. "Neurological notes on the art of education," in Hilgard, E. (ed.), *Theories of learning and instruction.* Chicago: Univ. of Chicago Press, 1964, pp. 78–110.

45. Pribram, K. H. "Reinforcement revisited: a structural view," in Jones, M. (ed.), *Nebraska symposium on motivation.* Lincoln, Neb.: Univ. of Nebraska Press, 1963, pp. 113–59.

46. Pribram K. H. "Some dimensions of remembering: steps toward a neuropsychological model of memory," in Gaito, J. (ed.), *Macromolecules and behavior.* New York: Academic Press, 1966, pp. 165–87.

47. Pribram, K. H. "The intrinsic systems of the forebrain," in Field, J., and Magoun, H. W. (eds.), *Handbook of psychology.* Vol. II. *Neurophysiology.* Washington, D.C.: American Physiological Society, 1950, pp. 1323–44.

48. Pribram, K. H. "The limbic systems, efferent control of neural inhibition and behavior," in Tokizane, T., and Adey, W. R. (eds.), *Progress in brain research.* New York: American Elsevier, 1967, pp. 318–36.

49. Pribram, K. H. "The new neurology: memory, novelty, thought and choice," in Glaser, G. H. (ed.), *EEG and behavior.* New York: Basic Books, 1963, pp. 149–73.

50. Pribram, K. H., Ahumada, A., Hartog, J., and Roos, L. "A progress report on the neurological processes disturbed by frontal lesions in primates," in Warren, J. M., and Akert, K. (eds.), *The frontal granular cortex and behavior.* New York: McGraw-Hill, 1964, pp. 28–55.

51. Pribram, K. H., Mishkin, M., Rosvold, H. E., and Kaplan, S. J. "Effects on delayed response performance of lesions of dorsolateral and ventromedial frontal cortex of baboons." *J. comp. physiol. Psychol.,* 45 (1952) 565–75.

52. Pribram, K. H., Spinelli, D. N., and Kamback, M. C. "Electrocortical correlates of stimulus response and reinforcement." *Science,* 157 (1967) 94–96.

53. Pribram, K. H., and Tubbs, W. E. "Short term memory, parsing and the primate frontal cortex." *Science,* 156 (1967) 1765–67.

54. Schwartzbaum, J. S. "Changes in reinforcing properties of stimuli

following ablation of the amygdaloid complex in monkeys." *J. comp. physiol. Psychol.*, 53 (1960) 388–95.

55. Scoville, W. B., and Milner, B. "Loss of recent memory after bilateral hippocampal lesions." *J. Neurosur. and Psychiat.*, 20 (1957) 11–21.

56. Sokolov, E. N. "Neuronal models and the orienting reflex," in Brazier, M. A. B. (ed.), *The central nervous system and behavior.* New York: Josiah Macy, Jr. Foundation, 1960, pp. 187–276.

57. Spinelli, D. N. "Occam, a computer model for a content-addressable memory in the central nervous system," in Pribram, K. H., and Broadbent, D. E. (eds.), *Biology of memory.* New York: Academic Press. In press.

58. Spinelli, D. N., and Pribram, K. H. "Changes in visual recovery functions produced by temporal lobe stimulation in monkeys." *EEG clin. Neurophysiol.*, 20 (1966) 44–49.

59. Spinelli, D. N., and Pribram, K. H. "Changes in visual recovery function and unit activity produced by frontal cortex stimulation." *EEG clin. Neurophysiol.*, 22 (1967) 143–49.

60. Symmes, D. "Effect of cortical ablations on visual exploration by monkeys." *J. comp. physiol. Psychol.*, 56 (1963) 757–62.

61. Talland, G. *Deranged memory.* New York: Academic Press, 1965.

62. Thompson, B. J., and Zinky, W. R. "Holography: a status report." *Res./Dev.*, 18 (1967) 20–25.

63. Walter, W. G. "Slow potential waves in the human brain associated with expectancy, attention and decision." *Archiv. für Psychiat. und Zeitschrift. für die ges. Neurologie*, 206 (1964) 309–22.

64. Waterman, T. H. "Systems analysis and the visual orienting of animals." *American Scientist*, 54 (1966) 15–45.

B 0
C 1
D 2
E 3
F 4
G 5
H 6
I 7
J 8